Globalization in World History

The idea of globalization is currently inescapable, though the term and the theory attached date back only to the 1990s. History helps clarify where globalization comes from, how it relates to broad processes of change, and why it rouses controversy.

In *Globalization in World History*, Peter N. Stearns argues that although the term is a relatively new one, the process of globalization has roots much further back in time. He shows how tracing this process of change can also help to define the concept of globalization as we understand it today. The book examines major changes in global interactions from 1000 CE onward, and defines four major turning points that have accelerated the process of globalization.

Issues covered include:

- The factors that have shaped the process of globalization – including economics, migration, disease transmission, culture, the environment and politics.
- How and why reactions to globalization differ across societies. Regions examined include Japan, the Middle East, Africa and China.
- The advantages and disadvantages brought by globalization.

The book is a vital contribution to the study of world history, and is a useful companion for students of politics and sociology.

Peter N. Stearns is Provost and Professor of History at George Mason University. He is co-author of *Premodern Travel in World History* (2008), and author of *Sexuality in World History* (2009), *Gender in World History* (2nd edition 2006), *Consumerism in World History* (2nd edition 2006), *Childhood in World History* (2005), and *Western Civilization in World History* (2003), all in this series. Other recent publications include *The Global Experience* (2005) and *World History in Brief* (2007).

Themes in World History

Series editor: Peter N. Stearns

The *Themes in World History* series offers focused treatment of a range of human experiences and institutions in the world history context. The purpose is to provide serious, if brief, discussions of important topics as additions to textbook coverage and document collections. The treatments will allow students to probe particular facets of the human story in greater depth than textbook coverage allows, and to gain a fuller sense of historians' analytical methods and debates in the process. Each topic is handled over time – allowing discussions of changes and continuities. Each topic is assessed in terms of a range of different societies and religions – allowing comparisons of relevant similarities and differences. Each book in the series helps readers deal with world history in action, evaluating global contexts as they work through some of the key components of human society and human life.

For Inanna Mae, welcome to the world

Globalization in World History

Peter N. Stearns

Routledge
Taylor & Francis Group

LONDON AND NEW YORK

First published 2010 by Routledge
2 Park Square, Milton Park, Abingdon, Oxon OX14 4RN

Simultaneously published in the USA and Canada
by Routledge
270 Madison Ave, New York, NY 10016

Routledge is an imprint of the Taylor & Francis Group, an informa business

© 2010 Peter N. Stearns

Typeset in Times New Roman by Taylor & Francis Books
Printed and bound in Great Britain by
CPI Antony Rowe, Chippenham, Wiltshire

British Library Cataloguing in Publication Data
A catalogue record for this book is available from the British Library

Library of Congress Cataloging in Publication Data
Stearns, Peter N.
Globalization in world history / Peter N. Stearns. -- 1st ed.
p. cm.
1. Globalization--History.   2. World history.   3. International
economic relations--History.   4. Economic history.   5. Human
beings--Migrations--History.   6. International relations--History.
7. Intercultural communication--History.   8. Culture diffusion--History.
9. Diseases and history.   I. Title.
JZ1318.S73 2009
303.48'209--dc22
2009019851

ISBN10: (hbk) 0-415-77917-0
ISBN10: (pbk) 0-415-77918-9
ISBN10: (ebk) 0-203-86606-1

ISBN13: (hbk) 978-0-415-77917-3
ISBN13: (pbk) 978-0-415-77918-0
ISBN13: (ebk) 978-0-203-86606-1

Contents

Acknowledgments

Despite its argumentativeness, this book owes a lot to the New Global Historians and the Toynbee Society in which they participate, including Bruce Mazlish, Wolf Schaefer, Akira Iriye and Raymond Grew. My thanks also to the Osher Lifelong Learning Center, which helped bounce ideas back and forth. Laura Bell aided immensely with the manuscript. My wife, Donna Kidd, helped with a number of ideas and great patience. Finally, the Routledge staff, including Vicky Peters, provided vigorous encouragement and practical help.

Chapter 1

Globalization and the challenge to historical analysis

Globalization: in its literal sense the "process of transformation of local phenomena into global ones ... a process by which the people of the world are unified into a single society and function together." This process is a combination of economic, technological, sociocultural and political forces, though globalization terminology is often used to focus primarily on economics – the integration of national economies into an international economy through trade, foreign direct investment, capital flows, migration, and the spread of technology.

The formal definition risks being too abstract (and the reference to "a single society" may be overdoing things a bit, at least so far). But the process has real human meaning. It refers (in the financial crisis of 2008) to Americans who wake up at 3 a.m. to check Asian stock markets, because they know these will influence and foreshadow Wall Street later in the day. It refers to global McDonald's, with 31,000 locations worldwide, all with a common emphasis on fairly greasy food served quickly and (in principle at least) cheerfully. It refers to a quarter of the world's population (regardless of the time zone) glued to televised accounts of World Cup soccer. It refers to the millions of American kids playing with Japanese toys like Hello Kitty or (not too long ago) Pokémon, or the charitable contributions from around the world pouring into disaster areas like tsunami-hit southeast Asia or Katrina-devastated New Orleans. It refers ... – the list is long indeed, with an impressive range of arenas and activities.

The term globalization is quite new, widely introduced only in the late 1980s/early 1990s, though the Japanese used an equivalent concept in the 1960s. (My computer spellchecker still does not recognize the word, and keeps urging me to remove it – but I'm writing a book about it instead.) The term, and the concept behind it, were not coined by historians, but rather by other social scientists, with economists in the lead. These theorists in turn, implicitly or explicitly, argued that globalization identified a phenomenon whose nature and consequences were quite novel, leading to very different inter-regional interactions and human experiences from anything that had occurred before. Most of them also contended that this global innovation was largely a good thing, producing not only a different but also a better world; but it was also possible to make the same claims about novelty but conclude that the results were unfortunate – the world is indeed different and getting worse. Primary attention, in other words, tended to focus on the quality claims associated with globalization, the list of advantages and drawbacks, which is indeed a vital topic.

Thomas Friedman, for example, an articulate popularizer of the globalization idea, came up with the dramatic statement that no two countries that have McDonald's restaurants have ever gone to war with each other – meaning that societies that successfully participate in global consumerism will become much more cautious about belligerence, because they will have other pleasures they seek to protect and a lot to lose. Others, convinced that the global economy and global connections will lead to new wars over access to scarce resources, also assume that globalization brings change, but simply paint an opposite picture of probable impacts.

What tends to get buried in these types of debate is the equally important question about the innovation claims associated with the globalization concept, which is where historians and historical perspectives come in. How new is globalization, compared to previous patterns of contact among societies in different regions of the world? What's the difference between a multinational corporation – one of the bearers of globalization today – and the international corporation of the late 19th century, or indeed the international trading company of the 16th century? No one can contest that contemporary globalization harbors unprecedented features – the Internet is purely and simply new; the capacity for a quarter of the world's population simultaneously to watch that same sports event is purely and simply new. But claims about globalization as a huge departure in the human experience go beyond these narrower examples, and they should depend on a very careful assessment about how the globalization process stacks up against earlier changes in contacts and their results.

Figuring out more explicitly when globalization began is also an essential component of determining what caused it. Some discussions of globalization seem to assume that it dropped out of the sky, with at most a few generalized references to changes in technology. In fact, of course, a variety of very conscious human decisions are involved, for example in determining not only what technologies to use but how local policies are meant to coordinate, or not coordinate, with potential international arrangements on issues such as immigration or foreign investment. Wrapped up in the discussion of the newness of globalization is an analysis of how its timing can be explained. One way to ask about origins, in fact, is to determine the point at which the motivations to accelerate global exchanges became so compelling that further expansion of actual contacts was virtually assured. It's at least possible that attention to causes and motivations will push chronology back a bit, without ignoring the importance of more recent developments, like the Internet, in shaping an additional stage in the globalization process. Root causes, in other words, may predate important but more surface manifestations.

Even the debate about the quality of globalization's effects – the debate about advantages and drawbacks – hinges in part on the assessment of novelty. McDonald's as an international restaurant chain is new, but the sharing of food habits and products across boundaries goes farther back in time (and did not turn out to prevent war). So are McDonald's and contemporary consumerism new enough for us to assume that older human tendencies, like war, will be submerged; or should we be more cautious in these assessments? The same applies to the pessimistic side: recent globalization probably has increased economic inequalities among different parts of the world, but the process of creating regional economic inequalities goes much farther back in time – so are we really heading toward some new kind of global perdition?

We need a more focused historical discussion to help sort this all out.

This said, we must also offer a few confessions about historians and historical study. Historians as a breed tend to love to fuss about origins, sometimes to the point of tediousness. Any study of globalization in historical perspective must talk about origins, entertaining arguments that the effective beginnings of globalization occurred earlier than current theorists posit. But the real point of the analysis is not, in fact, to argue that we have to push globalization's origins a few decades or perhaps a few centuries earlier. Rather, the goal is to use a discussion of globalization's relationship with prior patterns of inter-regional contacts to determine more precisely what is really new about the recent developments, particularly beyond specific technology, and whether the current changes constitute in fact a huge jolt of the unexpected or, rather, an acceleration of experiences to which many societies had already adjusted.

Historians (like most scholars) also like to argue. Thus one group, calling themselves the "new global" historians, urges that recent globalization is indeed a huge change, perhaps one of the greatest in human history. The group tends to opt for a slightly more generous time span than some non-historians prefer, pointing back to the 1950s or so for the onset of the contemporary current. But they're adamant about seeing the phenomenon as a great gulf between present and future conditions, on the one hand, and the bulk of the human past on the other. Indeed, they like to distinguish themselves from world historians, arguing that their "global" history alone captures the uniqueness of recent change instead of burying it in the catalogue of centuries. Against this, though somewhat less fiercely, another cluster of historians has begun to urge that it's the later 19th century, not the later 20th, that should be seen as the true globalization seedbed. Against both, one eminent world historian contends that it's around the year 1000 CE that human history divides between largely separate or regional experiences (before) and increasing contact, imitation, and convergence (after); and if this is true, more recent changes associated with globalization form merely the latest iteration of this basic and long-standing momentum.

Then of course there's a small but vocal contingent who argue that it's not globalization and convergence at all that are shaping our present and future, but an ominous "clash of civilizations" that will pit the West against Islam, with societies emanating from the Confucian tradition possibly a third competitive force. This group, championed by a Harvard political scientist, would not necessarily deny the importance of new contacts and globe-straddling technologies, but it would argue that the looming conflicts override this system in determining what will really affect most people.

Finally, and most recently, an important cluster of books has begun to emerge that really does venture a more systematic historical look at globalization, generally arguing that relevant changes should be seen as emerging in phases (one of the major studies is in fact entitled *The Three Waves of Globalization*). These books have the great merit of moving our vision away from an exclusive focus on essentially contemporary developments, as in the new global history approach. They do tend, however, still to focus primarily on relatively recent change. *The Three Waves*, for example, turn out to be the 1750s, 1850s, and late 20th century. This may involve a neglect of earlier possibilities, as in the argument about the trans-regional network that had emerged in 1000. It also, and in related fashion, tends to focus quite heavily on contributions or burdens brought to the world by purely Western commercial and technological initiatives, whereas a somewhat more open view places greater recognition on Chinese and particularly Islamic innovations. So debate inevitably continues.

This book seeks to add to the slim available literature in several ways: it emphasizes the transcendent importance of globalization, as against the clash of civilizations approach, while recognizing however regional variations and disputes at every point in the process. It picks up on the idea of stages or waves of particularly important changes, but adds greater attention to chronologically earlier precedents; and by the same token it puts Western involvement in a somewhat larger perspective. Finally, as against any single schema, it urges the need for continued debate, for recognition of the complexities in picking any point of origin. It's far more important to see the basic issues involved in assessing what globalization meant in any of its phases, and how it differed from previous phases (particularly, of course, how present changes relate to those before), than insisting on any single formula.

It is of course inevitable that the various existing approaches and debates, like any arguments, have some sterile and nit-picking features. At base, however, they are genuinely important in guiding what kind of past perspective we apply to what's going on today (which in turn is, at base, why history is not only worth studying, but must be studied). Judging the degree of change involved in a major phenomenon such as globalization is a key application of historical analysis, vital to assess the amount of adjustment and dislocation that can be expected. And of course if the clash of civilization doomsayers are right and globalization doesn't head the future agenda after all, it's even more important to apply as much perspective as possible on recent historical trends and their probable relationship to the future. Establishing a historical fix on globalization contributes as well to the thorny questions of costs and benefits, the other established debate which suffers when globalization is pulled away from historical roots.

There's an additional twist here. In my experience, even fairly sophisticated world history students, interested in globalization, don't easily understand the specifics involved in assessing change when such a big phenomenon is involved. I've several times asked my college class when, in light of their work in world history, they would argue that globalization began, and almost always they come back with 1000 CE. This reflects the emphasis I've placed on the acceleration of inter-regional interactions at that time, and it's a perfectly defendable conclusion. But it does not reflect (I fear) an adequate consideration of the options, or really a full understanding of how to measure the magnitudes of changes in a complex subject area like this. So I think a more explicit discussion will be useful, not in deciding the case once and for all but in facilitating more informed discussion and clearer awareness of the empirical and analytical issues. Other audiences can be involved as well, for globalization impinges on far more people than students alone.

This book, then, will consider major changes in global contacts and processes from 1000 CE onward, with particular attention to four major turning points: around 1000, around 1500, around 1850 and of course in recent decades. No one has yet clearly argued for globalization before 1000 (but as we will see there are some diffuse gestures in this direction), though even here there are a few issues to consider and certainly the need to establish a backdrop for the greater complexity in trading and contact patterns thereafter. The goal is to show how globalization in part flows from prior change – to see it as part of a sequence of developments, with some ongoing motives and impacts attached – but also, through the same approach, to highlight features that are demonstrably and significantly novel.

This approach will also open some other kinds of discussion that an all-or-nothing approach to globalization – either dramatically new or old hat – tends to obscure. In the first place, it can help sort out regional experiences. Every serious analyst of globalization, even the most enthusiastic, urges interpretation that recognizes the interaction of the regional and the global. And it's quite clear that different societies have different reactions to globalization, as a whole process and in terms of some of its constituent parts (like immigration, or consumer culture). A more explicitly historical approach shows how these differences develop, and even suggests that some societies formed basic commitments for or against globalization at different points in time. Japan, for example, made key decisions on relationships with the rest of the world after 1868 that have clearly conditioned its responses to the more recent rounds of globalization later in the 20th century. Parts of the Middle East and Africa, in contrast, have probably faced core issues more recently, while China arguably postponed full consideration of globalization until 1978.

The historical approach also assists in disaggregating globalization in terms of its constituent parts, each with a somewhat different historical background. Migration and disease exchanges, for example, are important parts of contemporary globalization, and as such they should be analyzed in terms of how they contribute to change; but as basic processes, they go way back in human history. Global environmental impact (as opposed to more purely regional results of human activity), on the other hand, and global movements to protect the environment, are much newer. Definable global political arrangements (as opposed to more traditional relationships among nations) fall a bit in-between, older than global environmentalism but younger than disease exchange. Looking at globalization as the accumulation of different types of connection helps to focus the relationship of current developments to the past.

For globalization is both an intensification of the range and speed of contacts among different parts of the world and an expansion of the kinds of activity intimately involved in global interactions. Both aspects help explain why global developments play an increasingly active role in shaping human lives, which is the key reason to study the phenomenon in the first place. They explain also why globalization, even if ultimately judged to be a novel force, is not entirely new.

We know most, of course, about the recent manifestations – the Internet use, the speed of jet travel, the global popularity of media stars like Britney Spears. But it was several hundred years ago that many Europeans developed such a passion for a product they could not themselves produce – sugar – that they not only organized new trade routes to obtain it but actually seized both land and slaves in distant places in order to assure its output. It was a century and a half ago that it became apparent that a bank crisis in one place – more often than not, the United States – could topple financial systems in other parts of the world. It was a century ago that a British economist, John Maynard Keynes, noted that "the inhabitant of London could order by telephone, sipping his morning tea, the various products of the whole earth, and reasonably expect their early delivery upon his doorstep," even as the wars in other parts of the world seemed to be "little more than the amusements of his daily newspaper." The question of when globalization began cannot be answered simply on the basis of our knowing more about the present.

Contacts among different societies have increasingly become the key focus in world history scholarship and teaching, for they commonly involve such interesting tensions and attractions and so often produce changes in all the societies involved. Globalization connects this core interest to the present, by forcing analysis not just of specific contact episodes but of how contact patterns built up into durable systems and motivations. Globalization today is partly the result of conscious planning, but it partly reflects the ambitions and daring of many people who knew they wanted to reach out for new goods or new ideas or new conquests without having any idea that what they were doing would some day amount to a new world system. By the same token, explicit resistance to globalization also builds on the past, on earlier efforts to argue that too much contact risked loss of identity and loss of control.

A historic tension

The pull to separate but also the pull to connect both go far back in human history.

Separation resulted from the wide dispersion of human bands, initially a function of the demands of a hunting-and-gathering economy. Hunting-and-gathering groups, usually about 60–80 strong, usually required upward of 200 square miles to operate – depending of course on climate and other conditions. This in itself tended to create substantial open space between one group and the next, which in turn could encourage the development of distinct habits and identities.

Furthermore, the same conditions impelled frequent migration, a pattern that took shape among early human species, well before the advent of *Homo sapiens sapiens*, and then applied to this latest species as well. For every relatively small expansion in population would force some members of a hunting-and-gathering group to move beyond its current territory, to look for additional sources of food. By the time *Homo sapiens sapiens* began to move out of its original home in east Africa, dispersion through migration developed quite quickly, as the species moved not only to other parts of Africa, but to the Middle East and thence to other parts of Asia and Europe, to Australia (using a land shelf extending from southeast Asia, that has long since been submerged but that for a time allowed a relatively small journey over water), and (by 25,000 BCE) across the then-existing land bridge between Siberia and Alaska and surprisingly rapidly thence to other parts of the Americas. By 10,000 BCE, before the advent of agriculture, the roughly 10 million people in the world had populated virtually all inhabitable areas. Several Pacific islands still lay vacant, including Hawaii, New Zealand was untouched, and Bermuda would not be discovered until European voyages in the early modern centuries. But there were small bands of people almost everywhere else. This meant, obviously, that huge distances began to separate different groups. A few, like the Aborigines of Australia, would be cut off entirely from other population centers until modern times. Others were less isolated, but might easily find contacts with people outside a specific region unusual and possibly threatening.

The isolation point should not, of course, be overdrawn. Few small hunting-and-gathering bands were entirely separated from larger regional networks. While local languages might develop (there used to be far more different languages in the world than there are today), most of them related to larger language groups, like Bantu, or Indo-European, which in turn meant that communication among many groups was not forbiddingly difficult. Within a single region, certain hunting bands might regularly come into contact for purposes of self-defense (or aggression), mate selection, or other social and trading purposes.

It remains true, however, that it is not entirely inaccurate to emphasize the decisive quality of dispersion and differentiation of the world's human population on the eve of agriculture. Sheer distance was challenge enough, in the long centuries when people could move about only on foot (even granting the superior walking ability of earlier humans, compared to their contemporary counterparts), or on crude boats. But distance also combined with dramatically different habits, localized religions, and linguistic patterns to make contact and communication extremely difficult, often promoting proudly separate small-group identities and no small fear of strangers. Larger contact networks – even far short of globalization – would have to contend against these localizing factors.

In certain ways, agriculture could make aspects of these localizing tendencies even worse, for it tied groups not just to a general locality but to very specific property, often an individual village. Hunters and gatherers, after all, had to move around at least within a circumscribed region, which could facilitate impulses toward wider migration. Agricultural villagers, in contrast, were often linked to specific properties passed from one generation to the next through inheritance and a family cottage. Deep cultural attachments to particular villages could readily develop, making even the next village down the road slightly suspect, and strangers from greater distances truly ominous. Of course some villagers traveled at least a bit, in order to market some goods or seek temporary employment elsewhere; and when crowding impinged, some would move away altogether. It's important not to overdo the local parameters. It remains true, even in the present day with buses and other modern amenities facilitating travel, that some villagers (often, particularly women) rarely if ever get more than a few miles from their home turf, seeing no purpose and possibly some real threat in exploring further.

Scattered populations and highly regional habits and cultures could thus be confirmed by the advent of agriculture. It would take much time and effort to build regular contact networks simply within larger regions (like China's ultimately fabled Middle Kingdom, or India's subcontinent), not to mention inter-regional connections. World history, in a real sense, began on a local level, and even today has not entirely escaped these confines.

On the other hand, reasons for wider contacts existed early as well, and at least some individuals pursued them even before we have any clear record of how they moved around. At the most basic level: local isolation never introduced so many genetic modifications within the species *Homo sapiens sapiens* that interbreeding could not occur, as happened with so many other species that were far more locally defined.

The most obvious lure to pull people away from purely regional interactions involved goods that could only be obtained through more distant ventures. Rare decorative materials might be a lure, like gold or precious stones. The advent of the use of bronze, after 4000 BCE, forced considerable travel in search of tin, one of the key alloys of this composite metal. People in the Middle East ventured into Afghanistan and possibly as far as Britain to seek regular supplies. Soon also, knowledge of valuable spices that could only be obtained from certain localities drove considerable long-distance trade. Once it was established that goods of this sort were worth the risk and cost of travel, other specializations could develop, including ultimately manufactured goods based on the traditions and ecologies of particular regions, which would expand this motivation still further.

Contact could also generate knowledge of food products that might be imported to the benefit of local populations. We know that somehow foods native to parts of southeast Asia (bananas and coconuts) were brought to Africa very early in the agricultural phase of human history, and once planted in Africa they became vital food staples. Similar kinds of benefit could result from learning about, and exporting, domesticated animals. China's knowledge of horses, and for a considerable time an ongoing source of supply, came from contacts with Central Asia; a southeast Asian pig was brought to Madagascar. The opportunity to learn about basic goods, beyond trade items, could easily spur a quest for wider ventures.

Ultimately, it became obvious also that other kinds of learning could result from long-distance ventures, when particular regions became known for particular kinds of cultural strength. It's hard to pinpoint when student and scholarly travel began – and patterns would long involve only a few individuals, not larger cohorts – but Greeks were visiting Egypt to learn about mathematics early in Greek history, and it was not too long after that when individuals from places like China began to go to India to seek Buddhist wisdom. Knowledge, in other words, added to trade and products in motivating outreach.

Harder to calculate, but attached to these more specific spurs, could be simply a quest for adventure and new experiences, without a precise calculus of what social or personal gains would result. The confines of life in villages or even early agricultural cities could seem limited, sometimes even stifling, and a few individuals undoubtedly looked to wider horizons for personal reasons. Details here are hard to come by, for almost none of the most ambitious early travelers left any record of their motivations. We know, for example, that a Phoenician named Hanno, with a crew, sailed through the Mediterranean and down the first part of Africa's Atlantic coast to Sierra

Leone and possibly as far as Nigeria – but we don't know why he did it, and what kind of personality would push him into what, for him, must have been the real unknown. The fact that fanciful beliefs developed about many less familiar parts of the world, populating them with mythical beasts and bizarre human habits, might convince many people that it was best to stick close to home, but it might also have challenged a few to go out and see for themselves.

Finally, of course, purely local conditions could generate pressures to reach beyond conventional confines. Population crowding, exhaustion of local resources, and military ambitions could push groups into patterns of migration or invasion that, in some instances, could move them considerable distances and produce a host of new (and often unwelcome) contacts for local populations. Nomadic herdsmen, from places like central Asia, were often the sources of these new connections, spilling over into incursions into the Middle East, India, China or Europe, as with the movement of Indo-European peoples into India and the Mediterranean before about 1200 BCE or, a bit later, the surge of Slavic migrations into Russia and east central Europe. These migrants might ultimately settle down, but for at least a considerable time they would challenge existing cultural and political conditions and provide new linkages with more distant regions.

Early contacts, whether for trade or scholarly discovery or adventure, could easily begin to trigger other changes, which in turn would encourage additional ventures to reach beyond the locality and region. This further process developed slowly, however, as so many people were enmeshed in local concerns that the motives and benefits of more extensive ventures were dauntingly out of reach.

It remains true that a real pull to develop some connections among relatively far-flung parts of the world emerged early on, and it recurrently tugged against the dispersion and localism of the initial world history framework. Neither the motivations nor the institutions or technologies existed to create a truly global outreach through the initial millennia of human development, but they could certainly produce experimentation and change. Localism long predominated, but not without recurring and sometimes productive tensions with people who saw benefits from wider horizons.

Further reading

http://en.wikipedia.org/wiki/Globalization

Appadurai, Arjun, ed. *The Social Life of Things: Commodities in Cultural Perspective* (Cambridge: Cambridge University Press, 1986).

Chase-Dunn, Christopher and Anderson, Eugene N., eds. *The Historical Evolution of World Systems* (New York: Palgrave Macmillan, 2004).

Curtin, Philip D. *Cross-Cultural Trade in World History* (Cambridge: Cambridge University Press, 1984).

Denemark, Robert A., Friedman, J., Gills, B.K. and Modelski, G., eds. *World System History: The Social Science of Long Term Change* (London: Routledge, 2000).

Frank, Andre Gunder and Gills, Barry K., eds. *The World System: Five Hundred Years or Five Thousand?* (London: Routledge, 1993).

Friedman, Thomas, L. *The Lexus and the Olive Tree: Understanding Globalization* (New York: Farrar, Straus and Giroux, 2000).

Hopkins, A.G., ed. *Globalization in World History* (New York: W.W. Norton and Company, 2002).

Huntington, Samuel. *The Clash of Civilizations?: The Debate* (New York: Foreign Affairs, 1996).

Mazlish, Bruce. *The Idea of Humanity in a Global Era* (New York: Palgrave Macmillan, 2008).

Mazlish, Bruce. *The New Global History* (New York: Routledge, 2006).

Osterhammel, Jürgen, Petersson, Niels P. and Geyer, Dona, eds. *Globalization: A Short History* (Princeton: Princeton University Press, 2005).

Robertson, Robbie. *The Three Waves of Globalization: A History of a Developing Global Consciousness* (London: Zed Books Ltd., 2003).

Robertson, Roland. *Globalization: Social Theory and Global Structures* (Newbury Park, CA: Sage Publications, 1992).

Chapter 2

Emerging patterns of contact, 1200 BCE – 1000 CE

A preparatory phase

Historians do enjoy finding evidence that crucial aspects of the human experience started earlier than we once thought, as noted in the previous chapter. This is part of their effort to elucidate the past and to bring it alive by making it unexpectedly relevant to more recent interests. Thus historians of medieval Europe, intrigued by the popularity of the Renaissance, long ago began to find "renaissances" in the 12th century. Interests in the origins of the kind of romantic love that so clearly began to blossom in the 19th century led some scholars to uncover it back in the later Middle Ages with the love poems of the troubadours, and even more systematically to locate it in the 18th century rather than a hundred years later. Modern mass consumerism, once thought to be a product of the Industrial Revolution later in the 19th century, turns out to have started in Europe in the 17th–18th centuries, well before industrialization, and now historians are discovering consumer revolutions as early as the 14th century. The sexual revolution hailed or lamented in the 1960s turns out to have started in the 1940s and 1950s – and so it goes on. The list of revisions of initial statements of origin, in the history of virtually every topic and every region, is a long one. Sometimes the resulting findings are superficial or debatable; sometimes (as with consumerism) they seriously reorient the ways we think about the past and about the causation of major change.

It's not hard, of course, to figure out when certain kinds of historical development start, like wars or reigns or presidencies. But the really important aspects of the past usually have more to do with trends, patterns and processes than with discrete events. Globalization is clearly a process, early inter-regional contacts form patterns. It's not easy to date their effective origins decisively. It does in fact often turn out that key developments start earlier than scholars first expect, earlier in fact than people noticed at the time. (For example, while people involved in the Industrial Revolution knew that something was changing, the actual label that defined change – the term "industrial revolution" – emerged only in the 1870s, a full century after the process began.) On the other hand, the impulse to find origins may sometimes tempt zealous historians to argue for beginnings that are more apparent than real.

This chapter juggles the first set of issues in the effort to put globalization into historical perspective: the distinction between undeniable and interesting inter-regional contacts emerging early in the agricultural phase of human history, and the fact that these contacts cannot be construed, by any plausible stretch of the imagination, as constituting a preliminary form of globalization. If we push globalization back to the first emergence of regular trading patterns, we risk losing all meaning – and that's the case with developments up to about 1000 CE. There were, however, some important precedents and motivations that can be identified as a backdrop to a more decisive set of changes in human contacts, and these form the focus of this chapter.

World historians, with their deep and growing interest in contacts, have devoted creative energies to uncovering and highlighting trade and other connections relatively early in human history. One result is the wide awareness of the so-called Silk Road (more properly, Roads) and the fascination with the exchanges and trade centers that formed its core. Indeed, the Silk Road has probably won too much attention, to the detriment of an awareness of other, arguably equally important, contact routes well before modern times. Not surprisingly, a few historians have gone on to argue that these early exchanges became so entrenched that they virtually guaranteed further and intensifying contacts later on. If this means that at least a brief survey of early patterns forms an important part of the backdrop to more in-depth analysis of globalization in historical perspective, then the implication is clearly valid. Indeed, some online definitions of globalization refer to entities like the Roman Empire or the Parthian Empire as globalization precedents, though usually without much elaboration. If the implication is designed to claim some early version of globalization before about 1000 CE, it is misplaced and in fact confusing.

The big contact challenge for most regions before 1000 CE, amid pervasive localism, was to build networks *within* larger regions – like the Mediterranean basin or the Middle East – that would facilitate trade and cultural and political exchange. Efforts to reach beyond the larger regions, though they did exist, had only passing significance for the vast majority of the human population. The trick is to sketch the intriguing connections and discuss their bearing on longer-term developments without so eroding an understanding of later, more decisive changes that globalization becomes a process virtually coterminous with the whole human experience. A case can be made that globalization was becoming inevitable by 1000 CE (though the case raises serious objections), but not before. Indeed, a key reason to sketch patterns previously is to provide a backdrop against which to measure later change, not to encourage a premature identification of globalization.

Types of early interaction

Migrations were surely the earliest human encounter with long distances. Undoubtedly, most migrating groups initially moved just a few dozen miles away from their place of origin, and the long distances were achieved over time as a result of movement by many successive generations. There were, however, examples of apparently rapid moves over many hundreds of miles. It seems likely that some groups of Native Americans migrated swiftly down the Pacific coast, from the Siberia–Alaska land bridge and the American northwest, by using coastal vessels, reaching various parts of South America. Even long-distance migration, however, did not set up structures of exchange. They brought people to new places and sometimes mixed different groups of people, but the migrants did not usually return – so no durable patterns of regional reaction developed beyond encounters between residents and migrants on the spot.

In contrast, trade, over any appreciable distance, whether for gift exchange or for profit, did bring back and forth interactions. It is not entirely clear when trade emerged, beyond purely local contacts. Sea shells from the Indian Ocean reached Syria by about 5000 BCE, probably constituting a gift exchange of ornamentation and obviously suggesting some movement across the Middle East from one coast to another – but we don't know whether this was a regular interaction or even whether any group or individual made the entire trip or whether the shells passed gradually from one locality to the next. Trade over a hundred to two-hundred miles also developed, for example in east central Europe (in present-day terms, from Hungary to Poland), not only for precious stones but for materials like flint, important in making early tools and weapons. The most venturesome early trade may have developed among peoples in southeast Asia, for example in some of the islands of present-day Indonesia, where boats developed capable of navigating in sections of the Indian Ocean. Primitive shipping also developed in the Persian Gulf region by at least 4000 BCE, with efforts to take advantage of favorable winds during certain months of the year to reach India and then return. Some of these Asian initiatives must have reached the east coast of Africa, explaining the crop exchange between the two regions. Boats probably initially served the interests of fishermen, but gradually their functions expanded, along with some improvements in design that moved away from the simple dugout canoes that first served seagoing efforts.

Crucial developments in the emergence of overland trade (including transshipments of goods initially brought by sea, for example from Indian Ocean ports in the Persian Gulf inland to the rest of the Middle East) involved the domestication of pack animals. Donkeys were domesticated by the 3rd millennium BCE, presumably in their west Asian place of origin. They spread widely to other societies. Their capacity to carry relatively heavy loads over long distances, though slowly and sometimes reluctantly, was a crucial advance for land-based travel. For certain regions, both in Asia and in Africa, the domestication of the camel had similar significance. These were humble advances, compared to the later technologies of globalization, but they greatly furthered connections among adjacent regions.

Several of the early river valley civilizations developed inter-regional trade. Mesopotamia, at the mouths of the Tigris and Euphrates rivers, exchanged with Harappan society in northwestern India (today Pakistan). Not only goods, but artistic symbols were part of this exchange, and there may have been cross-fertilization in religious ideas as well. Egypt began to launch shipping in the Red Sea by 2500 BCE, reaching the Arabian Peninsula (present-day Yemen) and also farther down the Indian Ocean coast of Africa. Egyptians received gold, ivory and slaves from Ethiopia, in exchange for manufactured goods. Trade with the Middle East emphasized spices, some of which had been shipped over from India. Here was an example of somewhat longer-distance trade that did not however involve direct connections; that is, it operated in shorter inter-regional hops rather than direct contact, in this case between Egypt and India. Several centers in the Persian Gulf, notably a center called Dilmun (present-day Bahrain), also served as transmission hubs for goods, such as precious stones, produced elsewhere. By the 2nd millennium BCE, a trading ship in the Mediterranean might carry goods from sub-Saharan Africa and northern Europe, as well as the Middle East or India, showing the range of contacts that sustained a lively commerce.

Trade also began to show up as a literary subject. The first-known epic poem, the Babylonian *Gilgamesh*, involves a travel theme. A ruler travels from Sumer, which is largely treeless, hundreds of miles to the interior seeking timber for his palace (the timber would then be floated downriver), and of course encounters many adventures in the process. The early Hindu holy book, the *Rig Veda* of the 2nd millennium BCE, features a story about pirates attacking an Indian merchant ship in the Persian Gulf, with Indian rulers sending armed vessels to retaliate against the pirates. Clearly, the excitement of contact caught attention early, and stories of this sort might stimulate other would-be adventurers.

These early ventures had some obvious limitations. For the most part, they operated between two neighboring regions, rather than over longer distances. (References however do exist to three-year expeditions, presumably all the way across the Indian Ocean and back.) Even the ventures between regional neighbors were also often interrupted. Migrations and invasions into the Middle East and India, for example, dried up seagoing initiatives around 2000 BCE for a considerable period of time – the newcomers, though triumphant over locals militarily, simply did not know how to run the more ambitious commercial operations. One particularly interesting initiative had a different fate: southeast Asians, with their superior shipping technology, were able to sail into the Pacific, reaching and populating some of the island groups of Pacific Oceania. But the connections were not maintained, and a separate Polynesian culture began to develop without any further linkage with its Asian progenitor or with the many technological and agricultural advances that began to occur in Asia itself. A more routine barrier resulted from prescriptive competition: not surprisingly, some of the people involved in trade worked actively to discourage others from joining in. Arab merchants who brought spices like cinnamon to Egypt in ships or overland caravans tried to convince the Egyptians that they did not know where the spices came from, or that they were dropped in the mountains by giant fearsome birds and that they could be obtained only by doing battle with dragons. Ruses of this sort formed another limit on regular trading activities. Finally, since goods were often trans-shipped rather than carried directly from production to use, a great deal of confusion existed about the actual sources of goods. Many Mesopotamians believed that items came from Dilmun that were actually produced in India, and there were many other similar misidentifications – reflecting real limits on effective contact and knowledge even amid significant inter-regional commerce.

Evaluations of merchants also suggest interesting hesitations about commercially based contacts. On the one hand, merchants were vital to the exchange process; on the other hand, many societies distrusted them, because of their profit motives and because they seemed to differ from the high-prestige aristocrats and state officials. One result, for example in early Greece, was a heavy reliance on foreigners to carry on the dirty business of commerce. But foreignness might simply increase the stigma involved, and sometimes suggested real danger in too much reliance on contacts outside one's own society. An Indian political handbook in the 4th century urged that trade should be promoted in order for rulers to earn tax revenues and acquire materials for war, but also starkly insisted: "Merchants ... are all thieves, in effect, if not in name; they should be prevented from oppressing the people." Ambivalences of this sort did not stop inter-regional exchange, but they suggested reactions that might constrain the whole process. Correspondingly, most cities in early civilizations were in fact centers for political and religious activities, with largely local trade and dependent on taxing peasants; only a few urban areas really focused on the longer-distance commercial opportunities.

It is true, of course, that some of the unevenness and hesitation over inter-regional contacts still apply to globalization today: tension between local identity and self-sufficiency, on the one hand, and wider outreach on the other builds on issues that emerged quite early on. But limitations were far more marked in the early periods than today, and the impact of the contacts that did develop was measurably less great in all but a few trading centers than would prove characteristic later.

One result of the narrow base and oscillation in inter-regional outreach was the fact that some really promising projects had surprisingly little impact. For example, the famous Greek traveler Herodotus reported that a Phoenician explorer deliberately went around the whole continent of Africa, with the sponsorship of an Egyptian pharaoh, to see if it was surrounded by water – the venture took two years. We cannot be sure if this actually occurred, but it would certainly have been feasible, and marks exactly the kind of initiative that one would expect of seafaring leaders like the Phoenicians – and exactly the kind of initiative that could have led to a permanent advance in Asian–African communications. But if it did occur there was no real result. No one else would venture around Africa until 1498 CE, which meant that African links with other parts of the world, though very important in the Indian Ocean and across the Sahara, were needlessly limited. Similarly, Phoenician expeditions into the south Atlantic, reaching the Canaries and Azores island groups, had no aftermath, as these islands were subsequently isolated from any contact for another 2,500 years.

On the other hand, the early patterns of inter-regional trading did begin to establish the kinds of motivation for at least medium-distance exchange that would sustain more ambitious and consistent efforts later on. Various groups developed a real stake in access to goods that could not be produced locally. Spices are obviously a core example; they not only enlivened foods (in societies where variety and freshness of food constituted real challenges), but they also contributed to other vital activities – cinnamon, for example, was used in Egyptian preparations for embalming the dead. Various kinds of consumers and producers, in other words, sustained this kind of trade even if they might not always have been aware of the inter-regional contacts involved. Not only goods, but other novelties attracted attention. Urban crowds in Mesopotamia, for example, could enjoy elephants and apes brought in from Africa – one poem wrote of "beasts from distant lands jostling in the great square"; and the role of exotic animals in motivating interest in exchanges would be a sustaining factor from this point onward. Governments and merchants had stakes as well, and they were quite conscious of the external involvement. Merchants could obviously win profits from distant trade. By the 3rd millennium, clusters of foreign merchants located in key cities, for example in the northern Middle East, were obviously both reflecting and encouraging awareness of the importance of commerce beyond the single society. Some merchant associations developed to help regulate inter-regional trade, for example to handle issues like the exchange of payments but also to help assure ethical standards. Governments played a vital role as well, working to stimulate trade but also developing a clear interest in assuring and, where possible, expanding its reach. They acted not only because of their own interest in diversifying available goods, in some cases including materials vital in the production of weapons, but also because of the taxes they could levy on shipping and trade caravans. Egyptian rulers, for example, were quite aware of the advantages Egypt gained from its access to the Indian Ocean and were eager to make sure that no other society unduly interfered or competed. It's even been argued that the Greek conflict with Persia, a bit later on, was less a clash of civilizations or a quarrel over landed territory, but more a function of Greek reluctance to accept Persian ability to cut off Greek contact with the Indian Ocean and its commercial riches. Motives of this sort, and their variety, suggest how trade-based contacts in early agricultural societies both reflected and furthered the kinds of thinking that would feed later, more elaborate inter-regional connections, ultimately including globalization itself.

The classical era

The advent of the great classical civilizations, from 1000 BCE or so onward, raises an obvious complication in even a summary analysis of the initial historical backdrops to globalization. The major civilizations now began to stretch over a large territory. In China during the Han dynasty, for example, it took forty days to travel from the capital to the most far-flung provinces, even on the relatively good roads the state now provided. Not surprisingly, the bulk of the energies of various leaders – not just emperors, but also venturesome merchants and cultural emissaries – went into developing internal networks that would take advantage of this new territory and work to integrate it into a (somewhat) coherent whole. Chinese leaders, for example, worked very hard to link north and south China, building canals to facilitate trade, sending colonists from the north to the south, and promoting use of a single language, Mandarin, at least in the governing class – despite or in fact because of the multiplicity of ethnic groups, languages and cultures of the mixture of peoples that now made up the Chinese empire. All the classical empires fostered cultural systems – like Hinduism and Buddhism in India, and Greek-derived architecture around the Mediterranean – that would provide new links, not necessarily attacking more local systems but seeking to supplement them with more overarching styles and values. Trading activities sought to take advantage of local specializations – like grain growing in north Africa in exchange for wines and olive oil from Italy and Greece – to promote greater efficiency and prosperity (and tax revenues) and in the process create a more coherent overall economy. Common social systems spread out, like patterns of slavery in the Mediterranean or the caste system in India, giving another linking device. Finally, periodically at least, outright empires sought to provide political unity to all or at least major parts of the chief civilization areas.

These efforts were quite successful for many centuries, and in some cases, particularly India and China, they created durable values and institutions that would provide internal coherence and distinction from other major societies for many centuries, well past the classical period itself and into our own day. Not surprisingly, the efforts took a great deal of energy and focus, and could distract from the comparable interest in reaching outside the new civilization areas. Indeed, to the extent that integration efforts promoted core identities for many people, they could actually discourage wider contact and breed disdain for societies and regions outside the home base. Greeks and Chinese both began to refer to peoples outside their own expanding orbits as barbarians, clearly inferior and worth little or no attention when there were so many exciting opportunities at home.

At the same time, however, the classical civilizations also advanced a more ambitious inter-regional agenda in several ways, even though the agenda never gained top priority. In the first place, the new empires brought in territories that had not previously been regular parts of the patterns of exchange. The Roman Empire, for example, building around the entire Mediterranean basin, now involved the whole of north Africa in regular contacts with southern Europe and the Middle East. Phoenician contacts had launched this inclusion, but the new Roman Empire made it an established fact. North African regions periodically broke off from larger political units – for example, from the later Arab Caliphate – but they would from this point onward always be economically and culturally linked at least to the Middle East. Rome's empire similarly involved new parts of Europe, such as France, in extensive trade and cultural exchange. Each of the classical civilizations was regional, but the region was now writ large, so that internal contacts already constituted a significant reduction of local isolation. This is why the creation of the great classical empires sometimes gets mentioned as a historical precedent for globalization.

There was even some tourism within the empires, beyond adventurers out on their own. Some Romans began to travel to Greece and Egypt, and occasionally into the Middle East, to see famous sights. The idea of "Seven Wonders of the World," like the Egyptian sphinx, originated in the classical period and helped spur travel for pleasure within the Mediterranean–Middle Eastern regions – another sign of the importance and widening reach of contacts within the huge territories now seen as part of a coherent whole.

Furthermore, the empires created an infrastructure that could facilitate even wider outreach by making trade and travel easier than ever before. Particularly important here were developments in the Persian Empire and its later successors, given the geographic centrality of this region to potential contacts between Indian Ocean and Mediterranean networks. With conquests beginning in 556 BCE, the empire itself achieved great size at least for a century, stretching from northeastern India (the Indus river region) to Egypt and Libya and the Mediterranean, though efforts to move significantly into Europe, or further south into northeastern Africa, failed. Exchanges stretched even more broadly, as Persian rulers at their height received gifts from sub-Saharan Africa (including elephant tusks), India and southern Arabia. The imperial government built an impressive system of highways, stretching over 8,000 miles. The great emperor Cyrus also established a series of carefully spaced inns, to house merchants and travelers on their journeys, with water reservoirs, and he set up the world's first postal and message service. A Greek later described the result: "With you [Persians], every way is easy, every river is crossable, and there is no dearth of provisions." The main purpose of all of this, of course, was to facilitate communication and trade within the empire – including the movement of military forces; as with the other classical civilizations, knitting the new, vast territory together and keeping it together was a challenging task. But the same systems could help merchants and visitors from other regions moving through the territory; more than ever before, the Middle East, including Persia, became an entrepôt for exchanges between east and west, a central point in interactions between much of Asia and key parts of Europe and north Africa. While the Persian Empire itself had a relatively brief life span, its systems were preserved or revived by later rulers and regimes – including Alexander the Great, the revived Persian regime under the Parthians, and subsequent Arab caliphs.

Similar developments took place in the Roman and Chinese empires. Chinese emperors began to build highways, at some points fifty feet wide, with trees planted alongside for aesthetic reasons. An official described the result as early as 178 BCE, noting that roads went "all over the empire ... around lakes and rivers, and along the coasts of seas, so that all was made accessible." By the time of the Han dynasty 22,000 miles of highway were available in China, providing internal linkages but also facilitating travel to the west, toward central Asia. A postal system was also operative, with fresh horses for messengers every ten miles. Rome constructed even more roads – 48,000 miles worth – and also invested heavily in seaports along the Mediterranean, particularly for the shipment of grain.

Finally, though building on internal infrastructures for overland travel but also the seaports in both the Indian Ocean and the Mediterranean, classical civilizations extended contacts with each other, which is the achievement world historians have picked up on particularly in their legitimate eagerness to show the early origins of inter-societal contacts.

The most famous linkage was the so-called Silk Road, which at its height brought products from China to the upper classes of the Roman Empire – and also to elites in Persia and the Middle East and in India. Exchange of silk from China westward began as a result of growing contacts and tensions with nomadic peoples in western China and central Asia. Chinese officials and merchants began to bring silk cloth beyond the country's borders as gifts to conciliate potential invaders, but above all in exchange for horses, called "heavenly horses" because of their superior qualities, which had a huge impact on the Chinese military and on Chinese imagination more generally. Ultimately the Chinese also imported alfalfa seeds, which allowed them a better agricultural base for sustaining the horses they were coming to depend on.

But for world history, the main point was the movement of Chinese manufacturing output toward other regions, stimulating not only new forms of trade but new tastes which could sustain international commerce for centuries to come. Nomadic leaders used the Chinese-exported silks for their own adornment and that of their families, but they simply could not consume all that the Chinese provided, so they began to pass the products west. Small amounts of silk reached the Middle East and even southeastern

Europe by the 6th century BCE, but significant exchange developed only in the 1st century BCE. Nomadic traders began to take Chinese products, headed by silk, and move them through several overland routes through central Asia and then into Persia, where other merchants would pick up the loads and use the excellent road network to distribute the goods more widely – with some of them reaching the Mediterranean where other merchants might buy them for sale to north Africa and southern Europe. Tastes for silk goods clearly expanded among upper-class men and women alike, with silk sashes adorning Roman togas and silk banners highlighting Persian military units. This was, in other words, a significant trade from the 1st century BCE until the political and economic deterioration of Han China and the Roman Empire. Not only did silk move westward, but obviously exchange depended on some two-way traffic that would repay the merchants for their trouble and ultimately provide value for Chinese producers as well; from the Middle East and the Mediterranean came various precious stones, "the eggs of great birds" (probably ostriches), manufactured carpets, furs, and even entertainers, as well as the horses the Chinese cherished so greatly.

Silk Road trade linked east Asia with other parts of the continent and with Europe for the first time, a major step beyond the more limited exchanges that had described inter-regional contacts previously. At the same time, however, the trade proceeded mainly through regional hops, of a few hundred miles each with re-exchange at several points, rather than by means of direct exchange from producing to consuming regions. In a larger sense, the Silk Road routes built on regional systems that had long connected northwest India (today's Afghanistan and Pakistan) to Persia and the Middle East, and China to central Asia. It was also true that (central Asian horses aside) the exchange goods that came into China were not as sought after, not as capable of developing new consumer tastes, as silk was in Persia and the Roman Empire; they tended to be seen as novelty items rather than staple luxuries. Indeed, the Romans, who wrote widely about the importance of silk, did not have a very systematic sense of what they could export in return. This imbalance between China and other parts of the world would long complicate long-distance trade, and it certainly constrained activity during the classical period itself.

Another set of routes served, like the Silk Road, to link different parts of Asia, Africa and Europe over long distances, with new merchant activity and new consumer tastes integral to the process. In this case, however, the sea – the Indian Ocean – rather than land served as vehicle, and India, rather than China, was the key player. Southeast Asia – what is now Malaysia, Vietnam, and Indonesia – was heavily involved in this network as well, providing products and merchants alike.

The quality of ships gradually improved by the 1st millennium BCE, though boats made from leather, papyrus and other materials continued to operate in parts of the Indian Ocean. Navigators from Sri Lanka apparently learned how to use birds, taking them on voyages and releasing the creatures so that they could follow them to land. Chinese invention of the rudder would ultimately facilitate sea trade in a more systematic fashion. Sailors learned how to use monsoon winds to help move through various parts of the Indian Ocean in appropriate seasons. A host of people were involved in trade: Arabs, Egyptians, Greeks, and Malays, as well as Indians and Chinese.

Spices constituted the core of the Indian Ocean trade. Chinese merchants sought cloves and similar items from southeast Asia and India, moving both overland and from the Pacific coast into Indian waters. Pepper, produced in India proper, became a crucial product. Greeks used it, partly for medicinal purposes, and it became a vital cooking item during the Roman Empire. Spices, incense, pearls and other materials from east Africa and the Arabian Peninsula blended into this trade as well, including African items like rhinoceros horn. Manufactured products gained attention. Indian cotton cloth won popularity, though the Roman Empire ultimately banned it because of its competition with woolen and linen fabrics. India also became another transit point for silks imported overland from China. The Chinese also had contacts with India by sea, at one point sending an expedition to buy a rhinoceros for the emperor's private zoo.

From the Mediterranean world, both merchants and government officials worked actively to promote these valuable exchanges, particularly by the time of the Roman Empire. Regular fleets set sail from the Red Sea coast of Egypt – upward of 120 boats, complete with Roman archers to help repel pirates; and colonies of Roman merchants formed in several Indian cities. Roman ships (staffed mainly by Greeks and Middle Easterners) also traded regularly with Sri Lanka and the Middle East, again from the Egyptian coast. From the Red Sea, goods were offloaded onto camels, which would carry them to the Nile and thence to the port of Alexandria, where they could enter standard Mediterranean trade. Romans, for their part, were able to put more items into this network than was true for the Silk Road, because ships could carry heavier goods. Thus Roman tin was sent to India, along with linen cloth made in Egypt and other products. Wine was particularly important, probably the most valued Mediterranean item in play. But even with this, the Romans faced a constant balance-of-payments challenge, because the commodities they wanted from Asia exceeded Asian interest in what they had to offer. Gold shipments were essential to correct the imbalance, and Roman observers worried that too much of their wealth was being siphoned off as a result.

Exchanges within southeast Asia also linked into the Indian Ocean network, often brokered by merchants from Malaysia or Indonesia. Inter-regional trade was not new in this area, but the growing links with Indian and Chinese systems gave it greater resonance. Raw materials were involved, including a number of fine woods native to the region and esteemed for their decorative qualities. But manufactured items were important as well, and some were now deliberately adapted to fit into long-distance commerce. Producers in Indonesia or Cambodia, for example, developed lower-cost incense candles or skin treatments, to compete with goods from the Middle East and the Mediterranean, particularly in Chinese markets. India exported to Vietnam cotton cloth, pepper, but also glass products and gold coins made in the Roman Empire; the Chinese sent maritime expeditions down the Vietnamese coast looking for a route to India. The Chinese also had an active interest in unusual animals, such as elephants, from the region. And again, regional products, including spices such as nutmeg, exchanged with Indian or Persian merchants, could make it all the way back to Mediterranean consumers.

Local and regional constraints

All of this has strong overtones of characteristics seen in economic globalization, though of course only parts of three continents, not all six inhabited continents, were involved. Consumers, though primarily wealthy ones, unquestionably developed tastes for goods that could only be brought in from a long distance. Clear trade routes were established, overland between east Asia and Europe, and by sea from China's Pacific Coast to the Middle East and east Africa (and by overland extension, the Mediterranean) that would often be used later on – the Silk Road, for example, crops up again in the Mongol period, and Indian Ocean connections remain vital to the present day. Merchants and key rulers alike knew that inter-regional commerce could pay off in profits, tribute and taxes, and their experience and motivations could easily carry forward into later periods. Small wonder that some historians, writing of the unexpected richness and variety of inter-regional trade by the early centuries CE, claim a virtually uninterrupted progress from these patterns, to the kinds of trade that would branch out in the 15th century, to even more recent connections – in essence, arguing for the origins of globalization in developments more than 2,000 years ago. There is no question that, centered of course in trade, some key habits and specific connections and processes were established by the time of the classical empires that would build into the global world we know today.

Setting a foundation, however, is not the same thing as launching the process. A number of limitations described even the most ambitious inter-regional enterprises, and these limitations must pull back from any premature globalization claim. In the first place, though this point is hard to establish with any precision, the range and excitement of the far-flung merchants should not distract from the fact that the bulk of social energies and imagination, even in the merchant class, continued to go into local and regional activities. Far more people were involved in building networks within the great empires than ventured into connections among major societies. And the key achievement of the classical period was the construction of new regional civilizations, above more purely local attachments – not the narrower bridges among these civilizations.

The links that did develop, furthermore, centered for the most part on interesting, certainly valued, but fairly superficial luxury products. Heavy materials, goods used by large numbers of people for basic activities, moved within regions or occasionally from one region to a neighbor – like the timber brought several hundred miles from the interior to the Mesopotamian coast – but not commonly in inter-regional trade. Expensive cloth – not the stuff of most people's clothing, or daily wear – spices, and a few other decorative items clearly helped develop new tastes but hardly worked into the essentials of life. A few substances did become part of wider rituals or consumer interests – like the spices used in Egyptian embalming, or the Roman tin imported in India, but they were the exception, not the rule.

Trade was, of course, the centerpiece of the interconnections, and while arguably this remains true with globalization, the narrowness of the trade impact in the earlier period was noteworthy. Technological exchange, for example, did not follow as clearly from commercial contact as might be expected. Chinese advances during the classical period, like the invention of paper, simply did not yet spill over to other societies, despite the expansion of access to Chinese products and commerce. The same applies to cultures and cultural apparatus. Extensive trade with India did not lead any other society, at this point, to realize the superiority of the Indian numbering system; separate numbering procedures, like the cumbersome numerals of the Roman Empire, continued to prevail. Religions and philosophical systems remained localized for the most part, spreading within the new civilizations but not much beyond them. Artistic influences were similarly limited, aside from some specific imitation of a few designs. Artists in northwestern India copied Greek styles for a brief period after Alexander the Great's conquests brought Greek rule to the region – the results were pictures of the Buddha dressed in Greek hair arrangements and costumes, for a little over a century – but there was no durable result, no real combining of styles. A few exceptions can of course be noted – Middle Easterners picked up some Indian stories that later became part of popular literature, and the game that ultimately turned into chess spread from India to the Middle East – but for the most part the range of interactions that we associate with globalization simply had yet to develop.

Inter-regional knowledge was also limited, even where products moved over great distances. The absence of direct travel, as opposed to shorter caravans followed by trans-shipment to another merchant group, played a key role here, along with the massive amount of time even a trip of a few hundred miles required. Chinese adventurers and emissaries went into central Asia, and later Chinese merchants and Buddhist students traveled to India; a limited number of Greeks and Romans moved through the Middle East and into parts of central Asia, and also into a few sections of sub-Saharan

Africa; and of course Roman trade with India brought direct exchange. Persians and Arabs, who might venture both east and west, may have known a bit about Europe and India alike, though the evidence is limited. But Mediterranean knowledge of China, and vice versa, was exceedingly vague, because, as far as we can definitely know, no Chinese ever ventured that far west, and at most one Roman group ever made it to China (and we cannot be sure even of this). Roman aristocrats might love silk, but they had little notion where it came from; their known world stopped at India, and only a single Greek writer, who had traveled to India, makes even a passing reference to "Thina" as a source of silk, adding: "It is not easy to get to this Thina: for rarely do people come from it." Romans indeed believed that silk came from plants or trees, save for one writer who claimed it was produced by giant spiders. Chinese authors knew a bit more about Rome than vice versa, describing it as a well-governed land with rich but honest merchants, but claiming also that Rome was the source of products like an ointment that made gold. Wild beliefs about regions that were vaguely known about but not directly visited – including claims about cannibalism or bizarre sexual habits – showed the extent of ignorance about even some neighboring regions, like central Asia or parts of Africa; and the same beliefs could discourage actual contact. Globalization, in contrast, while it still involves mutual prejudices, has greatly reduced the amount of fanciful exaggeration.

Finally, even the amount of inter-regional trade that developed spurred critics and skeptics – though arguably this has some echoes in diverse reactions to globalization today. If products were demonstrably moving farther than people did, this very fact created anxiety about the products as well. Roman moralists wrote scathingly against the vanity and wastefulness embodied in imported silks. Thus Seneca, in the first century CE: "I see there raiments of silk – if that can be called raiment, which provides nothing that could possibly afford protection for the body, or indeed modesty, so that, when a woman wears it, she can scarcely … swear that she is not naked." Other writers referred to silk as degenerate or indecent, in violation of all traditional standards for dress. And while Chinese authorities did not get quite so exercised about foreign products – partly because there was nothing as overwhelming as silk – they might note how little they valued distant opportunities. Thus the one Roman merchant mission that may have reached China, in 166 CE (it is at least mentioned in Chinese chronicles), brought gifts that did not impress the emperor, who refused to do any business with the emissaries. As a number of historians have noted, greater official interest at this point might have created not only a more direct but a more durable bond between Asia and the Mediterranean, but it was a testimony to mutual ignorance and the relatively slight importance of most actual long-distance trade that nobody cared to follow up. The two regions would remain without direct contact for another 1,200 years.

Not surprisingly, in this situation, the collapse of the great classical empires severely threatened the inter-regional linkages that did exist.

Overland travel became far more dangerous, because there were no strong states to protect against marauders, and this came close to shutting the Silk Road down in favor of shorter-distance exchanges. Merchants from Rome or China withdrew from the Indian Ocean, and while Indian traders took advantage of the opportunity to extend their efforts to southeast Asia, the range and volume of trade in this region also declined for a time. Commerce would revive, of course, and the Indian Ocean continued to attract attention, but there was no question that something of a crisis had emerged by the 3rd or 4th century CE.

In this crisis, finally, one other development began to take shape, with ambivalent implications for inter-regional contacts. As the classical empires deteriorated and then disappeared, with the collapse first of the Han dynasty in China, then of the Roman Empire in the west, both with ensuing disorder, several major religions began to spread more widely, their organization and other-worldly goals serving societies now in earthly disarray. Buddhism had already begun to move beyond India, and now reached actively into south-east Asia and China (and ultimately other parts of east Asia). Christianity broke beyond the Roman Empire, particularly toward northern Europe but also toward additional pockets in Africa and the Middle East. Soon, after 600 CE, a new religion, Islam, would spread most rapidly of all. All of these religions traveled on the strength of missionary zeal, a growing commitment to spread what was regarded as religious truth beyond the boundaries of any one society or people. The resultant processes of conversion and religious remapping served as one of the key developments in the next, post-classical period of world history.

The spread of world religions, in turn, had three relationships to the larger process of inter-regional contacts. In the first place, as the religions began to compete with more localized, polytheistic faiths, they reflected the wider contacts already developing among parts of Africa, Asia and Europe. Ethiopia, for example, was open to Christianity because of earlier trade links to the Middle East and eastern Mediterranean. Merchant activity often went hand in glove with religious proselytism and missionary work, as merchants helped bring religious practice as they set up trading communities and as their commercial success might suggest a level of dynamism that could be associated with an outside religion and thus provide another motive for conversion. Indeed, it can be argued that the unprecedented commitment to the idea of a universal religion, valid for all people, was a revolutionary development whose novelty reflected the experience of significant contact. Early defenders of the major world religions all debated this point – whether Buddhism as a reform movement directed at Hinduism should just be dis-cussed in India, whether Christianity was only for Jews, or whether Islam should be for Arabs alone. Leaders of the three faiths all ultimately decided, often after a period of hesitation, that the response should be ecumenical, that unlike all earlier belief systems the faiths should not apply to a single people or region alone. And this in turn suggested an awareness spurred by a sense of contacts among different regions and societies.

The same universal claims also generated further activity. The second point about the new religions is the fact that they could further contacts in turn. Belief in a single God or divine order, rather than divinities more specifically attached to a particular place, and the availability of doctrines and rituals that were also not place specific, could provide new assurance to individuals moving out of their locality of origin, for whatever region. The same faith that worked at home would be equally valid thousands of miles away. Expanding religions also provided new motives for travel, beyond the previous predominance of trade. Missionaries could be as eager as merchants to reach a distant spot. Religious faithful might seek study opportunities near spiritual centers like monasteries in India (for Buddhists) or hubs of religious scholarship like Cairo or Baghdad within Islam. Larger numbers of religious individuals might simply want to travel to holy sites, however distant – like Jerusalem, for Christians, or even more urgently, like Mecca for Muslims.

The emerging religious map also, however, set up some new divisions among regions with different religious predominance. The world religions overcame narrower cultural and political boundaries, but their variety, and in some cases mutual hostility, very definitely challenged any idea of a single world. Contact might be impeded by religious fears or dislikes, to a greater extent than had been true before. Individual travelers might hesitate before going beyond their religious community, or feel uneasy if they tried. The Mediterranean now divided between Christian and Muslim, and while the result was not always belligerent intolerance, the religious rift set up cultural barriers that have not been entirely overcome even in the present day. Certainly, when religious allegiances were at their height, the separation of beliefs and practices seriously complicated larger patterns of exchange. Here is a final reason to see the premodern centuries of the human experience, at least until 1000 CE or so, as contributing to, but measurably separate from, processes that might be considered actual versions of globalization.

Further reading

Aubet, Maria Eugenia. *The Phoenicians and the West: Politics, Colonies and Trade*, 2nd edn, trans. Mary Turton (Cambridge: Cambridge University Press, 2001).

Begley, Vimala and De Puma, Richard Daniel, eds. *Rome and India: The Ancient Sea Trade* (Madison, WI: University of Wisconsin Press, 1991).

Bentley, Jerry H. *Old World Encounters: Cross Cultural Contacts and Exchanges in Pre-Modern Times* (New York: Oxford University Press, 1993).

Casson, Lionel. *Ships and Seafaring in Ancient Times* (Austin, TX: University of Texas Press, 1994).

Ellis, Linda and Kidner, Frank L., eds. *Travel, Communication and Geography in Late Antiquity* (Aldershot and Burlington, VT: Ashgate, 2004).

Frank, Andre Gunder. *The World System: Five Hundred Years or Five Thousand?* (New York: Routledge, 1993).

Gosch, Stephen S. and Stearns, Peter N. *Premodern Travel in World History* (New York and London: Routledge, 2008).

Holt, Frank L. *Alexander the Great and Bactria: The Formation of a Greek Frontier in Central Asia* (Leiden and New York: E.J. Brill, 1989).

Hutterer, Karl. *Economic Exchange and Social Interaction in Southeast Asia: Perspectives from Prehistory, History and Ethnography* (Ann Arbor: University of Michigan Press, 1977).

Kearney, Milo. *The Indian Ocean in World History* (New York and London: Routledge, 2004).

LaBianca, Oystein and Schum, Sandra, eds. *Connectivity in Antiquity: Globalization as Long-Term Historical Process* (New York: Continuum, 2004).

Liu, Xinru. *Ancient India and Ancient China: Trade and Cultural Exchanges, AD 1–600* (Delhi: Oxford University Press, 1988).

Manning, Patrick. *Migration in World History* (New York: Routledge, 2005).

Mark, Samuel. *From Egypt to Mesopotamia: A Study of Predynastic Trade Routes* (College Station, TX: Texas A & M University Press, 1997).

Miller, J.I. *The Spice Trade of the Roman Empire* (Oxford: The Clarendon Press, 1998).

Potts, Timothy. *Mesopotamia and the East: An Archaeological and Historical Study of Foreign Relations c. 3400 – 2000 B.C.* (Oxford: Oxbow Books, 1994).

Ratnagar, Shereen. *Encounters: The Westerly Trade of the Harappa Civilization* (Delhi: Oxford University Press, 1981).

Ray, Himanshu Prabhas. "Early Trade in the Bay of Bengal," *Indian Historical Review*, 14 (1–2): pp. 79–89, 1987–88.

Smith, Richard L. *Premodern Trade in World History* (New York and London: Routledge, 2009).

Whitfield, Susan. *Life Along the Silk Road* (Berkeley, CA: University of California Press, 1999).

Wood, Frances. *The Silk Road: Two Thousand Years in the Heart of Asia* (Berkeley, CA: University of California Press, 2004).

Yingshi, Yu. *Trade and Expansion in Han China: A Study in the Structure of Sino-Barbarian Relations* (Berkeley, CA: University of California Press, 1967).

Chapter 3

1000 CE as turning point

The birth of globalization?

Something of a watershed in inter-regional contacts occurred about a thousand years ago. The date, 1000 CE, is simply a convenient marker – nothing really dramatic occurred in that year, or even that century, and few people at the time would have been aware of any particularly significant alteration or upsurge in global relations. But by 1000 CE a number of key changes had accumulated, over the course of about three hundred years; and after that date the changes would solidify and amplify, justifying the understanding, in retrospect, that a fundamental transition was under way.

One world historian, David Northrup, has put the case particularly vividly: before 1000 CE, the most important factors shaping human life and social institutions were separate, society by society, with contacts playing only a peripheral role amid regionally divergent impulses. After 1000 CE, in contrast, societies increasingly functioned as a result of contacts, communications and even deliberate imitations, so that world history becomes the story of convergence rather than separation. Of course, what happened by around 1000 CE built upon previous contacts, most notably in trade relationships and the motivations they had embodied, particularly during the classical period and then amid the initial spread of the world religions. But the new patterns were not merely an automatic extension of what had already taken shape: they involved real and measurable departures. This chapter, obviously, focuses on this theme of change, but also on some crucial limitations to change.

For the idea of a major break in world history, such that what went before must be handled society by society, whereas what went after can increasingly be handled in terms of mutual interactions, has direct bearing on the issue of globalization. If 1000 CE is the turning point for inter-regional convergence, then subsequent changes, however significant, must be seen as aftershocks, resulting from the momentum of the decisive shift. And indeed, many world historians do view globalization as simply the latest version of a process that is now a millennium old.

No one, to be sure, puts the label globalization on the changes that took shape during the centuries after the end of the great classical empires.

Among other things, the networks that developed were Afro-Eurasian, not truly global – for the Americas and Pacific Oceania remained isolated from the larger inter-regional currents. But the identification of a process that involved such intense and fruitful contacts that its further development became inevitable – so that the extension to the whole world, while itself a significant further change, built on established patterns – might justify the conclusion that the effective origins of globalization really date this far back in historical chronology. After all, the voyages that brought the Americas into the global picture for the first time were intended not to discover new lands but to shorten the connections between Europe and Asia – intended, in other words, to take advantage of existing inter-regional ties.

The idea of the 1000s CE as the beginnings of global linkage, in strong contrast to previous and more sporadic connection, risks becoming a historian's abstraction. The challenge is to demonstrate not only change, but significant change, and to show what this all meant in human terms. For not only is there no dramatic event to mark the divide between separateness and convergence; there is also no overwhelming new technology, no communications revolution of the sort we associate with more modern phases of globalization. The shift, instead, resulted from an accumulation of developments in shipping, in trade routes and in cultural outreach – and accumulation, though the basis for most major departures in history, is never as vivid as a single transformative invention or some upheaval in foreign policy or war.

Happily, nevertheless, the chronological divide is not just a theoretical construct or even an organizing device for textbooks (though that's true too, as historians increasingly realize the ramifications of the change), for it has a concrete human face.

It was only in the centuries after 1000 CE, for example, that wide-ranging inter-regional travel took shape. Whereas during the classical period there is record, and uncertain at that, of only one trip between Europe and China, by the 13th and 14th centuries a substantial number of travelers went from Europe or north Africa to east Asia. Some were missionaries, some merchants, some adventurers or job-seekers, and there were even some entertainers involved. The world's greatest known traveler, Ibn Battuta (b. 1304), operated in this context, with many trips from his native Morocco to the Middle East, central Asia, India, China and southeast Asia, and sub-Saharan Africa, logging almost 80,000 miles on his journeys overall. Travel of this sort reflected a new capacity to take advantage of established routes and contacts and a new interest in reaching out as widely as possible in the known world. It also supported further travel in turn, for some of the new adventurers, including Ibn Battuta, wrote accounts of their trips which helped a wider audience learn about other parts of the world and could spur some to outreach of their own. It was no accident that Christopher Columbus, on his own travels late in the 15th century, had with him a copy of the most famous European travel book to that point, Marco Polo's description of his journey to China. Long-distance travel was still the province of a relatively small number of individuals, and of course it was noteworthy that the more extensive ventures went west to east rather than vice versa; but the phenomenon was no longer simply a rarity, and that fact in turn signaled the beginning of a new era in terms of inter-regional contacts.

Mapping came of age by around 1000 CE, with increasingly accurate representations of Asia, Europe and much of Africa. Arab map-makers led the way, which reflected larger leadership in the processes of trade and travel. But map-makers from other societies joined in, based on knowledge of Arab maps and guides and on travel from their own home bases. Fanciful representations even of neighboring regions, common still in the classical period, gave way to more precise detail. Better maps, in turn, facilitated additional contacts, showing the attainability of far-flung destinations.

Dependence on long-distance trade also increased, another sign of change. Markets for Chinese silk continued to play an important role, which represented obvious continuity with the past. But the range of Chinese exports expanded, for example to include porcelain. Chinese consumers began to count on imports of tea and some other food specialties from southeast Asia. Imports of African slaves to the Middle East became a regular trade item (and ultimately, over several centuries, over nine million people would be brought in from eastern Africa). Indian cotton cloth became a valued commodity in markets as distant as Japan, gaining attention from European merchants as well by the 13th and 14th centuries. By the 14th century European interest in imported sugar (which could not be locally grown) began to surface, and would ultimately help spur increased European involvement in global outreach more generally. Some of the products now central to inter-regional trade also began to move below purely elite consumer levels, to involve wider reaches of the population. Correspondingly, some regions – for example, parts of China during the Song dynasty (960–1279) – began to depend heavily on production for the export trade. The impact of the inter-regional economy, with increasingly active exchanges among Asia, Africa and Europe, began to accelerate, moving beyond the levels of some surplus production and the interests of a few merchant groups.

Recent discoveries of ships from the period, which sank for various reasons, add specifics to the point about the growing range of trade and consumer involvement. The Belitung shipwreck, involving an Indian or, more probably, Arab ship, was found in Indonesian waters in 1998. It had been built according to Arab design, with Middle Eastern wood, though it had been repaired with materials from other areas. Its cargo consisted of some lead, a variety of Chinese ceramics from the Tang dynasty – mostly bowls, but also small jars, a few large basins, and some very artistic porcelains. Chinese coins were also carried. Star anise, another Chinese product, took some space, though there were no other spices. From the Middle East, possibly intended as gifts, were silver items, mirrors and other glasswares, along with dice and some cast-iron utensils. The ship is clear evidence of the direct trade between the Middle East and China by the 9th century; the ship had undoubtedly loaded in China and was bound for the Persian Gulf.

The Cirebon shipwreck, another recent discovery, involved a southeast Asian boat, also sunk off the coast of Indonesia. Here, too, the ship had taken on goods at Guangzhou or another southern Chinese port and was heading for the western Indian Ocean with intermediate stops at southeast Asian ports. The ship contained over 200,000 artifacts, including objects for Buddhist and Hindu temples. Chinese ceramics were again strongly represented, with bowls, platters, and pitchers, but also figurines and incense burners. Colored glassware included many items inscribed in Arabic. Various jewels and ornate daggers, mirrors and bells suggest ritual objects. Items belonging to crew members suggest a multi-faith, multi-ethnic crew of Hindus, Buddhists and Muslims.

The creation of a new network for interactions among different regions depended on the confluence of several specific changes: a new leadership role for Arab and other Islamic merchants and missionaries, extending an east–west axis from China and its neighbors to Europe and north Africa; the development of a number of additional exchange routes, running mainly south to north, that greatly expanded the geography of participation in active contacts; and the emergence of new technologies, particularly for sea travel, which both reflected and further supported the extension of effort.

Arabs as trans-regional leaders

By the 7th and 8th centuries, Arabs played an increasingly dominant role in Indian Ocean trade, using many routes and exchanging many products that had been in play before, but with increased intensity and range. They neither sought nor gained monopoly: Indians were still active, as were other peoples from the Middle East including Persians; traders from southeast Asia maintained participation as well. But the Arab role was noteworthy, and this helped extend Indian Ocean activity particularly down the east coast of Africa, all the way to present-day Mozambique. Arab trading settlements were established at ports and on islands down the coast, and merchants mixed with local elites to form a network of connections. A new language, Swahili (from the Arab word for "shores"), mixing Arabic and African (Bantu) tongues with some Persian words as well, emerged for this trading and governing community, a clear sign of the cultural accompaniments to more consistent commercial exchange. And Islam, the religion of a growing majority of Arabs, provided religious linkage as well.

In addition to the enhanced African connection, Arabs and other Islamic traders brought several new components even to established Indian Ocean routes. Arab conquests through the Middle East and north Africa, and into Spain and central Asia, provided a large, landed territorial base that helped link Mediterranean and Indian Ocean trade and provided a number of vantage points for ventures into the Indian Ocean itself. At various junctures between 600 and 1100, Red Sea expeditions, from the Arabian Peninsula or Egypt, provided a primary entry for Arab activities not only to Africa but to India, southeast Asia and beyond. At other times, the equally traditional basis of Mesopotamia and the Persian Gulf served as the chief focus for trading expeditions.

The high Arab and Islamic valuation of commerce and merchant endeavor provided a vital component, along with the spur of competition with Persian and other traders. Muhammed himself was a former merchant and noted the value and satisfaction of merchant life, second only to a religious vocation. While later Islamic authorities sometimes questioned commercial motives, concerned about the honesty of activities designed to make money, Islam overall was far friendlier to the merchant calling than any of the other world religions, or than Confucianism in China. The *Quran* explicitly equates honest merchants with prophets and martyrs. Trading and profit taking were perfectly compatible with religious purity so long as certain ethical standards were observed, including refraining from directly charging interest on loans, and so long as religious obligations such as regular prayer and charity were fulfilled. Indeed, merchant wealth so obviously contributed to the capacity for charitable activity, and also the ability to undertake the pilgrimage to Mecca, that it might be seen as a religious plus. And of course, in fact, expansion of trade directly encouraged Islamic missionary activity. The contrast with Buddhist concerns about the snares of worldly achievements, or Christian worry that too much interest in money making might distract from spiritual goals, was considerable. Of course Buddhists and Christians could be successful merchants as well, and by the 14th century Christian attacks on business were lessening, but the Islamic cultural impulse, the sense that trading success and religious devotion could go hand in hand, helped push Arab merchants to unusual heights.

Islam, and Arabic, provided other trading assets as well. A reinforcing pattern emerged in which expanding trade helped encourage conversion to Islam, not only along the African coast but in parts of India and southeast Asia, which in turn made it easier for Arabs to deal with local merchants as co-religionists. Ultimately, this shared religious factor would encourage Indian Muslims, Indonesians and others to become more active in inter-regional trade in their own right, but initially, obviously, the impulse came from the Middle East.

The same cultural umbrella made Arabic something of a common language throughout much of the Indian Ocean, which in turn helps explain how an increasing rate of contact could operate, given the many languages which flourished in the regions involved. Enough people knew smatterings of Arabic, and enough translators emerged who could use Arabic to interact with other language groups, to facilitate regular exchanges well beyond the level that had operated previously. Not surprisingly, at the end of the 15th century when the Portuguese explorer Vasco da Gama rounded the southern tip of Africa and set sail for India, one of his key moves was to find a Muslim interpreter who knew sufficient Portuguese to backstop interactions with Indian merchants.

Travel and trade in turn served as important elements of Arab culture as they evolved in the centuries about 1000 CE. A number of books discussed trade routes and served as travel guides, and there were also Persian materials that discussed travel, for example in China. The famous stories of *A Thousand and One Nights*, written during the Abbasid caliphate, used the character of Sinbad the Sailor to take readers through the Indian Ocean, encountering bizarre birds (ostriches) in Africa along with purchases of ivory elephant tusks, visiting ruby markets in Sri Lanka, and meeting menacing tribesmen in Indonesia. Later stories, like the *Tales of Abu Zayd*, similarly used Indian Ocean trade routes as the setting for various adventures. Offerings of this sort reflected the importance of Arab involvement in wide exchanges, and might have stimulated interest in these exchanges in turn.

Scholars like Amira Bennison have indeed argued that the expansion of Islam, and the intense belief in a basic Muslim unity across geographical and political borders, created a first example of a global community. The Muslim *umma*, or community, knew no clear boundaries, but embraced all believers. Common commitment to Islamic law, the *sharia*, along with the shared faith, created genuine ties across long distances. So did the *hadj*, or pilgrimage to Mecca, which additionally allowed believers from many different regions to share news and experience and enhanced a sense of shared commitment regardless of place. To a slightly lesser extent, common beliefs about the state, and the relations between religion and politics, spread widely, though particularly within the confines of the Arab caliphate. All of this was not mere theory. Muslim scholars, for example, could travel widely and participate actively in discussions of faith and law among groups of colleagues in any Islamic center (though there were divisions among different schools of thought, even aside from the major rift between Sunni and Shiite). Many traveling scholars earned money by giving lectures or working in local bureaucracies, again across a wide geographical reach. Of course the Islamic world, the *dar al-Islam* or land of Islam, was not in fact the entire world, even in Afro-Eurasia. Muslims also identified a *dar al-harb*, or land of war, outside the Islamic purview – which in the centuries around 1000 CE particularly referred to Europe and east Asia. But the sense of shared endeavor created vital links for Muslims themselves and a larger context for wider exchange.

All of this contributed to the crucial point, as far as the rest of Afro-Eurasia and not just the Islamic regions were concerned: that as Arabs gained a growing role in trans-regional trade, particularly in the Indian Ocean, they also helped expand its range, volume and impact. Islam itself came to recognize an intermediate zone, a *dar al-sulh* or land of truce, which linked Islamic trade to neighboring territories that were outside the Muslim community but with which active relationships were both possible and desirable.

Islamic energy pushed in a number of directions. Expeditions in the Red Sea, both commercial and military, began in the 7th century. By the early 8th century Arabs had directly captured territory in what is today southern Pakistan, and planted commercial colonies in Indian port cities all along the Persian Gulf and also in Sri Lanka. Along with the growing activity in east Africa, this led to varied and vibrant exchanges of goods among Africa, the Middle East and the Indian subcontinent, going well beyond the luxury level that had largely characterized inter-regional activity previously. Africa contributed ivory, gold, and iron as well as slaves. Middle Eastern products included rugs, tools, jewelry and cooking ware (iron and copper pots), while India offered cloth (particularly its fabled and colorful cottons), metal implements and decorative beads, plus the highly valued spices.

Exchanges pushed farther east, to Thailand and Burma but also to south China. By the late 7th century Arabs and Persians, as well as Indians and Malaysians, were listed by Chinese officials as ship owners working out of the port of Guangzhou. Arabs began importing Chinese porcelains, cloth, carpets and glassware to east Africa. Porcelain, indeed, increasingly became the most important single Chinese export, surpassing silk (which now began to be produced in some other areas, such as the Byzantine Empire) despite the fact that it was both fragile and relatively heavy to ship. By the late 8th century a significant colony of Arab merchants actually located in Guangzhou, where the Chinese allowed them to follow their own laws and establish their own system of judges. Disruptions occurred, to be sure; for example the Chinese periodically tried to close Guangzhou to foreigners, but the importance of trade, and the merchants capable of maintaining it, survived the interruptions.

Arab commercial forays (along with ongoing and often competitive Persian activity) brought involvement from other groups. Indian merchants began to settle in some of the Swahili ports of east Africa to oversee trade between that region and the subcontinent. Jewish merchants moved easily from the Mediterranean to China. As noted, Muslims in other parts of Asia began to gain their own growing role in Indian Ocean commerce.

Arab connections furthered additional innovations. Partnerships developed between Arabs and local merchant houses, which helped organize more detailed commercial interactions. Bills of exchange were introduced, which facilitated payments for goods of distant origin, instead of requiring more direct barter on the spot in a port city. Arab commercial law was recognized in a number of different regions, and the Arabs helped create a precedent in which commercial regulations might be seen as transcending individual political units – with the individual states agreeing because of the profits the larger trading system brought to local merchants, and their contributions to tax revenues.

This east–west network was reaching proportions that affected the daily lives of many producers and consumers alike. Significant numbers of people now valued goods that came from a different region, and while the emphasis still lay on personal and household adornment the range of goods, and the capacity to spread to consumers not in the top ranks of wealth, extended beyond prior levels. Key regions, particularly in parts of China, in turn came to depend on the production of manufactured items that would be sold in the trans-regional trade – to India, to the Middle East, to Africa and even beyond. China's role as a production center for other parts of the world, such an obvious part of globalization today, was established during the Tang and particularly the Song dynasties in the centuries around 1000 CE.

Not surprisingly, the same intensification involved transmissions that went beyond the ranks of the merchants themselves. Again, some precedent existed from earlier patterns, but the range and speed of these wider exchanges were quite new. Crops spread from one region to another on the heels of trade. Enhanced trade with India – even though it expanded on previous connections – now allowed Persians and Arabs to import sugar cane, saffron and various rice grains, that began to be grown locally and soon became staples of the regional diet. Knowledge of silk production was smuggled out of China – to the Byzantine Empire, for example, by some Syrian monks in the 6th century. Persia was also producing silk by this point. Chinese silks were still highly valued, but they now had to compete with regional production. New Chinese manufacturing methods for porcelain – introduced to allow a nonporous container for tea, which was becoming a popular Chinese drink at this same time – helped propel this good to its new prominence, particularly in trade with the Middle East. Here was an early example of how increased international exchange generated competition that reduced the product edge in one category, in this case, Chinese silk, forcing greater concentration on a new specialty – a pattern that would become commonplace as globalization accelerated. Cultural techniques were set in motion as well, as Arabs by the 9th century were introducing the superior Indian numbering system and the concept of zero into their own mathematics. Transmissions of this sort, becoming an integral part of inter-regional contact, prefigured the similar, if admittedly more extensive, amplifications that have become a routine part of globalization.

New technology

Arab commerce helped generate significant improvements in shipping technology, utilizing ideas from China and southeast Asia as well as the Middle East. The innovations were not earth shaking in the sense of dramatically reducing the time needed for transportation or communication, but they did support growing use of the seas, initially in the Indian Ocean and later elsewhere, and a higher volume in the exchanges of heavy goods. Movement of bulk goods, like grains and metal ores, became possible as never before. Along with the sheer expansion of east–west trade, the new shipping capacities provided another step in the network of changes that produced a measurably different kind of trans-regional network from any of the patterns that had been established before. What was developing was a more sophisticated technological tool kit for ocean-borne trade, increasing the reliability of travel and expanding the distances over which trade could be carried out successfully. The spread of these same innovations, part of the growing intensity of trans-regional connection, also allowed other peoples to begin to participate in more venturesome maritime travel, including additional groups from southeast Asia but also the Europeans.

Arabs gained new advantages as they learned navigational techniques and ship designs from Persian traders after their conquest of that region. Indeed a variety of Persian words entered Arabic and would later, from Arab influence, penetrate Western languages as well – words like *barge, lateen, helm,* and *anchor.*

Improvements in navigational devices were critical. Arabs directly introduced a device called the *kamal,* used by Arabs and possibly others, which superseded the use of fingers held parallel to the horizon line to locate one's position in relation to a known star. The *kamal* was fairly simple, with a card held by a wooden crossbar, but it did allow more accurate calculation. Sailors in the period also utilized a quadrant, a quarter-circle with a plumb line and markings to indicate position. Arabs also picked up and improved the astrolabe, a device initially introduced in classical Greece, translating Greek manuscripts on the subject into Arabic by the 8th century. Astrolabes allowed the calculation of heights of mountains or human structures, as well as accurately measuring the position of objects in the sky. Astrolabes facilitated land-based as well as seagoing transportation, determining latitude and longitude though only approximately. The Arab astronomer al-Faraghani developed tables for calibrating astrolabes to every degree of latitude, making the device easier to use. Written work on astrolabes spread through the Islamic world, from Spain to central Asia. Ultimately, through Spain, other Europeans learned of the device; the famous early English author Chaucer, among others, wrote a treatise on the subject.

Even more important was the introduction and dissemination of the magnetic compass. Here was an instrument that could indicate direction in virtually any circumstance, in contrast to the astrolabe which greatly aided positioning but was of little use in a stormy sea because it needed to hang freely to find the horizon.

Though some European historians once claimed that the compass must be of European origin, apparently on grounds that no other people could introduce such a clever device, it's clear that the instrument originated in China, at some point in the Han dynasty. It may initially have been used to help guide the arrangement of furniture, according to the principles of *feng shui,* but this is not certain. And it was the navigational use, becoming very clear by the 7th century, which was really important. By that point, the Chinese knew that an iron needle could be magnetized by rubbing it with magnetite ore, and they were also able to use intense heat to magnetize a needle in a north–south direction. The needle could then be floated in a bowl of water, where it would spin until it pointed. By the 11th century, compasses used needles suspended in water, but also needles held by a pin or a silk thread. A Chinese military treatise in 1044 described a compass, and during the Song dynasty compasses were being used at sea to take bearings, particularly during cloudy weather when stars were not visible.

Through trade contacts, or possibly by written descriptions that spread along land routes, the Arabs learned of the compass at least by the 13th century but probably well before. A story in 1233 told of how to use an iron, fish-shaped needle in a bowl of water to find direction. Another reference from the Red Sea, just nine years later, describes placing a magnetized needle on a reed to allow it to float. Ahmed ibn Majid was the first to mount a magnetized needle on a revolving support above a compass face, doing away with the need for water, thus making the device more portable, and providing a clearer set of directions. His work also included detailed instructions for the proper use of the compass at sea. By this time also, via the Arabs, Europeans were beginning to write about the compass; an English essay, by the Augustinian monk Alexander Neckham, first mentions the compass as a way to locate the North Star in bad weather; he probably heard of it in Italy. Trading city states like Venice and Genoa, and the crusades that brought European armies to the Middle East by the 12th century, were also involved in spreading knowledge of the compass. The first known example of a European compass comes from Italy sometime after 1253. Soon after this both Arabs and Europeans were rapidly improving the device, mounting the needle on cards showing the different directions and setting it on swivels in order to keep it level on shipboard. This technique, probably devised in Syria and initially used for suspending incense burners without spilling their contents, generated designs that were also exported to Europe. But the Mediterranean was hardly the only center of ongoing development. Indonesian and other southeast Asian sailors were appropriating the compass from Chinese and Arab merchants in the same period, and introducing their own improvements.

Increasingly accurate charts, along with map making more generally, added to the new navigational devices in facilitating oceanic travel. Pilot directions were written down, with workmanlike and highly practical precision, reflecting repeated commercial voyages but also facilitating their replication without the burden of significant uncertainty. Thus an Arab pilot, Sulaiman iban Ahmed al-Mahri, recorded directions around the Indonesian islands and on toward China in 917 CE:

> The journey from Sundib and Farandib to Shati Jam is made in the direction ESE, from Shati Jam to the island of Zanjiliya is due south

and from Zanjiliya to Najirashi, SSE. ... From Pulua Sanbilan to the islands of Pulua Jumar is due south and from Pulua Jumar to the mountain of Pulua Basalar, SE by E, although some say ESE. Then from Pulua Basalar to Malacca it is SE, and from Malacca to Singpur, and this is the end of Siam to the South, and there the Little Bear is 5 degrees above the horizon ... the journey from Singpur to Ban-agah, where the Pole Star is 4 degrees above the horizon, is N. by W. ... Then from Sharh-i-Naw to Cape Kanbusa, at 5 degrees P.S., is SE by E. From Kanbusa to Shanba at 7 degrees P.S. is NNE, and from Shanba to the Gulf of Kawashi at 10 degrees P.S. is NNW.

Charts of this sort, widely distributed among merchants from various bases in the Indian Ocean, both reflected and promoted increasingly extensive trade.

Shipping itself was the other main beneficiary of technological improvements, though they were less dramatic than in the navigational realm. A crucial development was the growing use of the lateen sail, both in the Indian Ocean and the Mediterranean. Most early sails, in the classical period and before, had been square, which worked fine when the wind was coming straight behind a vessel, but had severe limitations otherwise – often necessitating the use of oarsmen to propel the boat in other conditions. Lateen sails were triangular, which allowed them to be maneuvered to catch winds coming from various directions; and they could be placed at the front and rear of a vessel. Both speed and flexibility benefited greatly from this innovation. Historians dispute when and where the lateen originated, with some claiming that the later Romans and Byzantines introduced them, others pointing to Arab use well before Islam. What is clear, and of prime importance, was that the Arabs perfected the sail and extended its use, providing models from which seamen in other societies would learn.

Arab ships, called *dhows*, came to dominate Indian Ocean trade by 1000 CE. They were relatively large boats, with transverse watertight bulkheads reducing – though, as we have seen, not eliminating – the danger of sinking. Holes and gaps were closed with tree gum and coconut fiber. Wicker rails prevented waves from breaking over the ship's bulwark. Dhows had two masts, each with a lateen sail. They could move quite rapidly when the sails were spread wide, but they could also maneuver readily when the sails were raised in a high triangle, sailing in zigzag tacks into the wind. When guided by the use of the compass and the other navigational devices, and benefiting from the rudder-based steering that the Chinese had introduced, Arab ships seemed ideally suited to take advantage of wind patterns in the Indian Ocean, including down the African coast, but they could also be adapted to other settings. Many features of their design would spread to Europe as Arab and European trading contacts accelerated by the 11th and 12th centuries, and indeed the Portuguese vessels (*caravelles*) that began to introduce a new chapter in Europe's relations with the wider world by the 15th century were explicit adaptations of the dhow. In Arab hands, the dhows allowed faster and longer trips and the transport of bulk cargoes such as foodstuffs, metals and manufactured goods – like the Chinese porcelain that was becoming so widely sought after. Arab dhows could range up to 400 tons, with crews of 30 that provided some oarsmen to supplement primary reliance on the wind.

The next set of shipbuilding innovations came in fact from the Chinese. Chinese junks had been introduced in the Han dynasty, but their wider deployment and growing sophistication dated to the Song dynasty and its great trading outreach. Here, too, developments facilitated more complex and capacious trading ventures at the time – feeding the 11th-century turning point in trans-regional contacts – and at the same time provided models that other seagoing peoples could copy and adapt. European sailors would have their debts to Chinese as well as Arab shipbuilders.

Advances in Chinese shipbuilding began early in the Han dynasty. Chinese ships came to be known as junks, from the Malay word *djong*, or boat; the Chinese themselves did not use this term. Junks were strong, heavy ships, some of them quite large, and capable of sailing both in the South China Sea and in the Indian Ocean. Hulls were divided into watertight compartments, so that if one began to leak, the ship would not sink. (One result of this was that relatively few remains of early junks have been found, in contrast to Arab and Persian shipping, because wrecks were so rare.) The ships could carry heavy cargoes and large crews. Designs and capacities improved steadily during the Song dynasty, by which time some ships were built that were over 200 feet long (and some scholars argue they may have been even larger, at least by the 15th century), capable of carrying not only goods but considerable armed force and also gardens and animals for the provision of fresh food. The strength and maneuverability of the junks, including of course their use of rudders, as well as their massive size, were well ahead of the types of ship available in the same period in the Mediterranean. Here, clearly, was another set of innovations in transportation that reflected the growing importance of oceanic trade and stimulated further activity in turn.

New routes

The final basic innovation in trans-regional contacts, particularly important for Africa and Europe but also embracing Japan and southeast Asia, involved the development of feeder routes that connected additional societies to the Afro-Eurasian trading network. Many of these routes ran north–south – the most important one linked sub-Saharan west Africa to the Mediterranean and the Middle East – thus obviously helping new regions link to the fundamental east–west axis that the Arabs and others were extending.

Trade from west Africa across the Sahara to the north, particularly from the emerging empire of Ghana, began fairly early, by 600 CE or so, on the basis of African merchant activity moving out from growing cities. Africans brought goods from forested regions, including gold but also dried fish, copper and other items, in dugout boats in the delta of the Niger River, where they met nomadic traders for the Sahara who offered salt and other products. This pattern was soon joined and amplified by Muslim merchants, including Arabs, coming south. For a time, mixed settlements developed, embracing merchant groups from both directions. Travel times of three months or more were not uncommon. African rulers vigorously encouraged the trade, because of the new products it generated but more obviously still for the tax revenues they could derive. As in the Middle East, governments set up inns where groups of travelers could lodge. From north Africa came an increasing array of manufactured products, including glass beads and pottery, but also large stocks of horses, whose breeding was difficult in the sub-Saharan regions. Most of the exchange products came from north Africa or the adjacent Middle East, but even luxury Chinese goods and Indian glassware have been discovered in the west African centers. Gold continued to serve as the basis for the African offerings, but other products entered in as well, including ivory; archeologists have discovered a mid-9th-century pit with over 50 hippopotamus tusks, destined for export to the north. Slaves were also traded, though less extensively than along the Swahili routes in east Africa.

These exchange patterns led of course to wider connections and to frequent Arab commentary on African conditions. A number of Africans, including major rulers, converted to Islam and used north African bureaucrats to help run their vast domains. Relationships with Islam were tricky, however; there were few mass conversions yet in sub-Saharan Africa. Some regions were particularly resistant, in ways that had to be balanced against trade needs. Thus Ak-Umari, writing in the 14th century about the great empire of Mali, noted that the people in one gold-producing province were "uncouth infidels." But "the kings of this kingdom have learned by experience that as soon as one of them conquers one of the gold towns and Islam spreads and the muezzin calls to prayer there the gold there begins to decrease and then disappears, while it increases in the neighboring heathen countries." So they left these territories alone in return for a regular gold tribute. On the other hand, in other parts of Mali, and particularly the great town of Timbuktu, with 75,000 inhabitants, many scholars visited from different parts of the Islamic world; there were 7,500 students in all. And several African leaders, most notably Mansa Musa, traveled out of the region to Mecca, spreading the reputation for wealth in gold in the process. The opening of a major route from western Africa to the Mediterranean and beyond thus rested primarily on trade, but with considerably wider potential, particularly in terms of cultural contacts.

Other new routes developed as well, though with products for the most part of somewhat lesser value. By the 9th and 10th centuries, traders were actively working connections between Scandinavia and the Byzantine Empire, with Constantinople as a key exchange point. Presumably Scandinavian traders introduced the first ventures, using overland and river routes through what is now western Russia and Ukraine, with intermediary cities like Kiev growing up in response. They carried honey, furs, amber and craft goods, trading for textiles, pottery and glass, and spices, along with fine metal products. But Byzantine traders and Christian missionaries were soon active as well, and many Arab merchants became directly involved. In 921, Ibn Fadlan led a party from Baghdad as an emissary from the caliph, seeking to meet the "King of the Slavs." The king had sent a letter asking for someone who could teach them about Islam and set up a mosque. The trip covered 1,500 miles, through dense forests and along the Volga and Dneiper rivers. Fadlan's report provided information for Arab geographers and travel writers, and encouraged further contacts (though the Russians in the end decided against adopting Islam). Fadlan was intrigued by the appearance of the Russians: "I have never seen people with a more developed bodily stature than they. They are as tall as date palms, blond and ruddy, so that they do not need to wear a tunic nor a cloak; rather the men among them wear a garment that only covers half of his body and leaves one of his hands free." Many Russian habits, including even the ways they bargained and traded, seemed strange, but this did not prevent vigorous mutual engagement. The many Arab coins found in Scandinavia testify to the range of activity, which came to include some commerce in slaves as well.

Arab outreach also widened connections with central Asia, though here the routes were not entirely new but rather built upon earlier Silk Road patterns. Central Asian products found increasing markets, so that the region was no longer simply a passage point for Chinese goods. Various kinds of manufacturing expanded to take advantage of the export opportunities. Writing about 985, the Islamic geographer al-Muqaddasi cited a long list of exports, including rugs, lamps, various kinds of soap as well as fur, leather goods, and various food. "There is nothing to equal the meats of Bukhara, and a kind of melon they have called ash-shaq, nor the bows of Khorezmia, the porcelain of Shash, and the paper of Samarkand." Traders also moved north, connecting with tribes in Siberia and using sleds when possible. Here, long-distance linkages were unprecedented, and one tribe was cited as being so unfamiliar with the whole process that they would simply bring goods to an exchange point and then vanish, coming back the next day to collect what the traders had left in exchange.

New Japanese routes to Korea and China constituted another expansion of the overall system of connections, though the distances involved were less vast than in the case of the north–south routes in west Africa and eastern Europe. Links to Korea came first, and for a while the Koreans served as middlemen between Japan and China, but then the Japanese organized direct seaborne links to China as well. Trade involved products like timber and mercury from Japan, in return for manufactured goods from Korea and China (but also, through China, from places like India). Merchant groups and even artisans, particularly from Korea, moved along these routes as well, settling in Japan in some numbers. Cultural exchange followed, and, as we will see, Japan ultimately established fairly formal systems for finding out about Chinese ways. Buddhism spread, and although some Japanese objected, the contact system itself provided persuasive motivation; as one observer put it, looking at Korea, China and beyond, "All the states of the Western foreigners worship it [Buddhism] – how could Japan alone turn its back?" This process brought missionaries as well, particularly from China but also from India (in small number); and it widened the demand for goods from other parts of Asia, to serve Buddhist religious rituals.

One final set of routes opened or reopened in this period, though a bit more gradually. Western Europe continued to engage in some Mediterranean trade even after the fall of the Roman Empire. Gradually, more north–south activity developed within this part of the European continent, bringing English, German and Dutch merchants to the Mediterranean. Italian cities began to expand, based on their obvious advantages in linking goods from other parts of Europe with the wider reaches of the Mediterranean, sponsoring exchanges with Arabs and Byzantines alike. But southern French ports and merchants also played some role in connecting western Europe generally to interactions with Asia, as mediated by merchants in Egypt or the Middle East.

Overall, the development of new linkages enhanced both the impact and the complexity of patterns of interaction by 1000 CE. New parts of Africa, Europe and Asia were increasingly engaged, even as the primary focus rested still on east–west exchanges through the Indian Ocean. The geography of contact was much richer than it had been in the classical period, which meant not only the involvement of more regions and more people, but also a wider array of products and new opportunities for cultural connections as well.

Impacts: the pace of exchange

The emergence of a new trans-regional context under Arab stimulus, the innovations in the technologies of trade and travel, and the range of routes forming networks of contact among Africa, Asia and Europe added up to significant change in the availability of interactions among the major societies of these three continents. The resulting network generated important shifts in the nature of exchange, accelerating the mutual influences possible when societies encounter each other – building on, but surpassing, the obvious intensification of trade. Here is where the idea of a quietly revolutionary shift to trans-regional coherence comes in. Exchanges happened more quickly than before on various fronts, and over a wider range of activities. This kind of change was exactly what one should expect from the more specific shifts in navigation devices or regional trade routes – otherwise the claims of a new network would have little practical meaning. The key developments, in the heightened dissemination of techniques and ideas and the establishment of deliberate patterns of imitation, arguably represent a definable – if admittedly still early – phase of what we now know as globalization.

Techniques and tastes

Transfers of technological know-how and, to a lesser degree, consumer preferences clearly illustrate the possibilities created by the new network. Paper is a prime example. The product was invented in China by the first century CE – this is when we have the first examples of uses of the material for writing. Different methods for making paper proliferated in China, including ways to lower manufacturing costs. By the 3rd and 4th centuries not only the product but the production technologies were being passed into Korea and Vietnam, and soon thereafter to Japan – following on China's orbit of influence in the late classical period. It was striking, of course, that paper did not capture interest more broadly, given its huge advantages over all other writing materials in cost and ease of manufacture – but despite trade links to China in the classical period, mutual knowledge was simply not extensive enough to break the barriers of distance and unfamiliarity. India, it has been speculated, had some cultural reasons for aversion to paper, and knowledge of China was simply not intense enough in other parts of Asia for paper to have become a priority item.

This changed dramatically with the arrival of the Arabs and a new pace of interactions with China. Arab troops defeated a Chinese army in western China, in the battle of Talas River in 751, and took several prisoners who were skilled in the manufacture of paper. A factory was established, on the basis of their knowledge, in Baghdad. The product – far cheaper and more flexible than the animal skins previously used for writing in many parts of the Middle East – caught on rapidly. By the 10th century, mills were producing paper through the Arab world and beyond, in Persia, Egypt, and Spain, as well as Mesopotamia. By the 11th century, paper was spreading to non-Muslim Europe, with the first factory established in Sicily, relatively close to the Arab centers. The result, first in Islam and then beyond, was an explosion of books and records, vital to commercial transactions, administrative operations and religious training alike. Centers of learning in west Africa also quickly benefited from the literacy and scholarship that paper could support.

There are two key points here: first, a clearly superior product that had been available but not widely known in the classical period, now begins to move out into other societies in the hemispheric network of Asia, Africa and Europe at a relatively rapid pace. The dissemination process, admittedly, still took many decades, but the speed was far greater than anything that emerges from past examples of technology diffusion. Second, paper, because of its particular importance in supporting the spread of information, facilitated other kinds of exchange, such as the translation into Arabic of knowledge and scholarship from India, Persia, China and elsewhere – including earlier Greek scientific and philosophical texts. It became another component of the acceleration of communication among societies, in a process that would soon spread beyond the Arab world to Europe.

Obviously, the rapid spread of navigational devices like the compass, often partly on the basis of manuals written on paper, forms an important part of the acceleration of technology exchange. So, though less familiar, does the growing interest in finding up-to-date methods of manufacturing steel. India, in the classical period, had developed the most advanced steel technology, adding ingredients to molten iron that produced a harder but more flexible metal that was preferable for certain kinds of product – including sword blades. By the late classical period, steel blocks, or eggs, were being traded along the Indian coast and across the Persian Gulf to the Middle East. In the context of the kind of trading network that emerged by 1000 CE, merely trading for steel was unnecessarily indirect: it was better to learn how to make it oneself. Techniques of steel production in India began to be taken to the Middle East, and, with the expansion of Islam, well beyond. It was in the 12th century that the Muslim geographer al-Idrisi wrote, "The Hindus excelled in the manufacture of iron and it is impossible to find anything to surpass the edge from Hinduwani or Indian steel." Muslim scientists like al-Biruni, Ibn Sina and al-Kindi wrote about Indian steel in their studies of technology. Knowledge of steel production also spread east to Indonesia, but also westward to Spain, where Toledo blades became famous through the European and Mediterranean zones. Another Arab geographer, Ibn Hawqal, wrote in 977 that "Toledo, like Damascus, was known throughout the world for its swords."

Greater speed in the dissemination of technology, but also a greater sense of intentionality, so that experts in one society began to think explicitly about what they could learn from counterparts in another, marked an important new step in the history of inter-regional contacts and their impact.

Developments in the area of taste were in some ways less decisively new. After all, merchants in the classical period had already discovered that certain regionally specific items, once entered into inter-regional trade, could spark keen consumer attachments. Pepper from India was an established example for people around the Mediterranean basin. It was important, nevertheless, that the roster of consumer preferences that depended on long-distance exchange expanded noticeably during the centuries around 1000 CE.

Tea was a case in point. Tea use seems first to have developed in China late in the classical period, indeed after the fall of the great Han dynasty. The first dictionary reference comes from 350 CE. By the 5th century nomadic Turkic traders had carried tea into central Asia, and by the 6th century its use had spread to Japan. By the 9th century tea was one of the commodities regularly carried by overland traders from China to India. The migration of Turkic peoples into the Middle East helped spread trade in tea, with consumer tastes developing in Persia and among the Arabs, ultimately penetrating the Mediterranean as well. Tea reached Europe proper only a bit later, in the 16th century, introduced by Italian merchants as a health drink. Here was a clear case of the development of an inter-regional consumer interest, often paired with a certain sense of ritual and by the use of cups and vessels, often made from porcelain, which also depended on trans-regional trade and aesthetic standards.

Sugar gained ground independently, and proved to be even more important. Sugar cane was probably originally native to parts of Indonesia, but cultivation gradually spread to other parts of southeast Asia and to India. It was in India, by the 4th century BCE, that processes were invented to extract crystals from the cane, so that sugar itself, rather than cane chewing, began to gain attention. Persians, fighting in India, learned about sugar, which one emperor termed "the reed which gives honey without bees." Early sugar cultivators, however, tried to guard the secrets of their production methods, because so much money could be made in exports. As we have seen, sugar was one of the products involved in classical-era trade in the Indian Ocean.

The Arabs began to expand the impact of sugar, once they learned the production process from their conquests of Persia. Massive sugar-growing estates were combined with large refineries. Most of the production was for domestic consumption, but obviously Arab expansion spread awareness of the commodity to more distant areas, like north Africa, Spain and Sicily. Other Europeans began to encounter sugar by the 11th century. The first mention of sugar in England comes from 1099, but the product's popularity soared still further in the next century, as a result of European crusaders' exposure in the Holy Land. Eagerness for the product expanded rapidly, creating a demand that could only with difficulty be matched by exports from the regions capable of growing cane. An English king had difficulty finding any sugar for a banquet he was organizing in the 13th century. By 1319 sugar in England was selling at a rate equivalent (in contemporary terms) to $50 a pound. The beginnings of a globalization in the taste for sugar, obviously accelerating after 1000 CE, would have further consequences for trans-regional contacts later on, but the importance of this new phase of trade and mutual influence, even in matters of personal taste, preconditioned all the later developments.

Basic products like tea or sugar were not alone in inciting changes in taste. Trans-regional transmission of fashion moved forward in this period as well. The attractiveness of silk was, of course, already established, so there was a basis already set. But in this period certain African furs and feathers won attention as fashion symbols as far east as Mongolia – again, a tribute to the expanding range of exports. Tall hats introduced for women in China would gradually make their way to France, where they became stylish accessories for aristocratic women by the later Middle Ages – even though the women involved probably had no notion of the product's point of origin. Indian cotton textiles, as already suggested, probably were the clearest success story in terms of influencing broad consumer tastes. Indian artisans in several districts learned to respond to regional preferences in terms of distinctive patterns and colors, while establishing a common fascination with the vividness and flexibility of cotton cloth for consumers from east Africa to the Middle East and Persia, from central Asia to Indonesia and Japan. To be sure, some societies reacted against these foreign influences, as signaling excessive interest in luxury: various European centers tried to enact laws banning Chinese silks, and they would later turn against cotton as well on occasion. But these laws, not usually entirely effective, were themselves positive proof of the challenge of foreign influence.

Concepts and cultural imitations

A second area of increasing trans-regional influence involved certain kinds of cultural apparatus, and some larger cultural patterns, as regions learned from each other and certain areas, more recently venturing into more formal political structures, tried to accelerate their advance by deliberately studying and copying other societies.

The spread of the Indian numbering system, with associated features like the concept of zero and decimal notations, formed a particularly clear example of the new traveling power of improvements in intellectual toolkits. The superior numbering system, devised by Hindu scholars beginning as early as 300 BCE and already copied, within India, by Buddhists, reached Persia well before the middle of the 9th century. The Persian mathematician Al-Khwarizmi, writing in Arabic, described calculations with "Hindu numerals" in 825, and an Arab mathematician also spread the concepts just five years later. Older numbering systems survived in the Middle East until recent times, even in commerce, though Arab use of the numbers for book-keeping would encourage their adoption by merchants in other areas such as Italy. And by the 10th century, a distinctive West Arabic version of the symbols began to spread in north Africa and Spain. The first mention of the numerals in western Europe occurred in 976, and by the 980s Gerbert of Aurillas (later Pope Sylvester II), who had studied in northern Spain, began to spread knowledge of the numerals more widely. An Italian mathematician trained in north Africa, Leonardo Fibonacci, provided further impetus around 1200, as his training in accounting introduced him to the numbers which "very soon pleased me above all else," though absolutely routine use in Europe would await the middle of the 16th century. Finally, it was through later European influence that the system spread still further, ulti-mately to east Asia and other parts of Africa as well as the Americas. Not a quick or uniform global journey, to be sure, but an indication of the power of transmission that had newly developed from the Arabian center by the 11th century.

Other cultural influences, aside from the world religions themselves, had a somewhat more circumscribed range, typically involving neighboring regions rather than wider impact. Here too, however, there was measurable innovation, as certain societies self-consciously sent student missions to more powerful states, hoping to learn a variety of secrets for success. The process began before 1000 CE, but it ultimately fed into the larger sense of inter-regional connection.

Thus Japan launched a period of intense study of Chinese values and institutions in the 4th and 5th centuries, under the leadership of the powerful Yamato clan. Chinese writing was introduced, with Chinese scribes brought over to make copies of major Chinese books and to help interpret them. Later, Japanese students and scholars who were fluent in Chinese began to be sent directly to China to further the learning process. The resulting imports were considerable: Chinese script was adapted to the very different Japanese language, giving the Japanese a written culture for the first time. Both Buddhist and Confucian ideas were widely imported, with Buddhist missionaries initially taking the lead. Other Chinese cultural forms, from styles of poetry to martial arts and gardening, were brought over and integrated into Japanese life. Both architecture and painting reflected the growing Chinese influence. Japanese literature filled with references to Chinese classical writings. New tools and techniques were introduced as well, from Korea as well as China, contributing to rising agricultural output but also helping to launch a serious mining sector for the first time. Chinese legal codes established a more patriarchal family structure in Japan, ultimately worsening the position of women – though the most extreme practices, like foot binding, were not adopted. Following the Chinese example as well, Japanese aristocrats began to engage in polygamy. For a time, the Japanese royal court also tried to follow the elaborate ceremonialism of its Chinese counterpart. At one point the Japanese emperor even added "son of heaven" to his many other titles.

This opening to the outside was not unchallenged – just as later exposures to external influences, in Japan and elsewhere, would rouse concerns from various people eager to defend established identities. Many aristocrats, for example, fought against the attempts to set up a powerful, Chinese-style central bureaucracy. Indeed, attempts at this point to imitate outside political institutions largely failed. The Japanese leaders abandoned the practice of sending regular official visits to China in the 9th century, though trade and cultural exchange continued at a high level. Clearly, despite massive imports, Japanese and Chinese societies did not merge into a single pattern. Still, the long period of deliberate and extensive imitation transformed Japanese life in fundamental ways.

Other patterns of intentional imitation opened up a bit later. Russian commercial interactions with the Byzantine Empire, along with Byzantine missionary activity, led to substantial but essentially one-way exchange. From Byzantium, Russia would copy Christianity, including the Orthodox definition of the appropriate relationship between church and state, and with this a host of artistic forms, particularly in the religious realm. An adapted Greek alphabet, called Cyrillic, gave Russians access to writing for the first time. As in Japan's experience with China, Russian interest in Byzantine political systems proved hard to implement, but some ideas, particularly about the importance of empire, did take root and affected Russian political forms later on.

Western Europe, by the 11th century, was actively staking out patterns of imitation as well. Political leaders, though sometimes aware of the sophistication of the Byzantine Empire and Arab caliphate, did little to sponsor direct study. This was not true for merchants, who were eager to copy the successful methods of their Arab brethren; a key result was the importation into Europe of the idea of commercial laws that might transcend specific political boundaries. Students of science, mathematics and philosophy were at least as zealous, with many groups visiting scholarly centers in Islamic Spain or north Africa, as well as Byzantium. The goal of these missions rested in part on an interest in recovering classical Greek and Hellenistic materials, often better preserved in the Arab and Byzantine domains. But interpretations of classical science and philosophy entered into the picture as well, with Arab philosophers like Ibn Rushd (known in the West as Averroes), who worked on issues such as the relationship between faith and reason, playing a huge role in setting up leading intellectual debates. Arab achievements in mathematics also drew Western students directly, as with Leonardo Fibonacci; this kind of contact even brought Arab words like *algebra* into Western languages, in acknowledgement of the importance of their contributions. Arab work in medicine also gained wide influence.

The kinds of trade and religious contact developing by 1000 CE generated cultural and political imitations from sub-Saharan Africa (looking to the larger Islamic world) and southeast Asia as well. But it was the explicitness of the foreign study programs issuing from Japan, western Europe and Russia that were particularly interesting in going beyond the normal effects of extensive contact through the acknowledgement of the importance of learning from other places. This attitude, which would continue to burn bright in many of these same societies, at least recurrently, in later phases of inter-regional contacts, suggests the relationship between the most self-conscious initial programs of examining external cultures and institutions and one core aspect of what globalization still involves. Japan thus sketched its main response to contemporary globalization from 1868 onward, in part because its leaders could recall the success of the previous openness to the Chinese example in generating demonstrable gains without an ultimate loss of identity.

To be sure, the efforts around 1000 CE involved neighbors, not the more distant models that some societies have had to chase more recently. But the patterns set at this point help explain why, later, even more venturesome outreach would be conceivable.

The travelers and expanded inter-regional knowledge

The emergence of more venturesome long-distance travelers was a final example of the kinds of impact the new trans-regional network began to have, at least within a few centuries. The known travelers were obviously a small minority, but their initiatives helped to put a human face on the new routes and technologies for communication. They reflected the new levels of interest as well as the new opportunities. The consequences of their ventures added, at least a bit in the cases where vivid travel accounts resulted, to the available information on the wider world and could spur others – like Christopher Columbus – to further efforts later on.

While the most famous travelers of the period, notably Marco Polo from Europe and Ibn Battuta from north Africa, operated a few centuries after 1000 CE, the precedent for more venturesome travel was established earlier. It was by the 9th century, for example, that merchants and seamen from the Middle East, embarking from ports in the Persian Gulf, began regularly to cover the 6,000 miles to the Pacific harbors of southern China, a trip that probably took at least six months. A Persian book of early in the 10th century, *The Account of China and India*, began to put these experiences into written form, offering information and the sense of enticement that distant voyages could generate. Other books, mainly by Persian sailors, offered vivid titles like the *Book of the Wonders of India*, with stories about other parts of Asia as well as India and a dramatic sense of the exotic adventure and profit travel could bring.

Religion continued to spur travel as well, particularly given the pilgrimage goals of pious Muslims. As Islam expanded, trips of 400 miles or more, for example from central Asia to Mecca, became increasingly common, often involving individuals (including women) who otherwise would not normally be counted among the most venturesome. Religion and trade combined to supply regular caravans of camels or donkeys, moving through various parts of Asia, the Middle East and north Africa, and benefiting as well from the inns that were opened at set intervals throughout the region. By the 12th century, religious travelers from west Africa, crossing the Sahara and then moving east along the Mediterranean, added to the pilgrims to Mecca.

This was the context in which the greatest traveler of the age, Ibn Battuta, launched his amazing series of voyages. Initially motivated by the religious pilgrimage to Mecca, to which he (like many Muslims) added side trips to other cities in the region, Ibn Battuta clearly caught an unusually fierce appetite for travel, from his early 20s into middle age, when he finally settled down back in Morocco and plied his profession as a lawyer. Deep interest in seeing new things, continued religious motivation in exploring the expanses of the *dar al-Islam*, and a desire for professional adventure – Battuta often took up jobs in Muslim governments in places like India – all combined as motivations. At some points also, a fair dose of sexual appetite probably entered in (Battuta periodically married and then divorced women in some of his destinations, like the Maldive Islands) – all sorts of stimuli kept him going at an almost nonstop pace. The pace and the distances covered were truly unusual, but equally important was the fact that Battuta was working largely within a well-established system that illustrated how far the connections among major societies had advanced.

Pushing beyond the Middle East proper, Battuta visited Somalia on the African coast, and also (while in principle heading for India, where he hoped to get a job) went deep into central Asia, heading up the Volga River into Mongol-dominated Russia. Doubling back to the Byzantine Empire, on a multi-year trip, he did finally end up in India, staying (unusually for him) six years, and encountering a number of adventures with bandits once he tried to leave.

His next goal was China, but again he wandered around considerably in the process, hitting the Maldives and also Sri Lanka. His ultimate stay in China was his only prolonged experience outside the Islamic orbit, and his reactions were interesting (and not totally strange to some global travelers even in our own day, when societies have converged far more than they had at that point). He recognized China's achievements and importance, but he could not feel at ease.

> China was beautiful, but it did not please me. On the contrary, I was very worried by the fact that the heathen have the upper hand there. When I left my house, I saw countless dreadful things. That disturbed me so much that I stayed home and only went out when I was forced to do so. When I saw Muslims in China, I felt as though I was seeing my own kith and kin.

This was hardly the last time that an increase in global contacts would take people out of their comfort zone.

Battuta claimed to have traveled fairly widely in China, and despite his general lack of enthusiasm he did offer some excited comments about the qualities of the great Chinese ships. On the way home he stopped in Indonesia and other parts of southeast Asia. Then a final trip, in the mid-14th century, took him to the great empire of Mali in west Africa.

A final series of major travelers involved the growing number of West Europeans who began to make their way to China, using land routes, Indian Ocean connections, or some combination. Merchants and missionaries headed the list – the Catholic Pope sent several missions to China in the hope of encouraging conversions. But there were also scattered entertainers and others eager for some combination of adventure and profit.

The most famous, and certainly the most influential, of these European travelers was the Venetian Marco Polo, who used a previous trip by his uncles, from Persia to China, as a precedent for forging a major expedition of his own. Polo, with his uncles, crossed into western China in 1273, after two years spent covering the 1,000 miles from the Mediterranean to the Middle East and Persia; it would take another year to reach the Chinese heartland. (The long travel times involved in this sort of journey help explain among other things how language barriers might be negotiated: a traveler could pick up at least a smattering of a new language – in the case of the Polos, Mongolian – while negotiating the transit itself.) Although Polo certainly recognized that the Chinese were "idolaters," in that they were not Christian, his admiration for Chinese political and urban achievements, and consumer prosperity, overcame any sense of strangeness – in obvious contrast to Battuta's reactions. Polo's later account, widely read in Europe by would-be adventurers over many centuries, made Chinese superiority very clear – in turn a clear motivation for Europeans to learn more from the Chinese and to find ways through trade to gain directly some of the benefits of Chinese achievements.

Both trade and travel generated an even wider literature about distant places and the excitement of foreign lands. A century after Marco Polo's account, an Englishman calling himself Sir John Mandeville wrote a book simply called *Travels*. It was largely fanciful, though many readers thought it reflected real journeys, as it described amazing people (like those who grew only one leg, in Ethiopia, which they used as an umbrella when they were sitting down) and massive treasures of gold in Africa and Asia. Work of this sort continued to stimulate wide interest – Christopher Columbus carried a copy of *Travels*, along with Polo's account – with its implications of the vast wealth and excitement that foreign ventures might bring.

The combination of expanding knowledge and excited misinformation involved more than European public, in this age of new trans-regional contacts. Chinese readers now could learn at least a bit about Africa. Direct Chinese merchant contact with east Africa expanded in the early 15th century for a few decades. But even before then the interactions the Chinese had with Persian and Arab merchants who had also visited Africa (a small number of African slaves were directly traded to China), and the interest in African goods and exotic animals, produced some sense of what Africa was like and why it might be interesting.

Travel and inter-regional knowledge, then, though still limited by the standards of our own time, expanded rapidly, even creating some of the issues about oversimplification and regional stereotyping that globalization still can involve today. The results unquestionably set a basis for further activity, as the cycle of trans-regional contacts ratcheted upward.

1000 CE and the stages of globalization

The innovations linked to the accelerating levels of trans-regional contacts had costs and benefits – as has been true of every stage in the globalization process including right now. On the costs side, the 14th century saw an unprecedentedly rapid spread of contagious disease. A new round of bubonic plague – what would come to be called in Europe the Black Death – originated in western China early in the century. Within a few decades it had spread, thanks to trade, not only to other parts of China but through the Indian Ocean to the Middle East and north Africa, where it would carry away well over a quarter of the population. Another decade or so saw the same plague in Italy, and thence northward in Europe where it had the same catastrophic effects. Diseases carried from other parts of the world, with results in high mortality, were not novel – the later centuries of the classical period had seen inter-regional contagion. But an impact this rapid and quickly catastrophic was new in world history, though it would recur at various points later on. More extensive and swifter contacts had a price.

On the plus side, in addition to new goods and excitement, trans-regional contacts might begin to create some sense of shared humanity across the various political and religious divisions that obviously still marked the world. It was also in the 14th century that a Chinese observer, Wang Li, could make the claim that with new levels of exchange, "civilization had spread everywhere, and no more barriers existed. ... Brotherhood among peoples has certainly reached a new plane." Exaggerated, to be sure, as are some of the more optimistic claims about globalization today. But the fact that the notion could even be put forward might suggest a novel stage in human interactions.

So was all this – the networks that had developed by 1000 CE, and the consequences that would continue to build during the ensuing two to three centuries – a definable first phase of globalization? That a new stage of interactions was emerging, compared to the more fitful patterns of the classical era, seems incontestable (though some partisans of previous trade connections would put up a bit of a fight on this). Whether this amounts to a preliminary phase of globalization or not, however, can certainly be debated. It's a question of assessing the magnitude of change and the extent of connections to what would happen subsequently. Is there a direct link between the emergence of new networks and contemporary globalization? Or are the really powerful shaping factors of more recent vintage?

Many of the negatives are obvious. The trans-regional connections that were surging by 1000 CE were Afro-Eurasian, not global at all. The isolation of the Americas and Pacific Oceania was the huge exception to any claim of early globalization, but there were also parts of sub-Saharan Africa that were uninvolved. The geography of globalization had yet to be established.

Even in the Afro-Eurasian network, the times involved in effective contact were massive by contemporary standards – months, literally, instead of days, to get from one end to another. This in turn limited the impact and intensity of interaction. We have seen how long it took even for obviously effective new products like paper to spread from one society to the next. Speed was increasing, but there were no dramatic breakthroughs yet.

The technology of contact, most obviously, had yet to be revolutionized. Attention to what the changes around 1000 CE brought toward greater globalization calls some salutary attention to aspects of the process that are not simply technological – that involve policy, commercial organization and motivation, and not just machines. Still, the lack of new machines, despite more modest gains in navigation and shipbuilding, is striking.

The range of interaction was also limited, partly because of the time-of-travel factors, partly because of cultural or other traditional barriers. There was very little inter-regional political influence. As we have seen, efforts to copy neighbors in the area of political institutions did not prove viable, and nothing like international political standards emerged at all (save to the extent that, within major religious zones like that of Islam, larger religious criteria transcended the purely local). While the consequences of contacts were expanding – as in the explicit exchange of manufacturing techniques – the inter-regional process overall revolved more exclusively around trade than was the case with later phases of globalization.

Regional involvement in the network of exchange, not surprisingly, phased in and out. As we will see, oscillations between engagement and disengagement have persisted in reactions to globalization even in recent decades, but the pattern was striking in the aftermath of the new connections that developed around 1000 CE. The Japanese retreat from the most ardent imitation of China after a few centuries has already been noted. Enthusiasm cooled still further in the 13th century, when China (but not Japan) was invaded by the Mongols, which made Japanese leaders feel that their country had surpassed their now-vulnerable mentor. Interest not just in imitation but even in active trade outreach declined. For quite different reasons, as the Byzantine Empire decayed by the 14th century, Russian connections with the wider world also diminished. Oscillations of this sort also qualify the idea of a compelling network, despite the important changes involved.

On the other hand, the strides toward more regular, wide-ranging and meaningful connections were considerable. Outright globalization came closer to reality as a result of the innovations, from the specific changes in navigational capacity or trade routes to less tangible shifts like the new sense of excitement now associated with travel and with travel stories.

Particularly important were new dependencies and motivations associated with trans-regional exchange, along with the expanding realization of what might be learned through foreign imitation. A growing number of people really craved goods, like sugar, only available in many regions through imports. Urgent tastes of this sort could even motivate foreign policy, as when Spain and Portugal reached out to seize south Atlantic island groups like the

Canaries, in part, ultimately, for their potential role in expanding sugar production. (And by the 14th century they were even importing African slaves to
provide labor on the new plantations, another sign of how new tastes, translated into consumer demand for imports, could drive huge changes in distant
human lives.) Merchants in many societies gained a durable stake in inter-
regional trade, another steady force for additional connections in the future.

Motivation and dependency, in turn, explain the creation of additional
systems of trans-regional contact in the centuries after 1000 CE, particularly
as Arab political vitality and leadership began to decline. Not only did new
merchant groups, like Muslim Indians, pour into established trade routes.
China began to accelerate its seagoing activities in the coastal Pacific and
Indian oceans with their pioneering big ships. For a brief time in the early
15th century, the Chinese even mounted major expeditions all through the
Indian Ocean, reaching not only southeast Asia but also India, the Middle
East and Persian Gulf regions, and east Africa, in search of trade and tribute. Finally, for over a century during the period of Mongol conquests,
from the mid-13th to the late 14th, interlocking Mongol empires from China
through central Asia to the Middle East and through eastern Europe created
protected routes for land transportation, complete with imperial passports to
travelers to guarantee safe conduct. (This was the context for Marco Polo's
journeys and his service in the Mongol administration of China.) Mongol
tolerance of foreigners, indeed their active interest, encouraged new levels of
trade and travel, especially from Europe to Asia, and of technological
exchange. From the exchange in turn came two of the great technological
imitations in world history: the Europeans appropriated Chinese explosive
powder to create new weaponry (from as early as the 14th century) and
Chinese printing, which set the basis for an explosion of new communication
and the dissemination of ideas (from 1450 onward). Knowledge of paper
money, playing cards and a host of other items formed part of this circulation
under Mongol auspices as well.

Trans-regional contacts, in other words, did not depend on any one system
after 1000 CE. When Arab capacity declined, other agents and additional
routes replaced them, and the same pattern emerged when the Mongol
empires began to crumble and attention had to return to seagoing links.
Throughout these adjustments, the pace and consequence of contacts tended
to continue their acceleration.

The trans-regional networks did more than prefigure key aspects of globalization by creating import dependencies or habits of imitation. They also
provided additional societies with the technological knowledge to enter the
world arena on new terms – as southeast Asian merchants began to do in
Indian Ocean trade, or as Europeans were beginning to do on an even larger
scale by the 15th century. The networks motivated new policies and new
adventurers to take fuller advantage of the contacts now so firmly established –
as when European statesmen and explorers began to think about more direct

ways to reach India and China, and in the process accidentally opened a new chapter in the whole contact process.

The next phase of globalization, from 1500 onward, thus resulted directly from the trans-regional network. In turn, there is a straight line, in terms of patterns, technologies and goals, between this network and each subsequent globalization stage – including our own. Assessing the significance of change, particularly a collection of diverse shifts like those that created the trans-regional network – and the force of its connections to later developments – is always challenging. There's always the danger of downplaying the importance of later innovations, or assuming too much inevitability. Simply pinning a common label, like globalization, on discrete series of changes risks being misleading. But failing to recognize connections – as globalization historians have tended to do in neglecting this trans-regional phase, or in ignoring Arab contributions in favor of honoring western Europe – is also misleading. Globalization was not necessarily predetermined by 1000 CE or 1200 CE; it could have been diverted, and it certainly had not yet fully unfolded. But key directional signals were clearly established. The next step, after 1500, was a surprise in the sense of the unexpected, almost accidental, involvement of the Americas. But it was no surprise at all that a host of people wanted to take fuller advantage of Asian and African trade and sought to gain a greater role in inter-regional relationships – which was precisely how trans-regional activity began to morph into connections much closer to globalization outright.

Further reading

Abu-Lughod, Janet L. *Before European Hegemony: The World System A.D. 1250 to 1350* (New York: Oxford University Press, 1989).

Bennison, Amira K. and Gascoigne, Alison L., eds. *Cities in the Pre-Modern Islamic World: The urban impact of religion, state and society* (Oxford: Routledge, 2007).

Bloom, Jonathan. *Paper before Print: The History and Impact of Paper in the Islamic World* (New Haven, CT: Yale University Press, 2001).

Chaudhuri, K.N. *Trade and Civilisation in the Indian Ocean: An Economic History from the Rise of Islam to 1750* (Cambridge: Cambridge University Press, 1985).

Frank, Andre Gunder. *The Centrality of Central Asia* (Amsterdam: Vu University Press, 1993).

Frank, Andre Gunder. *ReOrient: Global Economy in the Asian Age* (Berkeley, CA: University of California Press, 1998).

Hourani George F. and Carswell, John. *Arab Seafaring: In the Indian Ocean in Ancient and Early Medieval Times* (New Jersey: Princeton University Press, 1995).

Mintz, Sidney W. *Sweetness and Power: The Place of Sugar in Modern History* (New York: Penguin Books, 1986).

Nakosteen, Mehdi. *History of Islamic Origins of Western Education* (Bethesda, MD: Ibex Publishers, 1984).

Pacey, Arnold. *Technology in World Civilization: A Thousand Year History* (Cambridge, MA: The MIT Press, 1991).

Chapter 4

1500 as turning point
The birth of globalization?

Developments around 1500, and the systems that resulted, clearly moved closer to full globalization. The inclusion of the Americas in patterns of contact and, soon, the first definitely recorded trip across the Pacific, created the possibility of growing links to virtually every major society. Pockets of isolation remained. Australia and New Zealand were not fully brought into the picture until the 18th century, and well after that small clusters of hunting-and-gathering tribes people in remote spots were untouched by even tentative contact. But isolation was now the exception, and most regions became ever more substantially involved with exchanges of goods, people, diseases and more. The new global geography was only part of the change, however. The intensity and consequences of connections shifted. Precisely because exchanges had more intrusive implications, some societies consciously decided to limit their involvement – a backhanded testimony to the fact that contacts now raised new kinds of identity issues, compared to the more casual patterns of the previous phase. New types of inequality arose within the global system as well, that would become durable staples, at least to some extent, from the 1500s to the present day. In several respects, then, the meaning of global connections began to take on new contours. As happened after 1000, momentum would continue after 1500, leading to further changes, particularly by the 18th century, that enhanced global activities.

Many global historians acknowledge the importance of the changes that began to take hold at this point. One leading practitioner of the new global history, Wolf Schäfer, who argues that massive shifts after 1950 have created a fundamentally different world based on globalization, admits that 1500 nevertheless opened a significant new chapter, which he calls "protoglobalization." If the really big stuff was still to come, in other words, the innovations of the 16th century nevertheless deserve credit for a considerable push.

Interestingly, in contrast, the historians who have been working to see globalization emerging in several stages, rather than one great contemporary swoop, have tended to downplay 1500 in favor of later key dates. To be sure, Robbie Robertson, writing of the "three waves" of globalization, introduces the first wave in the 16th century, when

human societies experienced a fundamental change in their interconnections. Previously isolated communities found themselves danger-
ously exposed to new global forces. Many societies were transformed by
the experience; others were enslaved. Many peoples did not survive.

But his account of the nature of change turns quickly to fairly general and
familiar developments, not irrelevant, but not focused very clearly on the
kinds of shift in global structures we would associate with globalization.

Yet another historical treatment, by Osterhammel and Petersson, while
making brief bows to the earlier impact of Islam and the Mongols and then
the rise of European sea trade and the inclusion of the Americas, really
delays any clear reference to globalization until 1750. Before then, in the
authors' judgment, while forces of integration were gaining ground, most
societies operated very separately. It was only with a further surge in European imperialism and the first fruits of the Industrial Revolution that anything like globalization became possible, in this view.

So there is a genuine analytical challenge, to pinpoint exactly what the
developments after 1500 set in motion, relevant to globalization, that had
not previously operated, as opposed simply to holding back and waiting for
a later, more decisive date. The concept of a "protoglobal" period – genuinely moving toward globalization but not yet fully there – may turn out to
make great sense, but it needs explicit definition beyond familiar references
to the rise of European-dominated trade.

In this chapter, focusing on the reasons to identify the next phase of globalization, or preparation for globalization, in developments that began in
the 1500s, we deal with the huge implications of the changes in global geography – the inclusion of the Americas and what this led to in terms of the
further globalization of human basics like diseases and foods. Here, along
with the later opening of the Pacific Ocean and its territories, was a massive
expansion of the theme of new contact routes, already visible on the smaller
trans-regional scale in the previous phase. We deal with shifts in globally
relevant technologies, though again without overdoing claims about dramatic breakthroughs. New forms of weaponry, most obviously, facilitated
forced entry of some societies into others, but there were also some changes
in transportation and communication that furthered the process of inter-
connection. We deal with crucial new global institutions, most notably new
business organizations capable of bridging among distant societies in new
ways. The consequences of these various changes included innovations in
migration patterns and the mixing of peoples, and the new or at least much
more visible pattern of global inequality which became part of the exchange
process from this point until the present day. Production patterns and consumer tastes were further reshaped by exchange, another familiar theme now
given new dimensions; food options globalized, with the mixing of Old and
New World staples. But there were also limitations to the power of global

change. Different regions participated differentially – indeed there was more conscious resistance than in the earlier phase, a sign that there was more to lose from heightened contact but also, still, ample opportunity to decide not to join in.

Finally, change must also be qualified by continuities from earlier systems. If the emergence of globalization is seen in a series of surges, each surge must incorporate some elements of the previous phase. In this case, many key motivations obviously persisted; they did not have to be reinvented. Furthermore, some of the specific forms of contact, for example around Indian Ocean exchanges and amid Asian export patterns, persisted, even as attention began to shift to innovations such as the involvement of the Americas. Precisely because so many contacts had succeeded amid the developments around 1000, not everything had to be reinvented even as the preconditions for globalization accelerated further.

One of the most obvious developments during the decades after 1500 shows some of the complexities of the new contact patterns in this period. Around 1000, as we have seen, great religions, headed by Islam, had fanned out over large areas, showing the power to disseminate common basic cultures more widely than ever before; but at the same time, the resulting religious map introduced new divisions in humankind based on religious preference. After 1500, the capacity of several societies – first Spain and Portugal, then France, Holland and Britain – to set up and operate overseas colonies at great distances from the home country demonstrated new organizational strengths directly relevant to advancing globalization. Bureaucrats could be sent out, rules established, and records kept from European centers to American or Asian colonies as never before, defying earlier regional separation. To be sure, most of the colonies were fairly loosely organized, with lots of dependence on negotiations with local leaders – particularly in Africa or Asia – but the ability even to project political connections over these distances had no precedent in world history. Yet the colonial systems, like the world religions, divided as well as connected. European colonial powers fiercely rivaled each other; the common fact of colonial control faded before the battles between England and Spain, and France and England. Colonies also introduced new and deep divisions between colonizers and colonized that would complicate global relationships through the later 20th century and that echo still today. New global capacities and new global battle lines, in other words, emerged simultaneously.

Technology

Guns, and particularly the naval cannon, played a major role in underpinning the new patterns of global contact. Force had helped shape trans-regional exchanges previously, but for the most part in a subordinate way. Arab armies, pushing across north Africa and into Spain, and through central Asia to western China, had helped establish key contact patterns before 1000. Later, the great Chinese expeditions of the 15th century generated some skirmishes as part of the effort to win tribute from societies around the Indian Ocean.

With gun-based military technology, however, force became more prominent in shaping global relationships. The new technology depended on the previous Chinese invention of explosive powder and European improvements in the metal casting through which this powder could launch projectiles over considerable distances and with some accuracy – guns, in short. The combination was ready to go by 1500. When Vasco da Gama, the Portuguese explorer, rounded Africa and reached India in 1498–99, signaling Portuguese entry into established patterns of Indian Ocean commerce, he actually had little to offer his Asian counterparts: the European goods he brought drew scant interest. The main result of his voyage was the evidence he could provide of opportunities for Portugal to gain direct involvement in the cherished spice trade. But when da Gama returned to India on a second trip, and as Portugal organized an Indian Ocean fleet under the aggressive Alfonso d'Albuquerque, ship's guns began to produce the edge that mere trade offers could not provide. Heavily armed Portuguese vessels, bombarding ports and local shipping alike, gained Portugal several trading bases on the Indian coast and intimidated other merchants, some of whom began to pay Portugal a tribute tax in order to continue their seaborne trade. D'Albuquerque, to be sure, supplemented guns with less technological coercion, executing or cutting off the hands of sailors who defied Portuguese control. But it was European gunnery, steadily improved from 1500 onward, that allowed Europeans to acquire a substantial share in global trade and facilitated additional connections, including, of course, the inclusion of the Americas.

Guns were a core part of the military package that allowed Europeans to gain an upper hand in the Americas and the Caribbean, often with relatively little resistance. Hernando Cortés, for example, the Spanish conqueror of Mexico early in the 16th century, while eager to negotiate with native Americans peacefully, noted the impact of the "discharge of our guns" when resistance was offered. In turn an Aztec observer, present when Cortés ordered a "great cannon" to be fired off, noted that "the messengers lost their senses and fainted away." They later told the Aztec ruler how

> a thing like a ball of stone comes out from its entrails; it comes out shooting sparks and raining fire. … If it is aimed against a tree, it shatters the tree into splinters. This is a most unnatural sight, as if the tree had exploded from within.

Motecuhzoma, hearing this account, reportedly was "filled with terror. It was as if his heart had fainted, as if it had shriveled. It was as if he were conquered by despair." With guns, in other words, Europe not only crashed the global party, but helped redefine its dimensions.

Guns were not the only new technology that reshaped patterns of contact. The capacity to cross the Atlantic and, soon, the Pacific on a regular basis required improvements in shipbuilding, though it also relied on the navigational devices and innovations that had developed in the previous period. The fact that an individual crew could circumnavigate the globe, led by Ferdinand Magellan (completed under Juan Sebastian del Cano after Filipinos killed Magellan), 1519–22, was a technological triumph as well as a triumph of a new level of human daring.

Increasing the size and versatility of ocean-going ships was a key gain, as well as doing away with the need for oarsmen. Ironically, Europeans would not introduce some of the advances the Chinese had made, notably the provision of watertight inner compartments, until the 19th century; and they never matched the size of the largest junks. But European ship designers did build on other Chinese and particularly Arab designs, to launch types of vessel that were superior in many respects.

By 1500, European ships, though small compared to the great Chinese junks, had improved their maneuverability thanks to the use of both square and triangular, or lateen, sails. The mixture allowed them to pick up winds from almost any direction, which in turn was vital to the ability to develop new sea routes. Square sails remained essential for taking full advantage of tail winds, but they were fairly useless in crosswinds; this is where the lateen sails came in, allowing the use of winds from the sides. Portuguese and other European manuals on shipbuilding improved steadily, which obviously both summarized existing gains and encouraged further developments. Not only European but also Indian and southeast Asian shipyards served the ocean-going vessels of the period. European access to some of the rot- and insect-resistant woods available in tropical Asia also played a role in the steady if undramatic gains in ships' performance.

Other improvements from the later 15th century onward involved modifications of hull design, again with the goal of producing ships capable of sailing in mid-ocean, well away from land. Famous vessel types such as the Spanish galleon were defined by particular types of hull as well as the configuration of the sails. Gradually, design changes facilitated larger cargoes. In the 18th century, for example, the carrying capacity of Dutch ships plying the Indian Ocean increased by 25 percent.

Further improvements in navigational devices were also crucial, though almost all of them utilized the basic inventions previously adapted from the Chinese and the Arabs. Capacities in navigation changed rapidly in the decades after 1500, as more and more seagoing voyages operated for weeks, sometimes even months, without the ability to determine directions by sighting land. Measurements of latitude – distances north or south of the equator – developed particularly. Navigators learned to calculate not only the direction of a ship, but also its speed and the speeds of ocean currents and winds, to deduce latitude in a procedure called dead reckoning. Globes and improved maps of the earth assisted this work, as sea charts showing parallels of latitude became widely available. Equipment such as astrolabes and quadrants were further adapted. A new kind of cross-staff, used to locate directional stars and then translate this determination into degrees of latitude, had developed from the older Arab *kamal*. Novel devices also allowed calculations to be made from the sun, with smoked glass inserted to prevent the navigator from blinding himself. Astronomical charts, kept rigorously confidential by ships' captains, calculated heights of the sun above the equator at noon for every day of the year.

The compass remained fundamental; Christopher Columbus noted that it "always seeks the truth." Sixteenth-century compasses involved a large magnetized needle fastened to the underside of a directional card, with the needle swinging freely on a brass pin. The whole apparatus was carefully kept level through the use of mounting rings. Local variations in magnetic field, that might produce errors in the compass, were increasingly charted by the 16th century, with new instruments available to compensate.

Timing mechanisms improved as well, for these were essential in calculating latitudes. Hourglasses filled with sand were widely used, and these timers also helped calculate a ship's speed. Sailors also began more regularly to chart courses and speeds in ships' logs, which in turn provided data that could be used in more general charts.

And of course refinements continued. By the 18th century the big quest was for the ability to measure longitudes (east–west positions). King Charles II of Britain set up the Royal Observatory in 1675 to solve the problem of finding longitude at sea, and in 1714 the government offered a large price for methods that would provide accurate determinations. Relying on a new ability to register time more accurately and minutely (with new clocks and then even watches that would keep time with no more than one second's error per month), a successful device finally emerged in 1768. A three-year voyage of Captain James Cook, 1772–75, which ranged the Pacific from the tropics to the Antarctic, would have been impossible without the new ability to gauge longitudinal position, with Cook referring to the new watches as "our faithful guide through all the vicissitudes of climates."

The various developments in transportation technology, both ship design and navigational improvements, did not directly do much to increase the speed of transportation, and this was a huge limitation in the framework for advances in globalization after 1500. They did, however, greatly increase the areas that could be reached by sea – and this could have some indirect effects even on speed. It has been estimated that sea routes extended almost 45 percent farther by the 1500s than they had in 1000, a massive advance and probably the greatest increase over any 500-year span to that date. For the first time, indeed, sea routes began greatly to surpass land routes in terms of service as major arteries of trade.

A direct result of technological change, plus growing experience, involved new abilities to move into previously uncharted territories. Europeans, headed by the Portuguese, learned that going out greater distances at sea – for example, in the Atlantic Ocean – though counter-intuitive, would allow ships to pick up new directional winds that would allow greater mobility in the long run. The Portuguese had no trouble sailing to the Canary Islands in the south Atlantic because trade winds blew from the northeast, but getting back to Europe was a huge problem. Instead of trying to force their way against the trade winds, Portuguese ships by the mid-15th century went far- ther out into the Atlantic until they could pick up westerlies that would move them back to Europe directly. Similar principles were used to get from Portugal around the southern tip of Africa, and the pattern would soon be applied to other parts of the world as well.

Speed, as well as flexibility, might benefit. While there was no basic change in the pace of ships in the Indian Ocean, new navigational devices, plus greater experience and greater daring, allowed sailors to use lower lati- tudes – the 40s or the 50s – to move more directly from Africa to southeast Asia, because the winds were steadier at these levels precisely because there were no intervening land masses. There were greater risks of shipwreck as well, but, for many, the shorter travel time was well worth the gamble.

The most obvious technological emphasis in the period, beyond the new levels of force available, involved transportation rather than communication, because enhanced trading capacity was the obvious immediate goal. Yet the most revolutionary single technological development at the outset of the new period, aside from guns, actually rested in the communications field rather than transportation: the invention of more efficient printing presses in Europe, after adaptations from east Asian models. Printing had quick and dramatic effects in Europe itself in transmitting knowledge and imagery and, fairly soon, helping to upset established patterns of culture by challenging traditions and spreading new ideas. The global impact of the same commu- nications revolution, however, is not so easily established – at the very least, it was considerably more gradual. The new printing technology spread slowly outside Western Europe; books and other printed materials had to be translated if they were to have significant impact beyond a single region; and books themselves were heavy, hardly conducive to speed in communication.

Yet printing did feed into this preliminary phase of globalization in several ways, though without the revolutionary impact it had in Europe itself. Colonies of Europeans, most notably in North and South America, did establish printing operations by the 17th and 18th centuries and certainly served as markets for books initially printed in Europe. An intellectual community arose by the late 17th century, interested in the same kinds of novel (a new art form in the West at this point) and scientific information. While trans-regional communities had developed earlier around religious materials, printing expanded the range and helped shift the focus toward more secular topics. Second, printing, as we will see, helped international trading companies and also colonial governments promulgate rules and guidelines for subordinates in distant places. More standardized information could be disseminated than ever before. Finally, as additional regions became aware of European developments, particularly in science and technology, they began to seek access to printed materials themselves. Russian Westernization, for example, involved a whole class of Russian aristocrats trained in French and thereby easily able to participate in larger scientific discussions. New edicts in Japan in the 18th century encouraged translation of Western scientific and medical books into Japanese. Printing, in other words, might combine with the acquisition of literacy in other languages or with translation services to facilitate the dissemination of various kinds of knowledge across established political and cultural boundaries. Not, again, a communications revolution yet, but a significant development that built new kinds of trans-regional contact.

Global inclusion: the Americas and Pacific Oceania

Changing transportation technologies were directly involved in the most obvious revolutionary development in trans-regional contacts after 1500: the inclusion of the Americas and, more gradually, Pacific Oceania in routine global exchange. Quite quickly after Columbus' confused voyage of 1492, where he initially thought he had found a new direct route to Asia, Europeans established a growing series of voyages to various parts of the Caribbean and the Americas, linking not only Europe but Africa as well. Existing experience in sailing to key south Atlantic island groups like the Canaries helped explain why Europeans extended so rapidly. During the 16th century not only South America but also North America, including the farther reaches of eastern Canada, became routine stomping grounds for European explorers, traders and growing handfuls of colonists. Quickly as well, a new slave trade from Africa crossed the Atlantic to fill growing labor needs – a hideous traffic in human beings, over unprecedented distances, that would ultimately mount to well over 10 million individuals. While the Americas were most obviously transformed by this new contact network, virtually every part of Afro-Eurasia was affected to some degree as well.

Utilization of the Pacific developed more slowly. In 1519, Ferdinand Magellan, a Portuguese seaman but sailing under the Spanish flag, rounded the southern tip of South America to launch into the Pacific – which the Spanish had discovered, by marching across Panama, a few years before. Magellan believed that Asia lay just beyond the Americas, and hoped to accomplish what Columbus had not managed. Instead, he let himself and his crew in for an arduous trip, far longer than he had envisaged. Supplies ran low, so that the company was forced to eat leather softened in sea water, while seeking to capture any rats or mice that remained on board. Ultimately, the expedition discovered Guam and then went onto the Philippines; and once there, sensibly decided that recrossing the Pacific was a truly bad idea and that it would be better to sail into the familiar waters of the Indian Ocean instead.

Quite quickly after this, the Spanish began to establish regular exchanges across the Pacific from Mexico to the Philippines, where they brought American silver. But full exploration of the vast Pacific developed only over a longer period, with British and French explorers taking a leading role by the 18th century. It was only at this point that additional island groups, like Hawaii, became seriously involved in trans-regional contacts, and that the northwest coast of North America was drawn in. Australia and New Zealand linked in as well after 1750.

Still, a major redefinition of the world's contact map was an established fact soon after 1500, and the further ramifications would merely extend the results. Knowledge of New World geography, and by the 18th century that of places like Australia, advanced apace. Charts of the major new oceanic routes, complete with calculations of currents and winds, were another obvious result, facilitating further exchange and gradually making the voyages more reliable. More broadly still, the sense of what the world was expanded as well, particularly among Europeans. Most important, the inclusion of the Americas, and then Oceania, had concrete results that both confirmed and increased the importance of now literally global contacts. Trade, already a crucial sinew of trans-regional exchange, gained new significance thanks to the new products available from the Americas. Diseases took on new global dimensions, with crucial impacts as well on migration patterns; and an unprecedented global food experience emerged as well.

Global consequences: trade, diseases, migrations, and foods

Expanded trade, and trade impact, was an obvious concomitant of altered geography. American production of silver, organized by the Spanish, quickly fed commerce, particularly between Western Europe and Asia, as the Europeans used the valued commodity to pay for goods that were otherwise out of their reach because of balance of payments issues. China, particularly, imported silver with great zeal, expanding its output of porcelain and other items in the process. Peasants expanded silk production, destroying forests in favor of plantations of mulberry trees to feed silk worms. Silver became so common that the country shifted to payments in silver even for ordinary taxes by the 17th century, putting greater pressure on peasants to produce more for the market, so that they could earn money for payment, and in general increasing commercialism and also social inequality throughout the empire. Here was a clear instance of how new global trade rebounded on internal economies, with obviously mixed results. By the 17th century, more Mexican pesos circulated in China than in Mexico proper, because of their defined silver content. Indian manufacturing also initially increased in response to European buyers with silver in hand, as well as expanded markets in other parts of the world. The growing trade through the Philippines, which is where Chinese merchants exchanged silk and porcelain with the Europeans, encouraged urban growth and large colonies of foreign businessmen in this island group. Expanding spice production prompted southeast Asians to reduce forest acreage.

A bit more gradually, global trade growth affected European conditions as well. Growing popularity of Indian cotton cut into traditional levels of wool production, but otherwise global trade on the whole stimulated manufacturing. Increasing amounts of wood and iron were essential to supply the merchant fleets and their armaments. Profits from world trade and expanding domestic production brought improved living standards to many (though not all) West Europeans, who began to expand their array of home furnishings in response while also enjoying the greater availability of tropical products like pepper and sugar.

Not surprisingly, growing dependence on global trade, or at least a growing thirst, prompted military clashes. This was not the first time that trade had motivated war – we have seen earlier examples even in the classical period – but the motivation increased and so, obviously, did geographic scope. Britain and Spain battled for sea supremacy off the coasts of Europe but also in the Americas. Clashes between Britain and Holland, and Britain and France, had deep roots in the effort to establish global trade advantage. What was essentially the first global war, in the mid-18th century, pitting Britain against France in North America, the Caribbean, and India, as well as in Europe itself, mixed goals of colonialism and global commerce.

The heightened global impact of trade was only part of the story. Global patterns of disease were transformed. The Americas and, later, Oceania became enmeshed in biological exchanges with the rest of the world that included germs as well as foods and animals.

Disease and migration

There were two phases to the disease story. The dramatic first phase involved the encounter of Native Americans with contagions like measles, typhus and smallpox for which they had no prior immunity, that were now brought in from Europe and Africa. The result, between 1500 and 1700, was truly awful, in that up to 80 percent of the native population died out. The same pattern occurred in the 18th century in the Pacific territories, though at this point Europeans, eager to seize lands, positively encouraged the process in some cases by distributing infected blankets. This first phase of global disease contact led to massive depopulation in the Americas, which opened territories for European settlers and also created the kinds of labor force needs that sustained the unprecedented slave trade from Africa. These new migration patterns, bringing people over great distances in a relatively short span of time, were themselves an innovation in world history, as opposed to the previously dominant pattern of more gradual overland movements, and began to link migration to this new phase of preliminary globalization.

The first disease phase, however, was not the end of the story. Significant and horrible as the mortality results were for the people involved, in the long run a second development was at least as meaningful. Because of the new mixing of peoples, by the later 18th century there were no large regions in the world in which this pattern of massive die-offs could ever recur. With the exception of isolated pockets of hunter-gatherers, mostly on remote islands, everyone in the world was now incorporated in the same disease pool, with similar resistances. What had happened in the disease phase of the Columbian exchange was a massive example of what demographers call a virgin-soil epidemic, when a previously separate population is exposed to unfamiliar diseases with high resulting mortality compared to the patterns current among peoples accustomed to the same diseases. By 1800 – three centuries into this new phase of preliminary globalization – the possibility of significant virgin-soil epidemics had ended.

At the same time – and this was the final aspect of this second phase – the acceleration of new contacts among peoples, now literally around the world, increased opportunities for contagions that were important though less deadly than the virgin-soil encounters. New European interactions with the tropics, both in the Americas and in Africa, brought mosquito-borne diseases, particularly to southern Europe: outbreaks of malaria and yellow fever increased in the 17th and 18th centuries, with significant results. New forms of syphilis spread, either from the Americas or Africa. Interactions between Russia and the Middle East brought epidemics northward. Conflicts with the Ottoman Empire around the Mediterranean promoted periodic incidences of typhus, spreading from one region to another. Europeans did make some progress in the 18th century by imposing new border controls over the movement of people and animals from the Middle East, which reduced certain kinds of contagion. Others cropped up, however. It was in the 19th century that cholera, historically a disease in the Indian subcontinent, began to spread to other regions; seven major epidemics, from 1832 onward, brought cholera all the way to Europe, and from Europe to the Americas. In the 20th century influenza added to the global list, linking various parts of Asia, Europe and the Americas through contact-inspired paths of contagion.

The obvious point is that, increasingly, global populations became part of a common pool of diseases and resistances, in what can legitimately be seen as a new biological phase of globalization from 1500 onward. Massive die-offs began to disappear thanks to global contact experience, but contagious diseases, with less dreadful but still significant mortality results, gained new purchase by spreading from one region to another. Here was a new global unity in a very basic sense.

Foods

Something of the same global baseline emerged in the area of foods. As with diseases, there were important precedents; results of contact had long yielded opportunities to exchange knowledge of basic crops and animals. The addition of the Americas, however, greatly extended the results of this aspect of exchange.

For the Americas and Afro-Eurasia, because of long human separation and very different biological experiences, had very different food pools, that now, quite quickly in some respects, began to merge. To the Americas came Afro-Eurasian grains, like wheat, and domesticated animals – the latter vital as new transportation resources as well as food supplies. Populations of cattle, sheep and horses expanded rapidly in the new environment, and American natives adapted swiftly to some of the new opportunities. Peruvians, for example, partly because of Spanish pressures, quickly adopted the cultivation of grapes and olives, thus picking up two mainstays of the Mediterranean diet, while preserving local products as well. Encounters were not always so fruitful, of course. Mexican natives reported that European bread tasted "like dried corn stalks," and they also disliked the pork fat that delighted Europeans; they long held out for local corn products. Over time, however, some fusion occurred, with native Americans using pork fat as an ingredient of tamales, giving them a lighter texture and greater flavor, while Spaniards in their turn picked up a taste for local beans and chili peppers even as they continued to cherish wheat.

Foods *from* the Americas had an even wider impact than foods brought *to* the New World. Key American crops, like corn and the potato (including sweet potatoes), offered tremendous caloric advantages to many parts of the world; the same held true for several American varieties of bean. Specialty products like chili peppers and pumpkins might spice diets as well, and, a bit later, the American tomato would have a huge impact.

Ironically, American foods, though carried to different parts of the world by European merchants, long had greater consequences in Asia and Africa than in Europe itself. Columbus, for example, brought corn seeds back from his first trip, but Europeans found corn useful only as porridge and only in cases of famine, and even today regard it primarily as a food for animals – "a more convenient food for swine than for men," as an English observer put it in 1597. Corn won a much warmer reception in the Middle East, where porridge had higher status; it was widely enough adopted as early as the 1520s to begin to have a favorable impact on population growth by providing new nutritional value. Corn was also adopted in northern India, while Portuguese introduction of corn to west Africa quickly formed the basis for a new staple crop. Several Chinese provinces picked up corn from India by the 17th century.

Chili peppers had a lively trajectory: Spanish colonists learned to love them, but most West Europeans rejected their heat. The Portuguese brought knowledge of the plant to India, however, where it quickly joined other spices in dishes like Indian curry. From India it spread also to Thailand and (via the old Silk Road route) to several provinces in China now known for spicy foods. Africans also began to grow chilis, combining them with spices arriving in the Indian Ocean trade.

The Chinese learned of the potato primarily through commercial contacts with the Philippines. Spaniards had imported the plant there in the hope of encouraging population growth. Additional food sources were eagerly sought in China, particularly in the famine conditions that developed around 1600. Sweet potatoes, particularly, brought greater caloric value than rice, with much less labor. Corn and peanuts also increased agricultural productivity and brought new flavors to several regional cuisines in China and other parts of Asia.

European use of American crops took longer to develop, partly because there was less pressure on existing food supplies, partly because of fears of adopting foods not mentioned in the Bible and therefore seen as possible sources of disease. But by the later 17th century adoption of the potato proceeded rapidly.

Food exchanges, on balance, served to generate greater global population growth, thus more than counterbalancing the results of global disease patterns. Chinese and, later, European populations surged particularly through the use of new foods, but there were impacts in the Middle East and elsewhere. Equally interesting, however, was the growing amalgamation of basic food sources around the world. Different cooking styles remained; food globalization at this point did not threaten regional identity in this regard. And, as we have seen, certain regions made distinctive basic choices, as with Europeans and corn, and Indians and chilis. Nevertheless, the advance of foods of American origin was a global phenomenon. Today, it is estimated that a third of all the foods eaten around the world derive from plants originating in the Americas – and a full 39 percent of foods consumed in China. Here was a set of global adjustments, demonstrating the new range and power of exchange that continues to define how the world works today.

Global organizations: the international trading companies

Along with technology, plus the essential revolutions in contact routes and through this the new patterns of global trade, foodstuffs and disease, organizational capacity offered fundamental innovation essential to the advance of globalization as a process. There are obvious mutual relationships here: new organizations depended on the improvements in transportation, modest as these were, and certainly on the growing enthusiasm for trade. But organization must be considered in its own right, for it was in the decades after 1500 that international business, as we would define it today, took a major step forward, becoming a permanent part of global interactions.

The capacity for conducting business transactions over long distances was already well established. Arab and other merchants, operating particularly on the Indian Ocean routes, had developed procedures to exchange funds or letters of credit as the basis for commercial transactions; this was a crucial part of the innovations that began to accumulate after 1000. The actual organizational structures of trans-regional business, however, were not so clearly delineated. Many interactions depended on kinship ties or other personal qualities that could indeed stretch across different regions but had some obvious limitations. The new international trading companies formed in Europe to take advantage of the growing opportunities for commerce in different parts of the world, sometimes in close association with colonial expansion, went beyond existing precedent.

In the first place, the trading companies that began to be established in 16th-century Europe organized a number of shareholders, which allowed them to build up large amounts of capital. They did not depend on kinship groups alone. The Dutch East India Company, for example, established in 1602, had two types of shareholder, the participants, or non-managing partners who invested money in the hope of a return, and the 76 (later, 60) *bewindhebbers* who both invested and combined to manage the operation. Investors came from a variety of Dutch cities, and raised an initial capital of over 6 million guilders. Almost 400 businessmen initially joined in, despite a rather high minimum level, of 3,000 guilders, even for participants.

High levels of capital permitted companies like the East India Company (known as Vereenigde Oost-Indische Compagnie or VOC in Dutch) to acquire a large shipping fleet, while at the same time the Dutch government gave it a 21-year monopoly on colonial activities in Asia. Sheer size and scope have led some historians to label the company the world's first multinational corporation. But other organizations, including several trading companies in Britain, though they did not have quite such a large investment base, had similar characteristics. Unprecedented size, then, constituted the first organizational innovation.

The second innovation was an increasing tendency to combine sheer trading activities, which earlier merchant groups had conducted though on a slightly smaller scale, with direction production activities overseas. This economic diversification, with strong political corollaries, moved the international companies beyond mere exchange, to a deeper role in the internal economies of various overseas areas. The Dutch East India Company fleet thus not only moved Indonesian spices back to Europe and to other parts of Asia, but also utilized armed force to seize trading facilities and land in Java and other parts of what is now Indonesia. Alliances were formed with local rulers to acquire a monopoly over certain goods, while the company also directly organized plantations to increase the output of key products. In the 1620s the Dutch outfit forcibly expelled a large native population from the Banda Islands, killing many, so that new Dutch plantations could be established operating with slave labor. The goal was to increase the output of nutmeg and cloves, both valued spices back home, while cutting the costs. In the process, companies like the VOC, in Indonesia, or the British East India Company really gained military and governmental capacities in key areas, essentially running colonies from corporate headquarters. When, in contemporary globalization, multinational corporations are accused of wielding political influence over foreign governments, they are essentially mimicking the power position of the international companies of four centuries before.

Size and economic potency, and direct control over production and labor as well as trade, combined with increasingly sophisticated management methods and financial techniques. The international companies could shift funds from place to place, exchange currencies, and contract for sales over extensive commercial routes. Branch centers regularly reported to the home office. The British East India Company, for example, was constantly updated about trade patterns, with regional reports that were carefully catalogued in the central archive back home while also copied for circulation to other branch locations. Accounting records reported sales and inventories for both foreign and domestic operations. An extensive personnel system sought talented recruits, though there was some preference for hiring the sons of shareholders; and the companies also tried to prevent vices such as excessive drinking or gambling. Great emphasis was placed on standardization: the British companies had elaborate "laws and standing orders" specifying the procedures to be followed for all sorts of routine activities. Here was a key move toward more impersonal, bureaucratic management applied now to the global arena.

Not surprisingly, the international trading companies branched out vigorously, trading not only with the home country but with many other locations. The VOC had trading posts not only in Holland and Indonesia, but also Persia, China, India, Taiwan, Thailand and elsewhere, and it also helped launch the Dutch colony at the tip of South Africa. It brought silver and copper from Japan to acquire silk from China and cotton from India, which were then traded to other parts of Asia for still more spices or brought back to Europe. By 1669, the VOC was the richest private company the world had ever seen, with over 150 merchant ships, 40 warships, 50,000 employees, and a private army of 10,000 soldiers. This was international organization on an unprecedented scale, with growing geographical range added to the other innovations in organizational structure, measurably increasing business capacity as a central ingredient in the process of mounting globalization.

Global inequalities

The global contacts that developed after 1500 quickly installed new patterns of inequality among many of the regions involved. Here was a final aspect of this stage of globalization, along with heightened exchanges, new technologies, and organizational forms. The inequalities in turn became impressively durable, and in several cases persisted into the 20th and 21st centuries. Contemporary globalization notoriously differentiates among regions, with some clearly profiting, others suffering obvious exploitation. Essentials of this disturbing pattern began to be installed five centuries ago.

Trans-regional contacts even earlier had surfaced inequalities among trading partners. Areas that routinely supplied slaves for inter-regional trade in return for manufactured goods were both demonstrating and accepting unequal bargaining status, rooted in part in differences in organizational and technological capacities, sometimes also reflecting less abundant agricultural resources. But these inequalities cut less deeply into internal affairs, and had fewer wide-ranging consequences than the systems that emerged after 1500. By this point, it has been persuasively argued by social scientists like Immanuel Wallerstein, regional inequalities linked trading advantages or disadvantages not just to commerce itself, but also to social and political structures. And the inequalities proved so pervasive that they easily perpetuated themselves, if not permanently at least over large stretches of time. Here, arguably, was a crucial contribution of this phase of globalization to globalization ever since – and also a key reason that the results of globalization continue to attract so much anguished debate.

Here's how the pattern developed. European governments and merchants, benefiting among other things from their superior weaponry, forced their way into the Americas, hoping to find great wealth. Spain and Portugal headed the parade, but ultimately Britain, France and Holland gained the clearest economic advantages.

Quickly enough, the European powers found that they could use the Americas as sources of relatively inexpensive raw materials and foods. Silver from the mines of the Andes was the clearest delight, as it served European markets while also giving merchants the wherewithal to buy cherished Asian spices and manufactured goods; but colonists quickly set up plantations to generate sugar, dyes, tobacco, and (later) cotton, all for export to consumers back home. Brazil and the Caribbean focused particular attention for plantation activity, but the southern colonies in British North America followed suit as well. From some parts of the Americas also, forestry products and furs also served market needs.

In return for these items, Europeans sold manufactured goods like guns and beads, and also expanded their craft industries to provide furniture, paintings, and fashionable clothing for the wealthy minority in the colonies. Profit came in three forms in this colonial economic relationship, as Europe learned how to gain wealth at the expense of their new holdings. First, the products Europe sold, because they were processed goods, commanded better prices than the colonial commodities did. As we will see, Europeans gradually learned how to expand their sales inventory, generating a wider array of manufactured goods. Second, the goods were carried, in both directions, in European ships, and while there was risk involved in this, there were also additional opportunities for earnings. And finally, the whole operation was organized, as we have seen, by European merchant companies, who had their own fees to charge. European earnings from this new global trade increased wealth for many, providing new levels of capital, new opportunities for consumer spending, and new sources of tax revenues for growing states. By 1650, for example, despite grinding poverty among a growing working class dependent on wage labor, the average British standard of living was three times higher than it had been in 1300.

The economies on the other side of the equation, initially concentrated in Latin America and the Caribbean, served almost as mirror image of the thriving European core. Revenue was being taken away, on balance. Individuals could gain wealth, to be sure, as plantation or mine owners. But the system depended on low commodity prices, which meant in turn low-wage labor. Use of slaves and semi-free peasant workers on estates helped keep pay levels down for the majority. Only small local merchant classes could operate, because the overseas trade was organized by Europeans; and there was no shipping industry to speak of, and only limited local manufacturing. Governments were weak – which meant that there were few controls over European activities or the operations of the landowners – among other things – because the tax base was constrained.

Some change could occur in this equation. Spain and Portugal slipped from their initial power position, in part because little manufacturing developed at home, and, of course, more aggressive competitors from northwestern Europe took their place. By the 18th century, regional trade and manufacturing in Latin America expanded somewhat, around the major cities.

But the basic inequality was very hard to escape. With growing investment funds and more powerful states, the rich – that is, countries like Britain – found it relatively easy to get richer. It was at least as hard for the poor regions to escape their poverty. Ill-paid workers often lacked skills for more than menial labor, and they certainly had scant motivation to strive for more. Governments were hampered in trying to spearhead change. The lack of a vibrant merchant group was an obvious problem. Estate owners had wealth, but often saw little reason to try to change the system that brought them individual profit. Notoriously, they typically preferred to use personal wealth to expand their own consumption levels, traveling to Europe and buying European art objects, rather than investing locally. The poor tended to stay poor.

Furthermore, the reach of this system of inequality tended to expand with time, affecting areas that were not held as formal colonies. West Africans, induced into the slave trade, became dependent on a global trade pattern that brought individual earnings for local slave traders and governments, but disruption and misery, and scant earnings, for the bulk of the region's population. Europeans, selling manufactured goods and operating the ships and commercial companies, made their disproportionate profits here as in Latin America. By the 18th century, parts of eastern Europe like Poland, exporting cheap grains to West European markets and depending on low-paid serf labor on the great estates, began to lock themselves into patterns broadly similar to those in the Americas. Imports of more expensive European goods, particularly for the wealthy, confirmed the unequal relationship. Even the Russian economy, relying on harsh serfdom and exporting commodities like furs, timber and grain, took on some of the characteristics of economic dependency by the 18th century. So did India, again during the 18th century, as the British gained increasing commercial control and reduced India's manufacturing capacity in favor of a focus on exports of spices, tea and gold. So, finally, did parts of Indonesia under Dutch control.

This was not, to be sure, a fully global system, as a number of regions managed to avoid entanglement at least until later on. East Asian countries, to take the most important case, either continued to profit from world trade or isolated themselves from extensive involvement. British colonies on the Atlantic coast of North America, outside the south, generated an active merchant class and extensive shipping and local manufacturing; they did not match European wealth, but they avoided dependency. Clusters of European merchants located in the cities of the Middle East, operating by their own laws, but active regional manufacturing and merchant ventures continued in this region.

Nevertheless, the tentacles of world-economic inequality were pervasive and hard to disentangle. European governments and merchants gained both experience and motivation that could push for expanding the basic system even further – which is precisely what began to occur in the 19th century. Observers in the challenged regions were often quite aware of their plight. An 18th-century Indian account described the pattern of exploitation:

> But such is the little regard which they [the British] show to the people of this kingdom, and such their apathy and indifference for their welfare, which the people under their dominion groan everywhere, and are reduced to poverty and distress.

Knowledge, however, could be cold comfort. Local leaders, deriving their own benefits from unequal global trade, often simply did not care to seek change, and even if they did, they found it virtually impossible, at least at this point, to modify the system.

Structural global economic inequality, and the attitudes of condescension or resentment that could swell in response, were firmly installed in this stage of globalization, a legacy that would prove extremely hard to shake off.

Continuities in Asia and Africa

The "waves of globalization" approach, logically pursued, means that each major new step builds on, though also transforms, steps taken earlier, rather than simply wiping the slate clean. It is not surprising, then, that along with new participants and trade routes, older patterns persisted as well, so that exchanges of different types coexisted and in combination increased the overall level of interaction.

Emphasis on these elements of continuity is all the more important in that many scholars in recent years have criticized undue fascination with the doings of Europeans and the opening of the Atlantic because it leads to neglect of the continued vibrancy of the trade and manufacturing operations in Africa and Asia that had been established earlier. Indeed, it is important to remember that in many ways Europeans, flush now with gold and particularly silver from the Americas, were trying to break into a preexisting system, with a primary goal of seeking greater access to Asian products. This in itself suggests that elements of the older, pre-European system might retain considerable vitality and even generate extensions of its own.

Thus overland trade ranging from the Middle East, to Persia, to central Asia, Russia and western China continued in the centuries after 1500, with little or no direct connection to the innovations involved in transatlantic and trans-Pacific commerce. Much of this trade depended on special merchant groups, linked by religion and kinship, as had been the case before. Thus Armenians fanned out from the Iranian city of Julfa, reaching the Ottoman Empire and Russia in the west, and India, Thailand and Burma to the east. Significant colonies of Armenian merchants operated in Burma alone. Overall, Armenians traded cotton, various food delicacies like sea slugs (valued especially in China), and other items. Indian merchants, often carrying textiles, moved northward from India into Russia, forming a large colony on the Caspian Sea. Again, kinship was heavily involved, as merchant families sent relatives to the outlying areas, expecting that they would return every five years or so and be replaced by other kin.

Indian Ocean trade also retained many older patterns. For all their efforts, and their superior weaponry, the Portuguese never managed to control more than 50 percent of the spice trade in the 16th century. They failed to break into connections branching out from the Rea Sea at all. This meant that large numbers of Arab, Persian, Indian, and southeast Asian merchants maintained many of the long-distance trading links that their ancestors had pioneered several centuries before.

As had previously been the case, Chinese activity in southeast Asia, both by sea and overland, remained extensive. Chinese expeditions even penetrated to the northern coast of Australia, seeking various foodstuffs including sea slugs. By 1600 over 30,000 Chinese merchants operated in the Philippines, and other large clusters scattered throughout southeast Asia.

European interference occasionally touched east Africa, but here too for the most part older patterns prevailed, with some new intensities. This was in marked contrast to the situation in west Africa, where earlier trans-Saharan emphasis was substantially replaced by the new lures of the Atlantic trade as mediated by the European merchants. In east Africa, trade along the Swahili coast continued to interact with the Middle East, and this included the slave caravans that maintained earlier connections. Exchange centers like Malindi grew further, centering activities by Indian merchants who connected east Africa not only with India but with southeast Asia. Indian textiles were exchanged for exotic African goods.

Japan, even as it fostered growing isolation in many ways, also built on some of its earlier trade connections in the 16th and 17th centuries. By the early 17th century about 10 percent of the Japanese economy depended on exports, with Japanese shipping reaching not only China but also southeast Asia.

These various dynamic connections confirmed the importance of earlier innovations and their survival power even in a new era. They remind us that the inclusion of the Americas and the new position of European outreach, though important, even in reshaping activities in Asia as well as west Africa, are not the only story. The multiplicity of patterns, both old and new, actually adds to the force of protoglobalization after 1500, even as it somewhat complicates the standard story. At the same time, the vitality of these older links, and the innovations that could still spring from them, seriously modified, at least for several centuries, the worst impacts of global economic inequalities. Not only could many Asian societies, headed by India and China, expand their production for European and (through them) American buyers, thus winning much American silver in the process. They and other parts of Asia and east Africa maintained significant opportunities for profit in production and trade, independent of the European-run commercial systems. They were not, as a result, forced into a stark choice between a dependent status or some attempt to avoid trans-regional interactions altogether.

The limitations of early modern globalization

The importance of global developments from 1500 onward, even amid the vitality of older systems in Asia and Africa, must not of course conceal the limitations of the systems involved. Full-fledged globalization moved closer, and there was stimulus for still further change, but this was not a globalized world in our contemporary sense. Two limitations stand out: the relatively modest changes in the technological apparatus, and the striking decline of overt imitation among societies.

The European capacity to sail across the Atlantic and Pacific, as we have seen, signaled some useful improvements in shipping and navigational capacity. Knowledge advanced about the geography of the Americas and, by the 18th century, Pacific Oceania including Australia, which resulted in more accurate charts which in turn facilitated transportation still further. But long-distance travel remained slow and often risky, and there were severe limits on the volume and range of goods that could be carried. Printing affected communication, ultimately with some global implications, but, aside from this, communication patterns remained little changed. It took a long time to get information about developments in one part of the world to other parts. Evolution, not revolution, describes the relevant global technologies in this period, with the obvious exception of the new power of guns; and while this did not prevent steady gains in trade contacts, it was an obvious constraint.

Even more interesting, because in so many ways it was counter-intuitive, was the extensive turn away from acceptance of significant cultural contacts or voluntary or deliberate imitation after 1500, in this case in contrast not only to what would happen later, but to what had happened in the previous preglobalization phase around 1000. Precisely because contacts or potential contacts increased, many societies either intentionally or implicitly pulled back from too much cultural connection, eager to preserve identities even in a gradually shrinking world.

Mutual influences did continue, of course. Islam continued its spread into southeast Asia, including the southern Philippines, early in the new period; and Ottoman conquests allowed new conversions in the Balkans. Christianity gained on the heels of European conquests and commerce. Missionaries gained considerable success in Latin America and ultimately among imported African slaves. Of course Christian ideas were mixed with older religious beliefs and practices. In Mexico, for example, Mayans and other Indian groups managed to preserve elements of some of their traditional gods and goddesses in the guise of Christian saints. But these combinations were exactly what would be expected from mutual influence. With Christianity and European control also came new artistic styles and new standards for family behavior. Many Europeans professed dismay at local sexual practices, and urgently promoted different patterns of dress and less independence for women. Again, not all of these influences were fully accepted, but there was change. In the Americas, further, the arrival of significant European groups brought Western culture directly, establishing complex relationships between American and European cultural practices. Some Christian conversions also occurred in other centers of European power, for example amid some urban residents in west African ports, or in Portuguese Goa in India.

Other signs of cultural contact surfaced. European painting styles and even fashions had some impact among the upper classes in India, and the name "Mary" even caught on for many Indian girls. Briefly, in the 16th century, European influence brought some Christian conversions in Japan, though these were later attacked. Chinese elites showed modest interest in Christian missionaries in the 16th and 17th centuries, so long as the missionaries carefully took on Confucian dress and manners. Europeans were valued for their knowledge of clocks and some other curiosities, though the outreach was not extensive. For their part, Europeans eagerly learned about some aspects of the societies they now encountered, for example importing exotic animals as well as potentially useful plants.

But limitations and positive avoidance were on the whole more important. Europeans, increasingly proud of their technological achievements, often felt they had little to learn in the cultural sphere from any other part of the world. They might be impressed with the wealth of other places and with the power of rulers, but this did not translate into active imitation of cultural values. Indeed, Asian societies, and particularly the Ottoman Empire, came increasingly to be regarded as a bit backward and decadent, though these stereotypes blossomed fully only in the 18th century. Interest in benefiting from Islamic philosophical or scientific achievements declined notably, though some historians have argued that what really changed was European willingness to admit they were still copying, for example in mathematics, rather than a full refusal to learn.

In turn, several other societies passed up learning opportunities or prevented them outright. Notoriously, at the end of the 16th century, Japanese leaders began to turn against European and other outside influences, while attacking Christian leaders and converts within their own society. They professed fear of potential Spanish influence (based on their knowledge of the colonization of the Philippines) and related Catholic interference in Japanese culture. They also sought to protect the established feudal social order from the disruption that would come with uncontrolled access to European guns. Travel by Japanese was strictly limited, thus curtailing contacts with Asia as well. Among Europeans, only Dutch traders (less feared at this point than the Spanish) were allowed very limited contact through a single port near Nagasaki. Significant developments continued within Japan itself, including fuller use of the Confucian ideas taken over earlier from China, but interaction with the outside world was severely curtailed for over a century.

Chinese authorities began to attack Christian missionaries in the early 18th century, despite their fairly limited impact, again in a desire to preserve cultural and social order from outside contagion. Ottoman rulers, though well acquainted with developments in Europe, on the whole also held back from much imitation, though without so many explicit prohibitions. Notably, European printing was not permitted within Ottoman realms until the 1730s, presumably in the interests of preserving Islamic ideas and Ottoman political control from challenges that might result from a wider dissemination of new knowledge.

All of this meant that even technology transfer, though it did occur, was slower and less complete, in Asia and Africa, than might otherwise have been expected. And an interest in learning from European science, which was beginning to advance rapidly in findings, methods and technologies by the 17th century, lagged noticeably. Interestingly, Ottoman rulers did begin to import European doctors, though in fact their knowledge was not notably superior to that of Islamic physicians at the time. But the broader reaches of science were largely neglected.

The consequences of global contact, so vivid on the side of trade and food exchange, were thus artificially limited by conscious policies and (as with Europeans) cultural aversions alike. The fact that societies could stand apart to this extent was already a sign of the limits of globalization, and the fact that they chose to do so was revealing as well. Neither European example nor European guns, so potent in some respects, drew many societies in at this juncture.

Exceptions did develop, even aside from the areas of direct European control, though mainly in the 18th century. Japan, for example, which after all had a model of successful imitation in its past, slightly relaxed its prohibitions by the middle of the century. Aware of European advances from the contacts with the Dutch (and from those Japanese employed to translate with the Dutch merchants), Japanese authorities began to allow translations of Western works in science and medicine (though, deliberately, not other subjects). This was a wedge that would provide the basis for further expansion in the next phase of globalization, when Japan entered world systems with a vengeance. Ottoman strictures, as we have seen, also relaxed a bit, though there was no focused imitation.

It was Russia, another society with a successful imitation record from the previous period, that most obviously stretched toward deliberate learning, again from western Europe. Russian leaders had reached out to Western architects as early as the 16th century, seeking benefits from Renaissance styles adapted to Russian traditions. Far more important was the deliberate Westernization effort launched by Tsar Peter the Great at the end of the 17th century. Peter wanted several items from current Western practice. He sought military and naval technology, and related manufacturing techniques in metallurgy and armaments, to try to make Russia a military power capable of competing in European affairs. He was interested in a more rationally organized and better trained bureaucracy. He wanted his upper classes to be exposed to Western scientific and technical education, and hoped this would lead to improvements in agriculture and other areas. A 1714 regulation thus ordained:

> The Great Sovereign has decreed: in all provinces children between the ages of ten and fifteen of the nobility, of government clerks, and of lesser officials ... must be taught mathematics and some geometry. Without certificates [of study] they should not be allowed to marry.

Peter hoped, finally, that these same upper classes would learn Western art and fashion, so that they would seem less backward to European visitors. To effect all this, he imported European advisors, including artisans; he sent

Russians themselves abroad for study; and he relied heavily on the trade brought by colonies of Western merchants in cities like St. Petersburg and Moscow. In no sense did he seek to make Russia fully Western: he did not try to imitate Western commerce nor did he seek to alter the social structure or lower-class religious culture. Still, this was a huge effort at imitation that would have enduring consequences, as subsequent generations of Russians debated the value of Russian versus a more Western identity and as many in the upper classes accelerated their travels and cultural contacts.

Again, however, this effort stands out in the period as the only large exception to a general impulse to avoid much cultural interaction, save where it was applied through the compulsion of colonial rule. Older patterns of imitation, for example of China by its neighbors, also receded. Cultural globalization was yet to come, and it could even be argued that it was temporarily in retreat.

The mid-18th-century option

By this point it should be clear that several types of debate swirl around the subject of globalization in historical perspective. The initial question, fueled by the fact that globalization theory was not initially devised by historians, was whether there was much history at all, or whether globalization was so new and so huge that all one needed to know about the past was that it was different, and globally backward (or blissfully free from the evils of globalization – the evaluation could vary, but the historical conclusion was in one sense the same). Now that historians are chiming in, new debates surface about when to see the process of globalization beginning, and how many phases deserve attention.

This study has contended, thus far, that it makes good sense to see changes clustering around 1000 as marking a clear beginning of what might be called a preglobalization process. This depends on a realization that developments before that point, though interesting, are much more tentative and preliminary – and this can be debated. Then we have argued that a next phase, though certainly linked to patterns established in the centuries after 1000, opens in 1500. This new juncture would launch additional developments that would again extend over several centuries, easily continuing into the 18th century.

But we have noted an important series of claims that would urge attention to the mid-18th century as another turning point, often instead of 1500. And the claims deserve some attention as part of a more refined list of historical globalization debates.

Thus a "short history" of globalization, by Osterhammel and Petersson, notes the emergence of a global colonial conflict in the mid-18th century. The Seven Years War pitted Britain and France in battles not only in and around Europe, but in North America and the Caribbean, and in India as well. The war would end with enhanced British power in India, as what had been an important set of trading outposts began gradually to turn into fuller colonial governance and also a reduction of India's manufacturing capacity in favor of British industry and Indian commodities contributions. There is indeed no question that Britain's global capacity began to increase steadily, as against French, Dutch and particularly Spanish involvements. But while this is an important power shift, it did not necessarily change fundamental global dynamics. One of the problems with some of the claims about the mid-18th century as transition is an undue focus on British leadership, rather than the nature of global contacts in a larger sense. The heightened British role can be granted without necessarily claiming that this altered basic global dynamics.

The British surge was not the only story, of course. It is also true that the later 18th century saw growing unrest in what historians are increasingly calling the Atlantic world, with colonial struggles in North America, Haiti and soon Latin America as well. And the Industrial Revolution, ultimately a process vital to globalization, began in the later 18th century. But while these developments undeniably occurred, and undeniably serve as important markers in world history, it is not clear that they decisively reshaped preliminary globalization at this point.

Another approach to the same period makes more systematic claims. C.A. Bayly, a historian at Cambridge University, argues that the later 18th century opened a decisive gap between what he calls "archaic" globalization and the modern version. Basically, Bayly contends that developments from the silk roads through the intensification of the trans-regional network constituted a definite form of "globalization," bringing serious contacts and consequences to the societies involved, which is an interesting claim in its own right. But, obviously, he also argues that all of this, even through the initial impacts of the inclusion of the Americas, constituted a system different from what globalization would come to involve later on.

What were the differences? Archaic globalization emphasized luxury goods for rulers and elites, often sought as part of a tribute system. Thus the Chinese periodically sought products from other regions around the Indian Ocean, basically to enhance the status of the ruling class. Emperors robed themselves in furs from Bangladesh, while seeking exotic animals for imperial zoos from India and Africa. Archaic globalization was also often disrupted by nomadic invasions, which forced alterations in trade routes and gave the whole pattern of trans-regional trade an oscillating quality. The trade itself was organized by merchant groups heavily dependent on family and religious relationships; African merchants, for example, were identified mainly through kinship clusters, and family groups also operated in central and southeast Asia, giving some sense of personal connection even over considerable distances. Participation in the same religion supported linkages as well, and also helped define the products sought, as in the ritual goods widely imported for Buddhist worship. Bayly highlights the extent to which these patterns persisted, particularly in Asian and Indian Ocean trade, for at least two centuries after 1500.

Two developments, he argues, both sponsored by West Europeans and particularly the British, fundamentally altered the situation around 1750, even though a few remnants of the earlier patterns would persist well into the 19th century. First, governments became more powerful and effective – particularly in Europe, but also in some other areas like the Ottoman Empire and, soon, the new United States. This allowed greater control over nomadic incursions and other disruptions of trade, such as piracy. Britain controlled the seas and provided new levels of security in the process, while the United States would play a key role in reducing piracy from north Africa. Trade and transportation became more reliable, as earlier oscillations came to a halt.

More important still was the emergence of larger capitalist enterprises – the great trading companies but also the workings of the slave plantations in the Caribbean, which increasingly replaced the more personalized, religiously based links that had sustained trans-regional commerce previously. The new operations were more fiercely profit driven than more traditional merchants had been. They increased the size of investments in inter-regional trade and production for this trade, and they were willing to introduce huge changes in labor systems to drive production up; in contrast, while the more traditional merchants had often indirectly encouraged more export activity, they had not directly organized the operations. The new ventures, also provided more impersonal management techniques, capable of operating over large distances without the need for personal connections. All of this meant that most dynamic international companies were ready by the mid-18th century to push global trade to unprecedented levels, with equally unprecedented impacts on local economies and local workers.

Finally – though Bayly himself does not deal with this additional facet – other historians would add to the claims about a mid-18th-century turning point by noting the increasing European, mainly British, activities in the Pacific, in beginning to impact Oceania, Australia and New Zealand directly and also in gaining new levels of geographic knowledge about this part of the world.

The arguments for a late 18th-century transformation are interesting and well worth considering. The key question obviously is whether most of these changes had not already been suggested by the transformations after 1500, such that it's the earlier date, not 1750, that offers the clearest break with the past. After all, the great trading companies and the new Atlantic slave system were both installed in the 16th century, with the more impersonal investment and management patterns emerging at that earlier point. The Pacific was crossed in the early 16th century as well, and Spanish use of connections between the Americas and Asia – particularly the Philippines – developed strongly thereafter. To be sure, all of this accelerated by the 18th century. Far more Pacific territory began to be involved in global systems, and the trading companies – particularly, the British East India Company's expansion of operations in India – did gain further scope. But this was, it can be argued, intensification, not a fundamental shift.

The idea of globalization unfolding in stages obviously must allow for further ramifications from each new phase developing in the decades or even centuries after the stage basically takes hold. This was true concerning 1000, and it was certainly true after 1500. Earlier patterns – like kinship-based Asian and African trade – will persist in the meantime, and historians like Bayly provide a real service in highlighting this extended overlap.

Historians often have to decide the date at which a significant change in process effectively begins and becomes self-sustaining. Does the Industrial Revolution, for example, begin in the later 18th century, when factory industry first spread in a few sectors of British manufacturing, or would it be better to put its inception later, when the system really began to define the British economy? Pinpointing the more capitalistic phase of globalization involves similar issues, forcing a decision between starting point and more mature roll-out. Of course, a compromise might involve accepting both dates, but this decision might begin to clutter the historical approach to globalization with an unduly complicated chronology.

There is a historical model, with a relevant precedent, that might allow scholars to have their cake and eat it too. If 1000 is taken as the first clear phase of globalization or preglobalization, it must be recognized that subsequent developments, and particularly the 150 years of the interlocking Mongol empires, not only intensified the trans-regional networks but also ushered in something of a transition toward the next clear phase. Under the Mongols, appetites for contact and travel increased and the process of technology exchange clearly accelerated, providing western Europe, particularly, with both the motivations and the technological means for its more forceful entry onto the world stage.

Similarly, developments around 1750, though clearly building on the post-1500 phase of globalization, began to move toward a next, later break. Inclusion of the Americas and the Pacific, the formation of new forms of international commercial organization, and the development of greater and persistent global inequalities – all the result of the 1500 phase – were still being digested, their impact steadily increasing as Bayly and others in a way suggest. The growing role of impersonal capitalism, though introduced in the 1500 phase, can readily be granted, as the international trading companies expanded their operations, along with the clearer decline of some of the older merchant forms.

But three other changes can also be highlighted, though two at least again constitute extensions of the implications of the 1500 phase. In combination with mounting capitalism, they do help explain why the levels of globalization that had surged after 1500 were about to change into a definable new global phase from approximately 1850 onward.

Change #1: toward a new consumerism.

Global trade has always closely related to consumer behaviors and motivations. From the silk roads exchanges through most of the activities on the trans-regional network, most relevant consumer involvements did stem from the elites, as Bayly suggests. From 1500 onward, while elite concerns continued to play a great role in supporting global trade, a wider range of consumers began to be involved. Several food imports first attracted this broader interest. Coffee, native to Africa, began to draw interest from urban publics first in the Middle East, then by the 1600s in Western Europe. Attachment to tea spread from east and central Asia to other regions, again with wider publics involved. Sugar of course was an even greater draw, with hosts of Europeans eagerly seeking the product by the 16th century (and with their teeth measurably suffering in the process, at least until the advent of better dentistry in the 18th century). Less specifically, growing Chinese urban prosperity, founded in part on the silver imports won in world trade, fueled new levels of consumer interest for both global and local products. By the 16th century, in other words, large numbers of people in several parts of the world – not the very poor, but not elites alone – were participating in a globally based consumerism that sustained production and trade in several commodities.

Inevitably, this initial expansion of consumer interests encouraged further elaboration. Dutch urbanites, in the 17th century, benefiting from their nation's success in global trade, indulged in a buying frenzy for tulips and pictures of tulips, one of the first consumer crazes in history. Tulips became a Dutch staple in the process, but the initial interest had actually been imported from the Ottoman Empire. By the late 17th century, popular interest in coffee, tea and sugar was also supporting a growth in table service – in pots, spoons, cups and saucers. Some of these were imported from China – and they now began to be called "china" in England; some began to be manufactured locally. But the larger point was that, fueled by global interests, consumer passions were expanding to embrace household items and other goods. The result, in turn, was a level of consumer expectation, and networks of shops to service these expectations, that were generating a real revolution in modern consumerism by the 18th century, and this would in turn play an additional role in supporting global trade in the future. Globalization, in other words, no longer depended on elite tastes and capacities alone, at least in the wealthier societies of the world. This was another factor that would simply expand when transitional developments led to a more decisively new stage in the globalization process.

Change #2: expansion of European manufacturing capacity.

We have seen that the establishment of the trans-regional network, around 1000, had among its several effects a concerted effort to reduce dependence on valued imports by developing more home-based capacity. Thus Arabs learned how to grow their own sugar. Thus Byzantines and Arabs alike introduced a silk industry to diminish reliance on goods from China.

As western Europe gained a growing global role after 1500, it quickly learned that there was profit to be made in exporting finished products and importing cheaper foods and raw materials. Initially, Europe's contributions in this regard depended heavily on the export of guns, to places like Africa, and artisanal products like decorative beads. Europe also encountered, however, the superior manufacturing capacity of several Asian societies, and gradually but logically its businessmen sought to reduce dependency by expanding local manufacturing capacity.

A key example involved India's printed cotton cloth, which was already a valued item in trans-regional trade before Europeans began to muscle in. For a time after 1500, as they became more familiar with Indian products, European businessmen and firms like the British East India Company were content simply to organize the export of Indian cloth, making considerable money not only in European markets but also elsewhere with the colorful fabrics. Along with Chinese silks, but for a less opulent consumer segment, Indian cotton became a definer of fashion. By the 17th century, however, some manufacturers were beginning to realize that there would be even more profit if Europeans could cut out the Indian producers and not only sell but also produce the goods themselves. By the late 17th century, European governments were also becoming concerned about the amount of money flowing out to India, and they began to pass laws limiting the permissible level of imports. This provided another spur to local manufacturers. But the European imitators faced several problems: the experience and artistry of Indian artisans were hard to match, and so were their low wages. Over time, the solution was the use of more machinery to cut costs, while producing a competitive fabric. The turning point was the later 17th century, when a number of factories were set up in Switzerland, France and elsewhere; there were over a hundred dye and print shops in Holland alone. Increasingly complex equipment was set up to do the printing, reducing the need for as much skilled manual labor. By the 1770s, use of copper plates and then, within three decades, rotary printing machines, completed the process of converting an import staple to a leading domestic product.

All of this was, as suggested, in one sense a standard result of global connections and competition; it had happened before and would happen again. In this case, however, the size of the consumer market and the fact that Europeans not only copied others' methods but increased the mechanization involved had larger consequences. The response to Indian cotton became part of the early industrialization process in western Europe, which was clearly under way, if not in the 1750s at least by the 1770s when the first steam engines applicable to manufacturing were being introduced by James Watt in Scotland. While the first decades of industrialization did not immediately alter basic globalization processes – though they did advantage British industry at the expense of traditional manufacturing not only in India but in Latin America and elsewhere – the revolution would ultimately have transformative effects. Here was another way that developments after 1500, encouraging further innovation by the 1700s, helped generate the next true phase in the uneven march of globalization.

Change #3: new attitudes about the world.

A few sectors of what we now know as public opinion, initially in parts of western Europe and North America, began to move toward a more inclusive definition of humanity in the later 18th century, which in turn would generate some strikingly new and potentially global standards for human treatment. This was a very tentative development, which conflicted with all sorts of old and new human prejudices, but it too would feed the next phase of globalization opening after 1850.

The idea of global humane standards was not brand new. The major world religions had recognized the spiritual potential in all humans, though this warred against the fact that each religion insisted on its own monopoly of truth, so that humans who happened to be in other religions were not spiritual equals. Some philosophers, for example in western Europe, talked about certain natural laws that would apply to all people. Individuals, like the 14th-century Chinese observer cited in Chapter 3, might occasionally write about the desirability of sweeping aside all boundaries in favor of a single humanity – he wrote in the excitement of the contacts that emerged with the Mongol empires. But a movement that explicitly operated from a sense of basic standards that should transcend political and religious barriers and apply to distant people with whom one had no other tie – this was a global innovation. And, unlike the other developments in the later 18th century, this one could not easily be predicted from the shifts that had begun to take shape after 1500.

The focus, gaining momentum, though sporadically, from the 1780s onward, was a new and unprecedented belief in the evils of enslaving other human beings and the moral responsibility of all decent people, whether involved in the slave system or not, to work for its abolition.

Slavery was of course a very old labor arrangement, and while various observers, including Islamic and Christian religious leaders, had criticized its excesses, no one had clearly enunciated global standards that sought to root it out entirely. In the 18th century, however, a combination of the unusually great exploitation in the Atlantic slave trade and the great American plantations – which brought some former slave traders and slaves to the attack – and what historians have described as a "new sensibility" born of variant strands of Christianity like Quakerism plus the ideals of the Enlightenment, began to generate the first potentially global crusade against a widespread human abuse. Soon, abolitionists were organizing massive petitions and other forms of pressure under slogans pointing to what they called the "principles of justice and humanity." They saw themselves as "friends of the slave of every nation and clime," and they talked of "the whole civilized world witnessing with horror" efforts to defend the institution of bondage. By the late 1780s up to 20 percent of the entire population of some British cities was subscribing to anti-slavery claims of this sort, and deliberate efforts to spread the word across political and geographic boundaries became the first example of the mobilization of globally applicable public opinion.

This new burst of humanitarian sentiment was no mere abstraction. By the 1790s it would begin to lead to concrete moves to limit the Atlantic slave trade and to end slave systems outright in a growing number of societies. By the later 19th century, the same kind of sentiment, though still aiming at surviving slavery institutions, would broaden to other areas of social justice, becoming part of a new kind of global politics in the next phase of globalization. At the same time, it is important not to overdo. The 18th-century antislavery sentiments did not immediately sweep over the entire world. They developed in Western societies at the same time as growing nationalism and new phases of imperialism created mutual hostilities and prejudices among various peoples: Westerners might attack slavery, but they also often deeply believed in the inferiority of African and Asians. Still, the emergence of a first idea of certain global rights – the French Revolution of 1789, after all, would proclaim the "rights of man," while the American revolution trumpeted that "all men are created equal" – was an important step. This added to the transition between the phase of globalization launched in the 1500s and the surge that would blossom after 1850.

Conclusion

Innovations and accelerations in global processes after 1750 were interesting and important, but for the most part they confirmed the durable shifts in global relationships that had developed from the 1500s onward. Just as the trans-regional network around 1000 created long-lasting connections and technologies that would not have to be reinvented, so the world systems emerging in the 1500s permanently altered world systems. New routes across the Atlantic and Pacific would only grow in significance, confirming the role of the Americas and the Pacific Oceania in global patterns from this point onward. The new business structures devised by the international trading companies would flow directly into new international corporations in the 19th century and, thence, into the multinationals of our own day. Exchanges of basic foods and the new disease patterns resulting from global contacts became permanent fixtures, reaching deep into ordinary lives in many parts of the world. While the days of institutional slavery were numbered, the importance of long-distance migrations would survive. Also durable, of course, were some of the structural inequalities the world economy established – many of the gaps between rich regions and poor still so troublesome today can readily be identified in the 1500s.

The new global period also set up conditions for further change – as had been the case in the earlier reverberations of the trans-regional network. International companies might readily seek new ways to increase their profits: it was in the late 18th century, for example, that managers in the East India Company discovered that they could make additional money selling Indian-grown opium to China, and ultimately this would contribute to a far-reaching change in China's relationship to the global economy. Consumer tastes might call for additional export production: as British manufacture of cotton fabrics increased, for example, it would ultimately require that other parts of the world expand the output of raw cotton, again with wide-ranging consequences. More generally, the increasing European capacity to use machines to rival traditional hand labor at home and abroad proved to be an immensely dynamic factor for the future. The importance of new global trade routes provided obvious motivations for more decisive innovations in transportation technologies, which could shorten carrying times around the world. Historians use words like "inevitable" cautiously, but it can be argued that the implications of the systems launched in the 1500s did indeed ultimately lock in the conditions that would birth another decisive phase in the global process. This in turn would mean that, in a basic sense, globalization itself had already begun.

Further reading

Adas, Michael. *Machines the Measure of Men* (Ithaca, NY: Cornell University Press, 1990).

Adshead, S.A.M. *Material Culture in Europe and China, 1400–1800: The Rise of Consumerism* (New York: Palgrave Macmillan, 1997).

Ballantyne, Tony. "Empire, Knowledge, and Culture: From Proto-Globalization to Modern Globalization," in A.G. Hopkins, ed., *Globalization in World History*, pp. 116–140 (New York: W.W. Norton & Company, 2002).

Bayly, C.A. "'Archaic' and 'Modern' Globalization in the Eurasian and African Arena, ca. 1750–1850," in A.G. Hopkins, ed., *Globalization in World History*, pp. 45–72 (New York: W.W. Norton & Company, 2002).

Benjamin, Thomas. *The Atlantic World* (New York: Cambridge University Press, 2009).

Bose, Sugata. *A Hundred Horizons: The Indian Ocean in the Age of Global Empire* (Cambridge, MA: Harvard University Press, 2009).

Chaudhuri, K.N. *The Trading World of Asia and the English East India Company* (Cambridge: Cambridge University Press, 2006).

Cipolla, Caro M. *Guns, Sails, and Empire* (Mill Valley, CA: Sunflower University Press, 1985).

Clunas, Craig. *Superfluous Things: Material Culture and Social Status in Early Modern China* (Honolulu, HI: University of Hawaii Press, 2004).

Crosby, Alfred. *The Columbian Exchange* (Westport, CT: Praeger Publishers, 2003).

Goldstone, Jack. *Why Europe?* (New York: McGraw-Hill, 2008).

Gunn, Geoffrey C. *First Globalization: The Eurasian Exchange, 1500–1800* (Lanham, MD: Rowman & Littlefield Publishers, 2003).

Kiple, Kenneth F. ed. *The Cambridge World History of Human Disease* (Cambridge, NY: Cambridge University Press, 1993).

Lemire, Beverly. *Fashion's Favourite: The Cotton Trade and the Consumer in Britain* (New York: Oxford University Press, 1992).

Linebaugh, Peter. *The Many Headed Hydra: Sailors, Slaves, Commoners, and the Hidden History of the Revolutionary Atlantic* (Boston, MA: Beacon Press, 2000).

Ogborn, Miles. *Global Lives: Britain and the World, 1550–1800* (Cambridge, NY: Cambridge University Press, 2008).

Osterhammel, Jürgen, Petersson, Niels P. and Geyer, Dona. *Globalization: A Short History* (Princeton, NJ: Princeton University Press, 2005).

Pilcher, Jeffrey. *Food in World History* (New York: Routledge, 2005).

Robertson, Robbie. *The Three Waves of Globalization: A history of a developing global consciousness* (London: Zed Books Ltd., 2003).

Schäfer, Wolf. "Global History," in Roland Robertson and Jan Aart Scholte, eds, *Encyclopedia of Globalization*, vol. 2, 516–521 (New York and London: Routledge, 2007).

Schäfer, Wolf. "How to Approach Global Present, Local Pasts, and Canon of the Globe," in *Globalization, Philanthropy, and Civil Society: Toward a New Political Culture in the Twenty-First Century*, 33–48 (New York: Springer, 2005).

Sherratt, Andrew. *Trade Routes: The Growth of Global Trade* (Oxford: ArchAtlas, Institute of Archaeology, 2003).

Stearns, Peter N. *Consumerism in World History* (New York: Routledge, 2001).

Stearns, Peter N. *Global Outrage* (Oxford: Oneworld Publications, 2005).

Wallerstein, Immanuel. *World-Systems Analysis: An Introduction* (Durham, NC: Duke University Press, 2004).

Wallerstein, Immanuel. *The Modern World-System I: Capitalist Agriculture and the Origins of the European World-Economy in the Sixteenth Century* and *The Modern World-System II: Mercantilism and the Consolidation of the European World-Economy, 1600–1750* (St. Louis, MO: Academic Press, 1980).

Chapter 5

The 1850s as turning point
The birth of globalization?

In 1902 an American banker, Frank Vanderlip, embraced a German economist's statement about what we might call globalization: about how

> the perfect and instant communication between distant parts of the world, the cheapening of transportation, the wider knowledge of every country, its products and its needs, have brought about an interdependence of nations that is now almost as great as the [domestic] dependence of one class or industrial workers on another.

Nine years later – though this seems misguided in retrospect, with a huge world war about to occur – a British peace activist claimed that global relationships made major conflict increasingly unlikely, arguing that

> international finance has become so interdependent and so interwoven with trade and industry that ... political and military power can in reality do nothing (as) ... the problems of modern international politics (have become) profoundly and essentially different from the ancient.

Again, the parallels with contemporary global optimists are intriguing. Despite the passage of a hundred conflict-ridden years, is this all part of the same scene?

Local and regional constraints

A growing group of historians specifically interested in globalization place the effective origins of the phenomenon in the middle of the 19th century. They differ from the larger cluster of world historians who add features to already-sanctioned dates like 1000 or 1500 to provide a larger historical perspective (though of course they would not deny the importance of preparatory developments prior to 1850). They certainly quarrel, if implicitly, with the advocates of 1750. But they also part ways with the "new global history" approach, which is so fascinated with the radical departures, the historical disconnects, of the past fifty years.

Thomas Zeiler puts the case this way. Admittedly, recent changes, particularly in technology, have accelerated globalization's pace beyond anything visible 150 years ago. But in terms of basic changes in transportation, new business networks and economic relationships, the real movement to globalization began earlier. The movement was "nascent and incomplete," and it was "interrupted by events of the twentieth century": "but movement existed, nonetheless." Zeiler sees changes taking shape before World War I as the "early era of globalization." It was fueled not only by new steamships but also the two great world canals, which sped commerce around the globe; and also by real breakthroughs in communications, with telegraph lines between the United States and Latin America and Europe, and British cables lines to Asia, allowing faster commercial interactions than ever before but also unprecedented exchanges of news. Great world's fairs, beginning in London in 1851, highlighted Western manufacturing, to be sure, but with growing attention to economic and cultural patterns in other parts of the world. "Global connections shrunk the world itself" – precisely the claim made about globalization more recently. It was also in this "early era" that not only the United States but also Japan made basic adjustments to globalization that have, with a few disruptions, defined basic orientations ever since. Japanese historians readily see this period, and not the more recent one, as the point at when Japan made its really fundamental global commitments, and the same could be said about North America. Global worries about Asian competition – defined in the words of the German emperor shortly after 1900 as a new "yellow peril" – and the first stirrings of concerns about cultural and economic "Americanization" accompanied these changes.

This chapter will amplify these claims, and add others, noting changes in patterns of immigration, the onset of new kinds of global connection in popular culture, and a really new era in political globalization with the emergence of capacities to define global standards in a number of areas – beyond anti-slavery – and the formation of international conventions on a host of crucial topics.

We will also, of course, deal with limitations in globalization's "early era" – because the global processes common today were not fully sketched. Even in advance, however, we must take up a still more fundamental question: if a really good case can be made for 1850 as globalization's inception, why has this date never been widely used in world history before?

Both European and world historians have conventionally seized on a period 1750 or 1789 to 1914 as an almost self-evident chronological unit in the human experience, with 1850s and early globalization buried within this larger scheme. The great British historian Eric Hobsbawm dubbed the period the "long 19th century," and virtually every survey history, whether Western or global in focus, has followed suit. Again, there's a bit of dispute about when to begin the "long" century. The date 1750 or so captures the early stages of British and then European industrialization, undeniably (if not then, at least ultimately) a major change in human history. As we have seen, a few voices for a first globalization phase have chimed in with a similar periodization. The date 1789 highlights the revolutionary era, launched a bit earlier but gaining new urgency with the great French rising of that year. And of course, regardless of specific inception, the two developments can be put together, with a long 19th century focused ultimately on the twin phenomena of economic upheaval – industrialization – and political and social challenge through the revolutionary ideas and precedents. Interweaving with both developments, though particularly with industrialization, the long 19th century also saw the further blossoming of Western imperialism, with Africa, Oceania and new parts of southeast Asia offering new jewels to European imperial crowns.

Ending in 1914 seems even more obvious: World War I was a huge event, disrupting lives and social processes around the world, though particularly of course in Europe itself. The generation that experienced that war understandably believed that it was a true watershed, the "Great War," and even later groups of historians picked up the same basic assessment. The brutality of the war, though foreshadowed by earlier conflicts like the American Civil War, was a marker in and of itself. More recent historians have also seen the war as the beginning of the end of European imperial dominance, thanks to the weakening of the major European powers and the unintended encouragement given to nationalist movements elsewhere, from Japan through India and Turkey to Africa.

The overall result is a really powerful set of historical assumptions, into which the idea of an intervening globalization process can fit only with difficulty. It is possible, of course, to envisage a scheme that would continue to argue for the long 19th century as a basic period, but with a new surge toward globalization coming in the middle. Given the importance that globalization has assumed today, and the fact that many people were claiming new and wide-ranging global connections even by 1900, this compromise seems dubious. In fact, aspects of the argument for a break around 1850 really assume that some of the features normally assigned to the late 18th century – particularly, the earliest stages of European industrialization – really gained full global importance only after mid-century, which makes the latter date preferable in indicating a real break in trends. Though British industrial competition had impact in places like Latin America and India earlier, mainly by driving down levels of traditional manual production especially in textiles, it was really only by the 1850s that a truly global dimension emerged, embracing for example China and Japan as well as south Asia. The age of revolutions angle is trickier, for it did move out earlier from origins in North America and western Europe, to impact Haiti and Latin America in the revolutions and independence movements between the 1790s and 1820s, and through nationalism affected southeastern Europe as well. But here, too, a fuller global roll-out of revolutionary principles, often highlighting nationalism, also awaited the later 19th century.

World War I takes on a partial new role in a globalization-based periodization as well. It did encourage some powerful countercurrents to globalization, in the form of nationalist and regional reactions seeking to limit globalization's impact and develop alternative economic structures. The war's importance is in this sense confirmed, partly on rather familiar grounds. Globalization hit a really rough patch between the 1920s and 1945. But obviously the results were not permanent, and a resumption of the trajectory took shape (at least in some crucial respects) from 1945 onward. World War I is a break, then, but it did not usher in a durable new structure, at least in global mechanisms.

Fortunately, the focus on globalization does not require a full consideration of all aspects of world history chronology. It suggests the possibility, however, of beginning to rethink conventional structures, to argue for a longer early modern period – 1450–1850 – based on the inclusion of the Americas, a new level of global exchange, and some shifts in global power relationships including a greater role for the West. The last century of this span, after 1750, with accelerated world trade, fuller inclusion of the Pacific regions, and some other changes, expanded several key themes of the period in ways that would provide transitions to the sharper departures of the 1850s and ensuing decades. Then, with the 1850s, came the real advent of modern globalization, with an important but not permanent disruption following World War I, and then a resumption with added acceleration from the later 1940s to the present. Again, this chapter does not depend on recasting world history so completely, but if globalization is the key change in modern world history (which is at least a defendable proposition) and if the modern form of globalization began in the 1850s, the new framework can certainly be suggested.

New technologies and systems

Transportation and communication formed the most obvious break between the protoglobal patterns of the previous period, and the global thrusts by 1850. Capacities for speed and volume in transportation followed from the application of industrialization's steam engine to both land and sea, with trains and steamships respectively. Communication was revolutionized through the telegraph, particularly when undersea cables moved the telegraph from a regional to a global device. The new technologies seemed obviously desirable, of course, because of the levels of global interaction already in effect – it seemed increasingly imperative to accomplish them more quickly. But the changes were so dramatic that they immediately supported a new level of connection, most obviously in trade but also in patterns of immigration, in the dissemination of news and in other areas.

Steamships were developed early in the 19th century, but they had no initial relevance to globalization. The focus was on coastal trips and travel along rivers, mainly for mail or to carry wealthy passengers. Early steamships used paddle wheels, which allowed them to reduce dependence on wind but which were very vulnerable to rough seas, where they could submerge or rise out of the water altogether, damaging engines. Heavy engines improved capacity, but they stressed the boat itself, often separating planks and causing leaks. Fuel use was high, requiring frequent coaling stops, another obvious barrier to global impact. (The first transatlantic effort, in 1818, had revealed the problem, as the ship, trying to reach Boston from Bristol, England, ran out of coal and had to finish the trip under sail.) A regular transatlantic service was established only in 1838, from Liverpool to New York, but the operation remained tentative. Only in the 1840s was the first steam shipping company, the Cunard Line, organized to handle regular trips between Europe and North America.

Initial gains in speed came, in fact, from a new, sleek sailing ship, the clipper, developed by Americans but applied not only to transatlantic routes but (by the British) for rapid transit from Asia to Europe, by which spices and teas could be rushed to market. Travel time was dramatically reduced, though the clippers were fairly quickly outperformed by improved steam vessels.

Globally competitive steamship operations depended on several changes which began to accumulate by 1850 or soon thereafter. Use of steel instead of wood provided a firmer basis for the engines themselves, largely eliminating leakage. Even more important was the replacement of paddle wheels by screw propellers, from the 1840s onward. This eliminated the problems posed by rough seas, as far as continued motor function was concerned, and also allowed the development of larger and more powerful engines. By the 1870s, more efficient engines, called Triple Expansion Engines, were introduced for ships, allowing steam to be used three times before being turned back by the condenser into fresh water for the boilers; and designs for the boilers themselves improved, allowing higher steam pressures. This meant that ships could travel far longer distances before refueling, effectively elevating steam shipping over sails for any activity requiring speed and/or high volume. By 1900 steamship routes criss-crossed all the major oceans, linking all the inhabited continents with unprecedentedly dense contacts.

The reductions in time of travel were immense; transatlantic crossings, requiring a month early in the 19th century, were down to little more than a week by 1900. Costs dropped as well, facilitating both commerce and passenger travel, whether for business, tourism, or migration. Other technological changes added in: by the 1870s refrigerated containers allowed fresh meats and other perishables to be shipped long distances, allowing places like Argentina and New Zealand to become meat suppliers almost literally around the world.

Trains, pulled by steam engines, also played a role in this surge of globalization. Transcontinental lines began to be completed by the 1860s, allowing movement from the Atlantic to the Pacific in both the United States and

Canada, and a bit later linking the Pacific coast of Russia to the Baltic Sea. The greatest impact of trains involved domestic transportation, of course, but long-distance linkage was an important facet as well.

Trains and steamships alike also began to open interior regions to growing global trade and contact. Steamships, for example, allowed riverboats to move upstream in places like Africa and China, which facilitated European military penetration but also encouraged trade. Many rail lines were built to do little more than link internal production regions to coast ports, to facilitate exports. Virtually all of Africa's railroads, constructed under European auspices, had this function; there were virtually no lines connecting different parts of the continent to each other. Coastal connections stimulated greater production of export products like coffee or vegetable oils, and also minerals. Similar patterns emerged in many parts of Latin America. The result, obviously, stimulated the production of foods and raw materials, which tended to depress prices through growing competition and, in the process, increased global economic inequalities vis-à-vis the industrial nations. Here was a massive downside of the globalization process, exacerbating trends already visible in the previous period; but globalization, in all its chronological phases, has always brought problems of equity and adjustment in its wake.

Communications technology entered the overall mix in new ways, adding an important new element to the infrastructure of globalization. Effective invention of the telegraph, in 1837, both in Europe and the United States, led within thirty years to trans-ocean linkages among all the continents except Antarctica. Links between Asia and Europe took shape in the 1860s – the Indo-European Telegraph Company, for example, was chartered in 1868, linking India to Russia and Germany as well as Britain, with routes through Persia – and telegraph connections between Australia and Europe were completed in 1871. Information, admittedly in small coded chunks, could now range more widely and rapidly than ever before: what used to take months was now a matter of seconds. Information about market conditions, including price changes, began to flow via the telegraph. So did news, items for the press, and soon news combines developed – like Reuters, in Britain – to funnel this news, widely based on a novel breed of international reporter. Costs of transmission tumbled. In 1866, when the first transatlantic line opened, the New York to London rate was a hundred dollars for ten words – hardly a wide-open invitation. Just twenty years later, thanks to growing international competition, the price had dropped to 12 cents a word. As the British poet Rudyard Kipling put it, writing of the deep-sea cables: "They have wakened the timeless Things; they have killed their father time ... Hush, Men talk today o'er (the occasions) And a new Word runs between: Whispering, 'Let us be one!'"

This was only the beginning, of course. By the 1890s, though at first slowly, international phone connections started to emerge, and radio communications also added to the mix. The inventor Guglielmo Marconi introduced wireless radio connections across the Atlantic in 1901. The range and speed of communication were intensifying.

Amplifying technology, for transportation and communication alike, was the impact of the great new canals, which obviated the need to sail all the way around Africa, in connecting Asia and Europe, or later around South America in connecting both East Asia and the Pacific regions of the Americas to the east coast of the United States or Latin America. The Suez Canal, linking the Red Sea and the Mediterranean, was first out of the blocks. Egyptian pharaohs had long before used a canal to connect the Nile River with the Red Sea, but this had fallen into disuse and obviously had narrower functions. Napoleon, invading Egypt in 1798, thought about a canal, but his engineers discouraged him. The project was revived by a French engineer, Ferdinand de Lesseps, in the 1850s, who won approval from the Egyptian government and chartered a French company to fund the work, which was carried out between 1859 and 1869 by teams of Egyptian workers. The resultant canal was 101 miles long, utilizing a few intermediary lakes but requiring no locks, because the sea levels at both ends are approximately the same. The effective distance between India and Europe was cut in half; from China to Europe by over 25 percent. The canal was an immediate success, and has continued to provide a huge service to global trade ever since its opening. Always intended in principle to be free to the ships of all nations, the canal long operated under British oversight, which was reluctantly ceded in the late 1950s to Egyptian authority. There have been few issues of freedom of passage, and the link has periodically been widened and deepened to accommodate larger vessels.

The Panama Canal project began, after several false starts, around the end of the 19th century. Spanish conquerors, aware of how much extra time it took to get precious cargoes from the Pacific coast back to Spain, projected a canal across a narrow part of Central America in the 16th century, but nothing ever happened. European interest revived in the 19th century, and the growing development of the United States west (including the California gold rush of 1848) increased interest in cutting transportation time as well. Another French company under de Lesseps took up the project in the 1880s, but by the 1890s the United States government assumed a dominant position, maneuvering control over a newly created nation, Panama, and completing the canal itself by 1913. (The connection was administered by the United States until an agreement late in the 20th century arranged to return control to Panama.) The canal cut 18,000 miles off a journey from the United States Pacific coast to the eastern seaboard, saving at least ten days' travel and greatly reducing costs, and over time proved vital in connecting Asian exports to United States markets as well. As with Suez, the canal demonstrated a new and intense interest in reducing transportation barriers, and of course it had the effect, along with the innovative shipping technology, in accelerating global contacts still further.

Key changes in policy added a final element to the framework for globalization in the later 19th century, though admittedly with some complexities. Headed by Great Britain, major European powers, and more hesitantly the United States, moved toward a pattern of reducing tariffs on foreign goods, on the assumption that freer trade would ultimately benefit all participants. Britain began turning toward this policy in the 1830s, confident in its competitive power as the world's first industrializer. Other major countries held back a bit, for example in trying to protect local farmers from too much competition from the cheap grains of North America; but there was a general interest at least in reducing barriers.

The second component of this policy shift involved the force European and United States imperialists began to apply to other countries toward opening their markets more fully. East Asia was prised open in a series of warlike confrontations. A small group of Western military pushed China to allow more international trade and penetration, beginning with the first Opium War of 1839. The specific goal was to prevent China from limiting sales of opium produced in India, which British traders used to win new profits and as a new means of paying for desirable Chinese goods; but the larger outcome of this and later clashes was to provide new opportunities for foreign merchants generally to engage Chinese markets and even set up production outlets. The arrival in 1853 of an American fleet in Edo (Tokyo) Bay, in Japan, followed by other British and American visits complete with threats of force, had a similar impact in pressuring Japan to allow foreign commercial activity. Korea also opened up in the later 19th century, while European imperial conquests in Africa brought new levels of foreign contact to the interior of that vast continent.

Imperialist pressure was double-edged, of course, in that the Western nations fiercely rivaled each other for the upper hand. New Western colonial holdings were hardly free zones for all potential global traders, for each imperial power tried to reserve the best pickings for its own nationals. And while resistance to imperialism within areas like Africa or India was difficult, given Western weapons superiority, many people resented Western controls and, understandably enough, often extended their hostility to international contacts more generally. Chinese leaders, similarly, long tried to keep international involvement to a minimum, because it was so closely associated with Western controls. Even in Japan and Russia, which on the whole adapted somewhat more successfully to the new context and avoided outright colonial status, there were many who wanted nothing more than to reclaim a separate identity and opt out of the global arena. Rivalries and hostilities, in other words, severely qualified the embrace of the new global technologies and policies. Nevertheless, Western assertiveness, backed by new levels of military force, did produce clear changes in the second half of the 19th century, compared to the patterns of the early modern period: it was literally impossible now for any large region to isolate itself from international trade and international visitors.

Impacts of the new speed and range of contacts, and the more open policies toward interaction, affected a wide variety of human activities. Trade and migration, both staples of trans-regional contacts already, took on additional contours and greatly expanded in volume. Diffusion of foods, diseases and technologies was also affected, though again a number of vigorous patterns had already taken shape. International business organization moved well beyond the levels of the earlier international trading companies. There were newer elements as well: a definable set of international political organizations and humanitarian standards entered the global arena for the first time. Suggestions of a new, global popular culture also emerged. A new surge of imitations was another crucial product of this launch of globalization, with formal student exchanges an important, and novel, component. These developments all made vital contributions to the ascending spiral of globalization, and in combination they helped to define how this global level departed from all previous precedents. But they all depended, as well, on the technologies and policies that simply made moving around the world easier than ever before.

Trade and international business

The main purpose of improved transportation and related policies involved enhancing global trade, though there were some military goals as well in this age of imperialism. The role of trade in globalization was not, however, simply a matter of volume. Government and popular orientations changed as well, and the 1850s mark a key departure here. It was in 1851 that the British opened the first of the great international trade expositions, the Crystal Palace exhibition in a specially designed, modern glass building. The exhibit touted its role as a display site for industry from "all nations of the world." In fact, strong emphasis rested on Britain's leadership in industrial achievement and on materials from the growing British Empire – which automatically gave it great global range, thanks to participation from places like India and Australia. But other nations did display, with the United States for example showing its new harvesting equipment. And many tourists visited the exhibition from major European cities. The precedent was established for international gatherings that would showcase technology and consumer products in a cosmopolitan atmosphere, while giving various nations opportunities to display their stuff. From the 1880s onward, beginning with an exhibition in Paris, world's fairs occurred about every five years, particularly in European and United States centers, creating great fanfare for the idea of a global economic community.

Levels of global trade reached unprecedented levels, with virtually all regions actively participating. Between 1870 and 1900, the shipping tonnage available virtually tripled. The total value of all exports and imports, worldwide, quintupled between the 1850s and 1900, virtually doubling again by

1914. British exports soared by 57 percent between the 1870s and 1900, but Britain's share of world trade actually dropped, as Germany, the United States, Italy and other societies began to get into the game, aided by the spread of steam shipping and the benefits of access to the canals. United States exports thus grew by about 200 percent between 1879 and 1914. African involvement in world trade increased, despite the end of traffic in slaves, as new transportation facilities helped move products like vegetable oils into the world market. Australia's reliance on world trade expanded steadily. Overall, world trade expanded by an average of 4 percent annually in the last half of the 19th century, a mark never before achieved; increasingly, as well, domestic economic performance depended heavily on the expansion of global activity.

Increasingly, trade was supplemented by the economic impact of various kinds of service provided internationally. Big banks, particularly from Europe and the United States, steadily augmented their holdings in other countries. European investment in the United States, for example, grew steadily, providing much of the basis for huge developments like the transcontinental railroads. British capital in the United States quadrupled between the 1870s and 1914.

Trade in modern weapons played an important part in this explosion of trade, greatly extending the export of guns that had figured in European exchanges with places like Africa in the previous period. Sales of artillery and repeating rifles to the empires of eastern Europe and the Middle East, for example, increased greatly. The United States became a major weapons supplier, particularly after the Civil War – many of the weapons used in civil strife in Japan in the 1860s, for example, came from across the Pacific. Between 1865 and 1870, 1.5 million American rifles were sold abroad. Germany extensively supplied the Ottoman Empire, while German and French firms, along with those from the United States, competed for sales to Latin America. China became a major importer of artillery, particularly from Germany, as well as small arms. Sales of warships also expanded steadily, with each improvement in firepower quickly registering in exports.

Growing international trade, of various sorts, fueled the expansion of international companies. While the overt political role of major companies did not rival the heyday of the trading companies of the 16th to 18th centuries, economic power in many ways increased. There were two major developments. First, large companies now set up supply bases in a variety of nonindustrial areas, often acquiring huge local influence in the process and at the same time expanding international sales operations for their finished products. Vertical integration, in other words, saw Western firms set up large mining or agricultural holdings in places like Latin America and Africa, while at the same time establishing branch sales offices for their finished products in many other parts of the world. In some cases, the results were very similar to what had occurred with the earlier trading companies. Thus the United Fruit Company, from the United States, founded in Boston in

1899, within seven years had acquired a 100 square miles of banana lands in Colombia, Cuba, and various parts of Central America, employing 15,000 people; it operated rail lines and shipping companies, and strongly influenced the politics of governments – often now called "banana republics" in the region; it even operated three radio stations to expand its influence.

The second development, in many ways even more novel, involved setting up production plants in various parts of the world, taking advantage of technological know-how while seeking to squeeze out potential local competitors and also reducing shipping costs. Singer Sewing Machine Company, for example, founded in the United States in 1851, began to go international in a big way in the 1860s. The company opened a branch sales office in Hamburg in 1863 and built its first foreign factory in Scotland four years later. It quickly discovered that having different production sites allowed the company to ride out particular economic and political pressures in specific regions – Singer's European production thus sometimes was used to compete directly in the United States, for example to blunt the demands of labor unions. By 1871 Singer's British plant was the largest factory in the whole country. A new facility in Polodsk, Russia, set up in 1902 also quickly became one of the largest industrial operations in the nation. The company carefully managed multinational patent filings in order to protect a steady series of technical improvements, thus beating back local competitors. Manuals and catalogues were developed in a host of languages, as Singer essentially organized a global change in the way ordinary families as well as manufacturing shops produced and repaired clothing. By 1929 the company had nine factories worldwide, with 27,000 employees outside the United States. This kind of production expansion, with major impact on local economies and consumer patterns, constituted a clear step beyond what international companies had previously ventured.

Expansion of trade, banking and international business had an inevitable corollary: the emergence of international economic trading crises. Traditionally, economic oscillations, which could be quite severe, depended on regional factors, notably bad harvests, and while these could spread beyond national boundaries they had only limited global repercussions. By the later 19th century this pattern was changing. First hinted in a short crisis in 1856, and then more extensively in 1873, economic downturns now typically resulted from speculative overinvestment by banks (often headed by firms in the United States): this resulted in a withdrawal of credit and shrinking levels of global trade, which in turn led to drops in production in both nonindustrial and industrial regions and a growth in unemployment. The pattern easily extended not only across national boundaries but across oceans. From this point onward – and the Great Depression of 1929 was only a particularly severe example – economic crises always embraced both Europe and the United States and usually had significant impact (or sources) in falling trade levels, both exports and imports, in Latin America, key parts of Asia, and other regions as well.

Migration

Levels of migration exploded in the later 19th century. The sheer amount of human movement added to overall globalization, even though migration as a phenomenon was not new at all. Furthermore, and not surprisingly given new population pressures and the new means of transportation, distances traveled by many migrants expanded dramatically. Increasingly migration meant a striking and rather sudden mixture of disparate cultures. Finally, again thanks to new transportation, a good bit of migration was now transitory, with significant numbers of immigrants returning home either briefly or permanently. This also altered the nature of migration, and provided new influences back home that had never before been common.

Millions and millions of people emigrated from the 1850s until World War I (when the flow understandably dried up for a while, not only because of war but because of economic dislocation and new regulations). The period formed the most intensive era for this kind of movement in human history to that point. Over fifty million Europeans went to North America, parts of Latin America, and Australia–New Zealand. About the same number of Chinese set sail to the Americas (particularly the Pacific coast regions) but also to southeast Asia and elsewhere. Thirty million Indians migrated (to various places, including southern Africa and the Caribbean), and there were huge flows from Japan and the Philippines as well (the Japanese, for example, became the largest ethnic group in Hawaii). Middle Eastern migration was less voluminous, but merchant communities moved out to Africa and Latin America from places like Lebanon, and there was some Turkish labor migration as well. Population pressures at home, new opportunities in industrial or commercial agricultural regions, but also the active work of industrial recruiters help explain this huge flow. Railroad and metallurgical companies from the United States, for example, sent agents out to places like eastern Europe looking for cheap labor, and there were few national regulatory barriers to interfere. Many agricultural and mining operations signed people up on indenture contracts, now that slavery was abolished, setting up contract periods of seven or more years and often transporting whole families in the process. This was a key basis for the movement of Asian workers to the Caribbean and parts of Latin America.

Obviously, the same data that show massive numbers also show huge distances, the largest ever for migrations that were at least partially voluntary. The movement of Asians to various parts of the world was striking, a major break with Asian tradition (at least, over distances of this magnitude) and a huge change in population composition and cultural interaction in places like the United States and Peru as well. New racial animosities were stirred in the process, as fears about labor competition were now supplemented by active distrust of so many apparently different cultures and habits. Chinese in the United States, for example, were often accused of encouraging prostitution and red-light districts, as well as other undesirable behaviors. New movements of Jews to additional parts of Europe and to the United States helped stir a surge in anti-Semitism. Globalization now depended heavily on unprecedented population mixing and the kinds of tension that could result.

New levels of migration, plus the new transportation facilities, also help explain new patterns of migrant returns. Some groups, to be sure, were content in their new locations or too poor to do anything about it. But other groups now exercised judgment as to how long they wanted to stay, and when cultural unfamiliarity or hostile prejudice or a reduction in available jobs made the host settings turn sour, they simply went home. In 1908, when the United States produced its first data on the subject, 70 percent of all immigrants from the Balkans and 53 percent of all those from Italy headed back home after a few years. The phenomenon was fascinating. Obviously, immigrants in other periods may well have wanted to go home, but simply could not. But it was also possible that the new conditions for immigration, including the long distances involved and the levels of ethnic tension (as well as periodic economic instability), heightened the desire – which now could be acted upon. A Hungarian song in the United States thus noted

> America is not my native country, I never had a happy hour there; I have wandered a great lot, But my heart became all the more bitter. ... Tuesday morning I went on a ship, I return to beautiful Hungary; God save America forever, But just let me get out of there.

Some long-distance migrants now never intended to stay, but simply to make money for a few years and return to the family back home – again, the possibilities for various motives and plans had never been more abundant in the immigration field. But the pattern of return migration actually could amplify globalization, rather than qualify it. For many return migrants, even those who had hated their experience, often brought new ideas and cultural patterns back to their native villages, affecting (and sometimes annoying) people there who had never had a thought of change. Some returnees showed off their wealth, which locals could find unpleasant – in one German neighborhood, a village section built on a hill was called "Amerika" because its residents looked down on everyone else. Others, however, displayed a new kind of informal democracy, challenging established status hierarchies. Behaviors of this sort, admittedly diverse, could be quite influential in an otherwise traditional community, linking it in new ways to more global patterns. Overall, levels of migration, but also the new complexities, forged novel ties among different regions of the world, making migration an instrument as well as a product of the new level of globalization.

Tourism

A brand new entrant to formal globalization involved the emergence of organized international tourism. Obviously, travelers (including religious pilgrims) played a key role in illustrating and furthering earlier phases of globalization, but the idea of extensive recreational travel, by ordinary people rather than heroic pioneers or selected elites, particularly beyond a single region, was a crucial innovation.

The phenomenon opened literally in the 1850s. A decade earlier a British cabinetmaker, Thomas Cook, had begun organizing travel within Britain, helping groups like temperance societies organize meetings in other cities. He gradually expanded his horizons: by the 1850s he was setting up travel arrangements to western Europe, and by the 1860s this included winter vacation opportunities in Switzerland. In the 1860s also he and a son visited the United States, and began to include this as a destination. The process also involved a trip around the world, as the Cooks returned from the United States across the Pacific and through Asia – and this world excursion became an annual offer from Cook's tours as well. Comparable developments spread to the United States, though somewhat later: the American Express Company was established in 1850, and as early as the 1870s was facilitating commercial shipments to international destinations, though particularly in Europe; only after World War I did a serious tourist department begin to emerge with global outreach.

The vast majority of travel of course remained domestic, in the later 19th and early 20th centuries alike. The international destinations that became at all common were hardly global. English middle-class people traveled at least occasionally to parts of western Europe. A growing number of wealthy Americans, plus many artists and intellectuals, went to Britain and Europe. But, as the Cook's world tour suggested, there was a trickle of travel that ventured more widely. Ambitious British tourists – not ordinary upper-class people, but not all professional adventurers – did begin to show up in places like Thailand for tourist purposes by the final decades of the 19th century. A variety of Europeans and Americans began to visit the Middle East, for sightseeing and cultural experiences, beyond the obviously well-established religious visits to the Holy Land. Hundreds of travel accounts were published in the 19th century, often involving accounts of European visits to the Middle East, Africa and Asia; and the letters travelers now could send added informally to the sense of connection to different parts of the world. Global tourism did not at this point reach dimensions that would have massive economic impacts, outside of some key European destinations like the Swiss resorts. But some precedents were established that would obviously blossom far more extensively after World War II.

Foods, diseases, and technologies

The opening of a new phase of globalization had less impact on certain key aspects of the human experience than it did in areas like trade and travel, largely because the fundamental framework had already been set in the decades after 1500. An important exception involved a new approach to diseases, initially developed particularly in western Europe but soon having global reach, that began to alter one of the oldest results of human exchange. And in the area of technology diffusion – not surprisingly, given the force of industrialization – a true global revolution began to take shape.

It would certainly be misleading to claim a watershed in global foods. This does not contradict the idea of a sweeping change in globalization levels overall, but it constitutes a reminder that not everything changes simultaneously, particularly when basic relationships had been established earlier. To be sure, trade in food was fundamentally altered, thanks to new shipping plus canning and refrigeration possibilities: a wider variety of foods could now be acquired from distant regions than ever before. The main impact was to provide greater quantities of certain foods, particularly meats, to at least the middle and upper classes; it did not alter the composition of daily diets beyond this point. As a result, nothing in the foods arena in the later 19th century really compared with the consequences of the earlier Columbian exchange in terms of the transmission of staple crops like the potato to new areas. There were a few interesting dietary shifts: global use of the tomato spread, for example. This new world crop had been picked up in southern Europe in the 16th century, but had been viewed with misgiving in most other regions. Many Europeans and North Americans for example feared that the tomato was poisonous, because it looked like some known poisonous plants. There was also a real problem for upper-class diners who used lead plates, for tomato acid could dissolve some of the lead and actually transmit poison in the process. But these issues – both the misimpressions and the use of lead table wares – were resolved by the 19th century, and from southern Europe the popularity of the tomato spread rapidly. The introduction of pizza, in the 1880s, and its gradual dissemination from its southern Italian home, was part of this process.

It was also true that certain cuisines began to globalize. It was in the 1840s that French cooking began to define elegant dining in elite American restaurants along the eastern seaboard. It was after the 1860s that Chinese restaurants began to take hold in the United States. First established simply for Chinese immigrants working on railroad construction, Chinese restaurants gradually began to win a larger clientele, developing foods that would appeal to other Americans, like chop suey, that used Chinese themes but with major adaptation to regional tastes. The expansion of diverse immigration from various parts of the world had similar impacts in other places. The huge surge of cosmopolitan food options awaited the later 20th century, but the process was launched during this globalization period.

Contagious diseases continued to spread across the globe, as had been the case earlier. Severe cholera epidemics occurred at various points from 1832 onward, with contacts from India and the Middle East to Europe and thence to North and Central America often involved. Influenza was another frequent global traveler, with a huge worldwide epidemic in 1918–19. Several yellow fever outbreaks involved contacts from Africa to the Caribbean and from there to east-coast cities in the United States and also to parts of Latin America such as Brazil. As with food, however, nothing as dramatic, or globally significant, as the Columbian exchange marked this new global period.

The big development in the global disease arena involved not the spread of contagion across borders, but growing efforts at scientific research, medical treatment and, above all, public health prevention. Research on cholera, for example, identified transmission mechanisms and, soon after 1900, led to successful cures. Even more effort went into sanitation measures in the cities, toward control of sewage and improved water quality. Together, these various approaches virtually eliminated cholera as a global disease by the 20th century. Medical and public health advances most commonly began in western Europe, but they were gradually applied in other regions; control of cholera after 1900 thus actively involved its traditional home in India. Western self-interest, aside from any humanitarian sentiment, motivated efforts outside the West itself. Thus greater public health efforts in African cities were necessary if only to protect Western business and diplomatic communities. Mosquito control was vital to the reduction of yellow fever, in turn essential to protect workers involved in building the Panama Canal. Disease patterns continued to vary greatly in different parts of the world, depending on the local environment and also the levels of wealth. It remains true, however, that certain aspects of medicine and particularly public health increasingly operated on a global scale and that, in turn, the connection between inter-regional contacts and the spread of fatal epidemic diseases loosened in this phase of globalization.

This was the context in which one of the most intriguing aspects of later 19th-century globalization took shape, though without a great deal of immediate impact. Fears about the spread of cholera from India, to Europe but also to the Middle East, generated new efforts at quarantine and public hygiene in many countries. But purely national responses were obviously inadequate to a disease that knew no borders, and, haltingly, an international component was sketched as well. Reform leader Muhammad Ali, in Egypt, involved the first international board in quarantine efforts for ships in transit, as early as the 1830s. The initial international conference for coordination occurred in Paris in 1851, and was followed by other periodic meetings on into the 20th century. Much conference time was spent in national wrangling, plus European efforts to portray their society as the superior guide for a disease-ridden "Orient" along with attacks on Muslim pilgrims as purveyors of contagion. Scant agreement resulted at first, as individual societies continued their own measures in seeking to prevent epidemics; globalization, here, was still tentative at best. Nevertheless, with the involvement of Russia and the Ottoman Empire along with Europe, the idea of societies living up to international standards of hygiene and disease control did gain new attention; and a Red Sea Sanitary Service was set up to try to assist Muslim pilgrims to Mecca in order to inhibit disease. The idea of imposing quarantine requirements on ships in periods of epidemics was discussed by the 1870s, though again there was as yet no real implementation. Still, the whole movement (along with an increasing number of scientific conferences discussing the nature of key diseases like cholera) represented a breakthrough in global thinking, and would lead directly to the establishment of world health services in the 20th century. Here, clearly, the later 19th century launched, however timidly, a vital component of globalization more generally.

Global change was even clearer cut in the area of technology diffusion. The tenor of the world's fairs already suggests how international technology exchange accelerated. Never before had new inventions passed so quickly from one region to another.

Of course there were constraints still. Early in the Industrial Revolution Britain tried to prevent its new industrial equipment from being transmitted to, or copied by, foreigners. A few pioneering ventures saw daring French entrepreneurs smuggling steam engine parts out on precarious boats across the English Channel. But secrecy simply did not work: British businessmen and skilled workers poured into other countries looking for chances to set up factories or build railroads, despite official prohibitions. And the British government abandoned its futile defensive efforts by the 1840s. Even after this, of course, individual businesses that jealously guarded secrets, plus patent protection and other devices, could slow technology transmission. And many countries simply did not have the capacity to build some of the more complex equipment, like train locomotives, on their own. Technology levels would continue to vary even in a more global age.

Still, designs moved fast, both because entrepreneurs in other countries took up the challenge of imitation and because Westerners themselves brought machines around the world. Within about thirty years after train lines began to be established in Britain, for example, Western engineers were setting up railroad systems in places like Russia, India and Cuba, and by the 1870s the movement spread to China. Japan, beginning to become an unusually active global participant by the 1860s, provides an interesting example of the new speed of dissemination. By that decade, after only a few years of interaction with the newest Western technology, the Japanese proudly announced that they could build their own steamships. Railroad engines had to be imported still until about 1900, when again the Japanese began to produce their own. Revolutionary new technology was now spreading in a matter of decades. In contrast, as we have seen, it had taken several centuries around 1000 for knowledge of paper production to begin to disseminate widely; and while the pace later picked up a bit, the Japanese learned of guns, after 1500, only two centuries after Europeans had introduced them (and then, of course, after a brief interest, decided this was not a technology they really wanted). The new pace and extent of technology exchange was a fundamental component of the wave of globalization after 1850, and obviously the momentum would carry easily into the 20th century and beyond.

The emergence of global political institutions

Global impacts in phenomena like technology and disease were familiar from earlier periods, even though dimensions changed significantly after 1850. At least as significant were areas in which global initiatives took shape essentially for the first time.

A crucial case in point: wide-ranging global innovation began to occur in the political sphere. In 1863, the United States called for an international congress to deal with the problem of mailing letters or packages outside a single country. Up to that point, someone who wanted to get a letter to a foreign nation either had to entrust it to a traveler – the safest recourse – or had to buy stamps from every country through which the letter would pass. This made it cumbersome, at the least, and often effectively impossible to use postal services beyond national boundaries; and this, in turn, was hardly compatible with the needs of an increasingly globalized economic and cultural system, not to mention the growing desire of immigrants to communicate with folks back home. Following the initial discussion, the Prussian (later German) postal minister, Heinrich von Stephan, took matters in his own hands, and forged what was initially called the General Postal Union through the Treaty of Berne (Switzerland) in 1874; the name of the organization was changed to the Universal Postal Union in 1878, and this still holds true today though the institution now functions as an arm of the United Nations. The principles were simple and clear: all nations agreed to maintain a standard rate for international mail, regardless of destination; they agreed to honor the stamps of the country from which the mail was sent, with the home country keeping the revenues but with the assumption that the balance sheet would even out over the long haul. For the first time, a person could drop a letter in a mailbox in the neighborhood, to any country in the world that had a postal service, and have a reasonable expectation that it would reach its destination without further effort.

This simple measure – so simple that today most people assume the general reliability of international mail service, aside from a few cases of national disruption, without further thought – illustrates the new kind of political discussion that, even in an age of intense nationalism, was proceeding across borders. Initiatives came from the West: the premise was that if Western statesmen could agree on an international program, it would easily apply worldwide. But no single country orchestrated the operation. Most important, this kind of agreement was fundamental to a new level of global exchange. Like the technological improvements in shipping, it both reflected the rising needs for smooth connections, and furthered those connections in turn.

Furthermore, the model could easily be applied to other areas. Almost simultaneously with the postal effort, for example, an international convention was forged concerning telegraphy.

And the list of practical political arrangements expanded steadily in the later 19th century. In 1883, for example, a Paris Convention on Industrial Property permitted citizens of signatory countries to file for international patent protection within twelve months of the original application date. The convention made the patent and copyright systems of one country available to individuals from any other signatory country: they could file for protection of their invention or work even if they were not citizens. Furthermore, so long as they filed promptly, the initial date of their national filing would be honored internationally, protecting them against a copycat invention introduced in another signatory country a few months after their own. Only eleven countries initially signed the agreement, entirely from Europe and Central America; but the list steadily grew, and today 178 nations adhere to the convention, with a few others, like Taiwan, though not signatories, honoring its provisions. Even more than with the postal agreement, this arrangement was hardly foolproof: a number of nations, even when signatories, allowed imitation of devices or materials without payment to the inventor or author. But the principle of international coordination, in a fundamental aspect of economic performance, was a huge change, and it did have significant protective consequences.

Considerable international discussion also applied to maritime law and the limits of purely national action on the seas and in the exploitation of ocean resources. The same principles were applied toward the end of the 19th century to attempts to limit purely national claims on activities in the Arctic and Antarctic.

International scientific societies began to take off for reasons similar to the commercial conventions: global coordination became increasingly necessary and desirable. Starting in Europe, statisticians began to discuss common procedures and categories across national lines. An American naval official in the 1850s triggered an initial meeting of meteorologists, and this led in the 1870s to an International Meteorological Association, which focused on gathering data from ships and from national weather services to improve basic stores of information and, ultimately, facilitate better forecasting in an area that, obviously, did not respect national boundaries. Here again were initiatives that have persisted, ultimately folding into larger frameworks for international collaboration such as the United Nations.

Another ambitious extension of international politics involved attempts to set standards for behavior in war, again developing in the same time frame as the other innovations in global politics. In 1859 a Swiss-Italian banker, Henry Drumont, became appalled at the lack of medical attention to wounded soldiers, on all sides, during the Italian wars of unification. He wrote a book urging new international standards in this area, which in turn caught the attention of celebrities like the French writer Victor Hugo and the British nurse Florence Nightingale, who began to take up the cause. The French government, pressed by Drumont, provided support as well. The result was the first Geneva Convention, signed in 1864, providing standards for the treatment of wounded soldiers, prisoners of war, and the like. A number of countries, initially in Europe, signed on quickly, modifying national legislation to permit the application of these international standards. And the roster of signatories, and their geography, expanded steadily; Japan, for example, pledged to observe the convention by the 1890s. The convention was closely related to the establishment of the International Red Cross (in 1863), that initially focused on providing medical treatment to combatants but gradually expanded to other humanitarian activities. The convention itself was periodically renegotiated and enlarged – an agreement early in the 20th century, for example, provided standards for the treatment of civilians in war zones; and later extensions tried to limit the use of certain kinds of weapon, as with an early 20th-century ban on throwing projectiles from balloons and later efforts to prohibit the use of poison gas.

Another ambitious effort – suggesting how the goals of global political coordination tended steadily to expand – came a bit later as a result of discussions that began in 1899, triggered by interest on the part of both American and Russian statesmen. A Permanent Court of Arbitration emerged early in the 20th century, based in The Hague, The Netherlands, and designed to help disputing nations sort out their differences without recourse to war. The court served particularly to interpret disagreements about treaty provisions. It provided the basis for even more extensive international legal efforts that developed after World War I, and that produced the International Court of Justice (often called the World Court) and other tribunals.

Clearly, growing global activity, in trade and conflict alike, required serious innovations in politics as well. In many ways, of course, the new set of global political agreements and institutions failed to keep pace with actual events: efforts to limit war damage, for example, paled before the brutal weapons technologies deployed during World War I. Dispute settlement was important, and the idea of permanent institutions to facilitate the process was truly novel, but it would be hard to argue that greater harmony settled in as a result. The fact that many of the most ambitious efforts were Western, at least in inspiration, was another limitation. Many countries felt left out of the process or positively threatened by agreements that, for example, seemed to confirm Western advantages on the seas. The fact remained, however, that a global political apparatus was being established, and that it had no real precedent in any previous period in world history.

The apparatus, finally, was not a matter of government action alone. A growing number of international non-governmental organizations (as they are now called, or INGOs) began to form by the 1860s, though with a clearer surge in the 1880s – a bit after the first push for state-to-state efforts, but in the same spirit and covering an even wider range of topics. As with the official ventures, these new organizations assumed that cross-border coordination was essential to promote their goals; national action alone would not suffice. And they assumed that there were some common standards, or should be, that had global applicability and that should be sustained by coordinated political effort.

Thus in 1864 Karl Marx formed the first Workingmen's International, designed to promote labor solidarity (and Marxist principles) across borders. The First International assumed that labor interests transcended nation-states, and that capitalism, itself an international force, needed to be confronted on the same turf. The International initially focused on European and North American unions and socialist parties, and it foundered on ideological disputes within a decade. But a Second International formed in 1889, and the principle of at least some collaboration among different worker groups has been sustained in one form or another from that point to the present day, with attention focusing increasingly on global inclusion rather than a largely Western cast.

Feminism, another new social force, began to try to go international in the 1880s, though, as with labor, the more concerted action continued to focus within rather than among individual states. A Swedish woman, Marie Gregg, organized a first International Association of Women in 1868, and during the 1870s a number of international congresses involved delegates from North America and Europe. Three new organizations formed in the 1880s, aiming particularly at voting rights and protections at work but hoping more broadly to mobilize public opinion to "produce the necessary revolutions in the minds of people, the people of the whole civilized world." As with most such efforts at the time, actual participation was largely Western, but efforts increasingly extended to identify at least individual members from places like China and Iran. The International Council of Women, one of the new groups, spoke explicitly of reaching out to women of "all races, nations, creeds and classes," while appealing to a "universal sense of injustice, that forms a common bond of union" among "women of all nationalities."

Global organization and membership were not, of course, the whole story here. Equally important to a sense of global politics broadly construed was the expansion of the idea that there were, or ought to be, some globally applicable humanitarian standards, whether the subject was labor conditions, gender conditions, or wartime behaviors. Ideas that had first inspired the campaigns against slavery (which continued to run strong, even as abolitionism spread) expanded to other topics. A British clerk helped organize an international campaign against the mistreatment of African labor in the Belgian Congo. Around 1900 a fierce effort was directed against the real or imagined seizure of women for prostitution in other countries – what was called the white slave trade. A host of international meetings and grass-roots organizations combined to fight the menace.

And these definitions of global humanitarian principle were not idle exercises. A new World Purity Federation formed in 1900, and soon there was an international agreement to fight the global sex trade (1904), with a new International Bureau set up to monitor. Global outrage prompted individual nations, accused of harboring enslaved prostitutes, to take action to defend themselves against further international embarrassment. Argentina, for example, often singled out, passed an increasingly rigorous series of laws to prohibit prostitution, hoping to clear the nation's name from global stigma. Other global (if de facto still largely Western) campaigns mounted against alleged mistreatment of minorities in the Ottoman Empire (first Bulgarians, in the 1870s, and later Armenians). Not only organizations but also the new mass newspapers eagerly crusaded against brutality and denial of rights, beginning to establish some force for a world opinion that could motivate actual diplomatic policies. Other targets of new global pressure, often expressed through the judgments of Western observers but then picked up by local reformers, included the foot binding of women in China and veiling in Egypt. Here, too, a widespread sense might develop that changes in traditional practices were essential to measure up to "civilized" standards – though the same process could generate reactions in favor of proudly separate identities. Chinese reformers, for example, readily cited foreign (largely Western) standards:

> The bound feet of women will transmit weakness to the children. ... Today look at Europeans and Americans, so strong and vigorous because their mothers do not bind their feet and, therefore, have strong offspring. Now that we must compete with other nations, to produce weak offspring is perilous.

In a similar vein, though a bit later, in the 1920s, the new leader of Turkey, Kemal Atatürk, cited global standards in attacks on traditional costumes and headgear, including women's veiling: "Gentlemen, can the mothers and daughters of a civilized nation adopt this strange manner, this barbarous posture? It is a spectacle that makes the nation an object of ridicule. It must be remedied at once."

Finally, spilling beyond politics, the same kinds of effort to reach across borders began to generate a new surge of global charity, another unprecedented expression of the intensifying connections among societies worldwide. The very fact of international capitalism motivated some of the leaders of international companies to spread their largesse beyond single countries, particularly by the early 1900s. Andrew Carnegie, a Scotsman who made his fortune in American steel, sponsored libraries in many countries. John D. Rockefeller established a foundation with an explicit global mission "to promote the well being of mankind throughout the world," with particular emphasis on medical and scientific research and public health programs, but with funding as well for education and international student exchange. The new Rockefeller Foundation fought yellow fever and tropical diseases in Africa and Latin America, while founding a new medical college in China. Even aside from big business, encouraged by media reports certain kinds of national disaster began to call forth giving from ordinary citizens in many different countries. Some of this, of course, translated earlier transnational ideas about Christian or Islamic charity, but the targets now spread beyond co-religionists to any group singled out for global attention.

Global politics and humanitarianism added important ingredients to the process of globalization overall. Though not yet as effective or as consequential as more familiar categories like global trade, they could nevertheless affect state policy and individual behavior alike. They expressed and furthered a new sense of unity among different peoples. And of course they provided a direct inspiration to the even larger array of political and charitable efforts that would attach to globalization later on. Here, without question, a vital new aspect of globalization was born in the later 19th century.

Cultural globalization: some new steps

Trans-regional connections had often generated mutual cultural influences across political and even religious boundaries. The great world religions themselves had deliberately worked to spread cultural standards, in art and law as well as in spirituality. So the idea of cultural interaction was hardly new in the late 19th century – less novel, certainly, than the emergence of certain types of global political action. Still, a number of developments in several cultural fields suggested a new level of cultural globalization, with the hints of novel global standards in consumerism and entertainment particularly interesting – and, often, with institutions to match. Crucial changes took shape a bit later than the first stirring of global politics – patterns began to emerge in the 1890s and 1900s for the most part – which may be an understandable lag in a period when assertions of regional and national identity also gained new attention. But the changes were significant, and they set the stage for the fuller development of global consumer culture and other manifestations in the later 20th century.

A host of new examples of trans-regional cultural influence emerged. European artists, striving for innovation, took inspiration from their new access to Japanese and African art in the later 19th century, and this helped forge dramatic new styles like Impressionism. Vincent Van Gogh, for example, deliberately imitated Japanese nature paintings as part of his developing repertoire. What began to be called "modern art" was a European product initially, but it had global reference points and would gradually attract artistic interest from other regions. Already before 1900 many United States and Latin American artists flocked to centers like Paris to train in the new styles.

Many societies began to sponsor study missions to centers of science and technology in western Europe and the United States. Even before the Japanese government made a full commitment to reform, in 1868, a number of leaders took study trips abroad. They were particularly interested in gaining technical information – Japan's capacity to build steamships on its own by the 1860s resulted from this imitation – but they acquired other guidelines as well. The Japanese who visited the United States struggled to understand political institutions like the American Congress: it seemed odd to have such partisan dispute in the halls, followed by signs of friendship among the same politicians after hours. Relatively egalitarian treatment of women, at least by Japanese standards, also seemed strange: one observer noted that Western women seemed to receive the deference Asians granted to the elderly. But other signals, beyond the purely technical, resonated more positively. Future educational leaders like Fukuzawa Yukichi began to argue that Western approaches to teaching and knowledge were superior to Confucian traditions in two crucial respects: the importance granted to science and the willingness to cast aside past wisdom in the light of new discoveries. When Japan turned to education reform in 1872, it quickly imported a number of Western authorities, including a Rutgers University faculty member, to head up its educational operations, turning away from this degree of dependence only after a decade.

Japan was a particularly eager provider of study missions, but other societies began to send students abroad as well. After long hesitation, China began to sponsor students at Japanese, European and American universities by the 1890s. The result was an increased flow of scientific and technical information, but also access to other ideas. Several leaders of the China republic under Sun Yat-sen, after the 1911 revolution, had trained in the West, and while they hoped to avoid certain Western features like some of the social tensions associated with the Western version of industrialization, they were enthusiastic about democratic ideas. Western educators themselves, including Christian missionaries, began to make a special effort to reach out to women as well as men. Several new universities were formed in China, with access available to women, while American institutions like Wellesley College, around 1900, began to recruit women students from prominent families.

Colonial systems encouraged foreign study as well. Many Indians spent time at British universities, including the future nationalist leader Mohandas Gandhi. Groups of African students clustered at British and French universities. Former colonies also got into the act. A number of eager students from the United States flocked to France and Germany, hoping to pick up the latest findings in science and medicine. Indeed, the whole idea of a research university in the United States resulted from experience with German models, as new institutions like Johns Hopkins were founded with this pattern in mind and other established centers began to convert toward the same goals. Latin American novelists often spent time in Europe or New York, and even as they developed some characteristic regional cultural themes they kept a close eye on the latest Western styles.

A new level of cultural globalization thus depended on the unprecedented amount of formal and informal study, involving a wide range of subject matter.

But cultural globalization also went well beyond student and policy levels, reaching wider ranges of popular behavior. Particularly important, both at the time and in terms of implications for the future, were the new foreign influences on popular consumerism and leisure.

Between the 1850s and 1900s, a number of major cities began to imitate the Western department store (which had originated in Paris a few decades earlier and spread quickly in Europe and North America). Russian department stores opened in the 1850s, catering of course to the wealthy but offering an unusual profusion of goods and styles, mainly imported from the West or developed along Western lines. Department stores in Tokyo, and in Western-influenced Chinese cities like Shanghai, by 1900 featured Western goods and also musical and artistic offerings, often involving foreign styles. Not everyone was attracted, of course, even when they had some money to spend. Many Chinese and Japanese long shunned the department stores as foreign implants. But there was growing influence nevertheless.

Western clothing styles, even more broadly, began to compete with local fashions, because they seemed more "up to date" and in some cases because they were more practical – safer, for example, than flowing robes when people were working around new machinery. Japanese enthusiasm for other specific products, like tooth powder, showed a similar openness to items and habits that were beginning to become global.

The globalization of sports clearly began in the later 19th century. This involved the spread of games from one region to the next – mainly from Western centers outward. It embraced a growing popular passion for imported sports, forming implicitly global audiences around deep new enthusiasms. And it involved international organization as well.

Thus the modern Olympic Games were launched in 1896, under the impulse of a French enthusiast who saw sports as a source of international harmony. Pierre de Coubertin boasted that the first games, held in Athens, were "modern" – highlighting competitions like track and field and bicycle races – but also "international and universal." In fact, the early Olympics were almost exclusively Western – with athletes coming from Europe and North America. Even more than most of the early global organizations, this one long harbored a tension between international statements and a rather narrow regional focus. But the principles were important, and obviously over time the Olympics would greatly expand its global potential.

Specific sports interests, however, were initially more important than the Olympics movement in the effective global arena. Two sports, specifically, began to spread out from their initial homelands toward more global participation and audience. American baseball, emerging in the United States by the 1840s, began to gain popularity in parts of Latin America and the Caribbean, and also in Japan, by the 1890s, with extensive amateur involvement and spectator interest. More strikingly still, British football – known in the United States as soccer – began to gain attention in the wake of British colonial and business expansion. Groups of expatriate British amateurs, mostly businessmen and diplomats, began playing soccer in Argentina in the 1860s, for example. Upper-class Argentinians soon followed suit, seeing status in this exciting foreign pastime. By 1900, interest was spreading more widely, toward popular participation and spectator enthusiasm. National leagues were established in many parts of Latin America and, soon, elsewhere, and international competition began as well. Major teams in Argentina, for example, played counterparts from Uruguay and Brazil, to growing audiences and (as one Brazilian woman put it) the "roar of the crowd's enthusiastic applause." By 1904 an international federation was established to oversee the game globally, and national leagues continued to spread into the 1920s, by which time virtually all major regions were actively involved. Never before had a single game captured such widespread, and often passionate, global attention.

Soon after 1900, finally, but as part of the same basic global current, the new medium of motion pictures emerged, allowing international sales of entertainment packages produced in a few major centers. European films quickly won some export interest, but by the 1910s it was Hollywood that emerged as the clear global center of the movie industry. Even before World War I, it was estimated that between 60 and 75 percent of all films shown in Britain came from the United States, mainly around cowboy and Indian themes but also with star-crossed lovers and various kinds of desperado. Major American studios set up branch offices in Latin America, South Africa, Australia and elsewhere, and by the 1920s young people not only in these areas but also in countries like Lebanon began experiencing American film fare as part of their basic recreation. The United States, with a huge national market and the capacity to develop films with wide appeal across specific cultural and ethnic lines, had a clear advantage in this new medium. But Hollywood was never American alone, as actors and directors came from other parts of the world to participate, and often star, in the new genre.

Partly because of movies, but also thanks to other United States commercial exports, observers in some quarters began to identify a current of "Americanization" as part of the global cultural package by the early 20th century. A grumpy British journalist noted how many of his countrymen were eating American breakfast foods, wearing American clothing, using American machines, and even reading American-style newspapers. Several Europeans worried that American "newcomers have acquired control of almost every new industry created during the past fifteen years," and even bemoaned what they called an American "invasion" or "the Americanization of the world."

But while United States involvement was crucial, and set the stage for even greater influence in the future, cultural globalization was a broader phenomenon, with dissemination from many different sources. The first soccer team in China, for example, was organized in the northern city of Harbin, thanks to Russian influence in the city. And it was Russian inspiration in Harbin that also sponsored the first Chinese movie industry, with quick national interest following from this initially foreign inspiration. As cultural influence broadened, all sorts of transmitters could play a role in furthering the process.

Continuities and limitations

The tremendous innovations of the later 19th century, beginning with the new technologies, make a powerful case for a major new phase of globalization. Without denying the power, however, it remains important to acknowledge both persistent and novel limitations to the whole process. It is also vital to recognize that elements of the previous phases of proto-globalization – the developments that had taken shape after 1000 and after 1500 – also persisted amid change; important elements of globalization were not entirely unprecedented.

We have seen, for example, that basic patterns of food exchange built largely on the earlier Columbian exchange: while access to additional styles of cuisine was interesting, and while the gains of previously ignored foods like the tomato were significant, the basic work of sharing food staples and domesticated animals had already been accomplished. Nothing in this period compared to the impact of access to corn and the potato several hundred years before.

Continuity also included some surprising echoes of earlier commercial networks, along with the fanfare of heightened global trade and new types of international company. Historians have recently emphasized, for example, how, under the cover of British imperialism, merchants from India extended some of the patterns they had launched almost a thousand years before. Indian merchants thus increased their contacts with eastern and southern Africa in the period, benefiting from common British control both of India and of colonies like South Africa. British protection and the advocacy of open markets helped Indians expand their trade connections, planting larger colonies of local merchants and shopkeepers in various parts of Africa along with new levels of indentured labor. India's global role expanded, in other words, despite the brighter glare of British imperial gains, but along lines already sketched in Indian Ocean trade.

Continuity most obviously describes many of the key patterns of inequality that still bedeviled world trade in the decades around 1900. The imbalance between Western industrialization and the lack of industrialization almost everywhere else sharpened the gaps, to be sure, but the basic issues were not new. Most of Latin America thus continued to serve the global economy by providing foods and raw materials. The range of products widened to include new staples like coffee, bananas or copper, and of course formal slavery was abolished; but sending out inexpensive exports, with shipping and commerce largely organized by foreigners, while depending on core societies for many manufactured goods, remained the basic pattern. The biggest new ingredient was growing foreign indebtedness, as societies that tried to expand exports by borrowing money to build train lines and modern ports found themselves beholden to Western banks in ways that only deepened economic dependency. Many African countries worked hard to replace slaves, in international trade, with new products like vegetable oil, but again the reliance on cheap exports (and in turn on low wages) and more expensive imports continued. The expansion of Western imperialism in Africa from the 1860s onward saw even greater pressure to develop raw materials exports as mining expanded and additional areas were brought into cultivation of crops like cotton. Again, however, elements of the basic relationship of African economies to the global commercial system had already been established.

Though regional inequalities were not new, their greater severity constituted an obvious limitation to the patterns of globalization that were now unfolding. Many people could reasonably conclude that globalization harmed their societies, and might seek alternatives. Other constraints impinged on transregional contacts as well. The surge of globalization coincided with a rising tide of nationalism. There was irony in this fact, some of which persists in the present day: the very decades in which the intensity of exchanges increased saw growing commitment to the new idea that each nation had a distinctive (and, some advocates would argue, superior) culture and that each should be served by a separate government. Nationalism in some senses responded to the increase of pressures from the outside, serving as a more modern statement of distinctive traditions and identities; and the fact that nationalism now spread virtually everywhere was itself a global development, however complex. By the end of the 19th century significant nationalist movements were arising not only in the West and Latin America, where the phenomenon had begun, but also in India, Turkey, among Arabs, and, increasingly, among some African leaders as well. Multinational empires, like the Ottomans or the Habsburgs, were under growing pressure to collapse into separate smaller national units – almost the reverse of the globalization process. Western nations divided between the impulse to form international arrangements across boundaries – as with the Postal Union – and the impulse to seek every selfish advantage against other national competitors. Not surprisingly, many features of the globalization process would collapse, at least temporarily, with the violent explosion of national rivalries that constituted World War I.

In fact, finally, while all regions were involved in many aspects of globalization by this point, clear divisions developed among levels of commitment. The late 19th century was the period, for example, when Japan made its basic decisions about joining the global community, after many decades of partial isolation. Openness to foreign standards and active engagement in world trade did not come easily. Some conservatives questioned the whole move; other people worried about loss of precious identity. Japanese leaders, particularly by the 1880s, did try to make sure that citizens would be taught some special political values, including loyalty to the emperor so that they would not be entirely Westernized; and there would be later hesitations as well. But the fundamental commitment was clear: Japan would be part of a wider world and would introduce the reforms needed to make it effective in that role. Less decisively, business and political leaders in the United States made similar decisions. The nation had never been isolated, but for several decades in the mid-19th century it was preoccupied with internal expansion and fiery domestic issues such as slavery. But the commitment to international business, shared consumer standards and more active diplomatic engagement expanded greatly between the 1870s and 1900, and, as we have seen, the nation began to play a strong role in global consumer culture as well. As with Japan, some hesitations would return: at various points and for various reasons, many Americans would have renewed hesitations about aspects of globalization. But the fundamental national decision was already in place.

This pattern of commitment did not, however, apply to all regions. Western Europe, of course, had assumed an active global role for some time. But involvements from places like China and the Middle East were more tentative, and domestic opinions were more divided. Many features of globalization, after all, were being forced on these regions, not more spontaneously adopted. Obviously, there were businessmen and reformers all over the world who adapted readily to globalization, but there were also many countercurrents. To take a humble example: while some Egyptians began to campaign vigorously against the veiling of women in the name of global standards, others, including many women, argued that precisely because of global interference Egypt must proudly maintain veiling as a sign of its distinctiveness. Concerns about the drawbacks of too much involvement in Western-dominated trade or imperialist politics provided more concrete reasons for resistance. A basic decision to commit to globalization had yet to come – and in some countries, may not have come even today. The pattern was varied.

The Great Retreat: 1914–45

World War I was a huge blow to globalization, because it effectively divided much of the world into warring camps. There were some unexpected new links. Soldiers from India and Africa used by Britain and France gained exposure to novel experiences and ideas, among other things learning more about European nationalism and what this might imply for their own countries. New groups of writers from places like the United States had meaningful encounters not just with war but with western Europe. In the main, however, the war encouraged disruption and new levels of divisive national commitments.

Divisions continued after the war, as a variety of societies decided that globalization, or at least key aspects of it, had brought dangerous consequences to regional interests. The United States, reacting to its unexpected involvement with European conflict and diplomacy, pulled back into isolationism, reducing its diplomatic commitments with other regions. New laws also severely limited immigration, reversing the older trends, in a wave of cultural antipathy to foreigners. Larger economic and cultural involvements continued full tilt – this was only a partial withdrawal – but the national mood was not pro-global. Spurred by revolution, the new Soviet Union also rethought globalization. In principle communist leaders maintained the commitment to the international organization of labor, and indeed formed a new workingman's International to spread revolution more widely. But actual Soviet leaders, and particularly Joseph Stalin from the late 1920s onward, talked about developing a separate socialist system and pulled away from most international arrangements including basic aspects of world trade. Cultural influences from outside were also carefully limited. When the Soviet Union would later expand, through its conquests and de facto empire after World War II, it continued to encourage substantial economic, political and cultural separation from the more general global systems. By the late 1920s and 1930s new leadership in Japan and Germany also looked toward the formation of separate economic systems to reduce dependence on the Western-dominated world economy. Japan began to carve out a new empire in East Asia and the Pacific, calling it the Co-Prosperity Sphere: the goal was to have sources of raw materials, cheap labor and markets independent from the larger global system. Germany hoped to use conquests in eastern Europe similarly to reduce interactions with other societies in favor of a Nazi-dominated empire. Nazi culture deliberately fought international influences like modern art. Other key regions, to be sure, made no such formal moves to set up alternatives to globalization. But in many parts of Asia and Africa core issues increasingly revolved around nationalist struggles for independence, and while this was by no means necessarily anti-global, it hardly placed a global agenda at the top of the list.

Beneath the surface of major events like war, revolution and the rise of fascism, in other words, a fundamental current in world history, for a quarter-century or more involved concerted efforts to modify, replace or evade globalization. Globalization hardly ended in consequence. International sports and movie interests persisted. Global trade and the big international companies continued at high levels of activity, though of course oscillating with internal economic conditions. Some new nations, like Turkey, vigorously introduced reforms aimed at adjusting local culture, including education, toward more global standards. It was in the 1920s, despite important countercurrents, that several United States universities first established regular study-abroad programs – these aimed, to be sure, at western Europe (particularly France and Italy) but they did embody a basic belief that, even in an age of growing nationalism, exposure to cosmopolitan experience should be a vital part of American elite education. International politics saw some vital innovations, extending and ambitiously redefining the types of global politics that had emerged before 1914. The League of Nations, as a deliberative body designed to reduce conflicts, expanded the idea of coordination, and both the League and other agencies increasingly, though slowly, opened to non-Western participation. Older separate agencies, like the International Labor Office (not the communist group, but an organization formed before World War I, designed to encourage better labor conditions across borders and to collect relevant statistics), now became part of the larger League operations, with increased effectiveness as a result. International non-government organizations, like some feminist groups, gained in intensity as well, partly because they could now lobby the League for support.

But the dominant trends no longer favored globalization. The League of Nations failed in its largest goals, unable to deal effectively with growing nationalist conflict. The Great Depression that opened in 1929, though a clearly global phenomenon, pushed most countries to new levels of tariff protection and other selfish measures that actually made the disastrous economic spiral worse than it would have been otherwise. A number of countries, even before the depression, introduced new policies of import substitution, which protected local industries with high tariffs and government subsidies in order to limit dependence on imports of products like textiles and automobiles: this was the policy in Iran and Turkey in the 1920s and in key Latin American countries in the 1930s. The results encouraged new levels of regional manufacturing and could reduce some of the sting of Western-dominated trading patterns, but at least for the moment the innovations were non-global if not anti-global.

Thus, in the wake of World War I and the depression, huge changes emerged in key aspects of globalization. Economic disruptions and the rise of high national tariffs thus reduced the average annual growth of world trade during the decades between the wars from the 4 percent characteristic of the later 19th century, to a mere 1 percent.

Other innovations dramatically cut into global travel, and here the consequences have lasted to the present day. The post-World War I years saw the rise of modern passport and visa requirements. To be sure, the rise of some forms of passport goes well back in world history. Various states had often issued letters to travelers to try to promote a good reception, and basic safety, in other countries. The idea was to help favored travelers, not hinder them. Thus King Louis XIV of France began to issue encouraging letters to court favorites in the late 17th century, calling them *passé ports*, because they might help travelers when they reached a foreign port. By 1800 most European countries had developed some passport system, and some tried to require visas of foreign entrants as well. The Habsburg monarchy attempted with some success to regulate travel across its borders from the Middle East, partly to protect against contagious diseases. The United States began to try to register immigrants, though they did not necessarily have official papers from their countries of origin. But the system was still haphazard: it was only in 1858, for example, that Britain stopped issuing passports to people who were not British citizens. The United States did not grant the Department of State sole authority to issue passports (as opposed to individual states or private firms) until 1858, and even then many Americans traveled abroad without documentation.

In the heyday of immigration and foreign travel in the later 19th century, in fact, what passport system there was totally broke down because of the frequency of travel and the rise of new means of transportation. France abolished passports and visas in 1861, and most European countries followed suit.

It was World War I that altered this permissiveness decisively. Fearful of spies and foreign agents, most European countries introduced strict passport requirements during the war, initially terming them temporary measures. The United States began to try to prevent anyone leaving the country without a passport in 1918.

The result was, at the least, a significant complication to the movement of migrants and travelers. When combined with new immigration restrictions, as in the United States during the 1920s, the result significantly reduced the international movement of peoples. Once firmly established after World War I, the idea of a government's right to prevent unauthorized departures and entries, and the steady increase in the paperwork involved in any kind of international travel, became a significant new component of global interactions. The new system did not prevent renewed global networks, but it definitely did not encourage them, and some feared groups of travelers might be totally left out, at least in terms of legal activity, in the process. The rise of the modern passport was both a symbol and, at least for a time, a new reality in reactions against the easy globalization of the later 19th century.

The extensive retreat of globalization does not challenge the idea of the later 19th century as the point of origin of modern globalization overall. Rather, the retreat confirms how much had changed, to the point that, spurred by the disaster of World War I, so many countries now believed that they had to think about how to recover greater autonomy. The larger period 1850–1945, thus, can be seen in terms of the rise of globalization punctuated in the final decades by various though incomplete reactions to the contrary.

Even with the retreat, several key aspects of globalization were vastly stronger in 1939 than they had been in 1839.

Yet the retreat was quite real as well. One consequence was that, when globalization resumed a forward march, it might seem newer than it actually was, an innovation more than, at least in considerable measure, a resumption of earlier trends. Another consequence was that, after the horrors of the depression and yet another world war forced growing realization of the disastrous consequences of some of the anti-global movements like Nazism, many leaders now had a new reason to seek more global solutions, to develop alternatives to the anti-global trends of two really challenging decades. Both aspects, finally, set up the next phase of globalization, a focused resumption of global initiatives after World War II that would finally spill over into a real global torrent, as earlier thrusts resumed and additional innovations added still further range and intensity.

Conclusion

Technology breakthroughs in transportation and communication alike, new approaches to global health issues and the massive acceleration of technology diffusion, really new areas of global interaction in culture and politics, and crucial commitments from key nations like Japan – the list of fundamental innovations is substantial, and might easily justify the idea that the post-1850 period is indeed the crucible of modern globalization. Add to this the considerable redefinition of established exchange areas like trade levels, the activities of international companies and migration, and the impression gains further heft. To be sure, the checklist by 1900 is hardly identical to what it would become by the year 2000. Constraints and regional hesitations and then the substantial pushback that developed after World War I must be added to the mix. Even with these complications and the appropriate recognition of key developments that had occurred earlier, a valid hypothesis remains: was this not the period when the dimensions of globalization became so wide-ranging, acquiring such massive momentum, that later phases of the process, though adding very real changes, in essence would follow inevitably, or at least with a high level of probability, amplifying trends that were already clearly in play?

And if the answer is yes, maybe the challenging task of rethinking recent world history periodization cannot be avoided: with the crucial break in the 1850s, followed by ensuing sub-periods even to the present day defined in terms of ebbs and flows of an established process. Globalization, seen as an extended modern development, may even compel us to change the textbooks. We may need to begin to identify the centuries of protoglobalization that extended to the mid-19th century, when a real break occurred, given the decisive onset of modern globalization, then followed by important but lesser shifts in the efforts at resistance, 1914–1945, returning to renewed commitment from 1945 onward.

Further reading

Baldwin, Peter. *Contagion and the State in Europe, 1830–1930* (New York: Cambridge University Press, 2005).

Fletcher, Max E. "The Suez Canal and World Shipping, 1869–1914," in *The Journal of Economic History*, Vol. 18, No. 4 (Dec. 1958), pp. 556–573.

Grant, Jonathan A. *Rulers, Guns and Money: The Global Arms Trade in the Age of Imperialism* (Cambridge, MA: Harvard University Press, 2007).

Hobsbawm, Eric. *Age of Empire 1875–1914* (New York: Random House, 1989).

Iriye, Akira. *Cultural Internationalism and World Order* (Baltimore, MA: The Johns Hopkins University Press, 1997).

Kenwood, A.G. and Lougheed, A.L. *The Growth of the International Economy 1820–2000* (London: Routledge, 1999).

Metcalf, Thomas. *Imperial Connections: India in the Indian Ocean Arena, 1860–1920* (Berkeley, CA: University of California Press, 2007).

Rennella, Mark. "American Travelers and the Transatlantic Voyage in the Nineteenth and Twentieth Centuries," in *Journal of Social History*, Vol. 38, No. 2 (2004), pp. 365–383.

Schivelbusch, Wolfgang. *The Railway Journey: The Industrialization of Time and Space in the 19th Century* (Berkeley, CA: University of California Press, 1986).

Stearns, Peter N. *The Industrial Revolution in World History*, 3rd edn (Boulder, CO: Westview Press, 2007).

Torpey, John C. *The Invention of the Passport: Surveillance, Citizenship, and the State* (Cambridge: Cambridge University Press, 2000).

Withey, Lynn. *Grand Tour and Cooks Tours: A History of Leisure Travel, 1750–1915* (Newton Abbot: Aurum Press, 1998).

Zeiler, Thomas. *Globalization and the American Century* (New York: Cambridge University Press, 2003).

Chapter 6

Globalization since the 1940s

A new global history?

A globalization guru tells the following story. In 1988 a United States government official traveling to Chicago was assigned a limousine with a cellular phone. It was his first experience with the novelty, and he was so pleased to have a new communications option literally at his fingertips that he called his wife just to brag. Nine years later, in 1997, the same official was visiting a remote village in Côte d'Ivoire, in west Africa, that was accessible only by a dugout canoe. While he was there a Côte d'Ivoire official told him he had been asked to contact Washington, and handed him a cell phone for the purpose. And if the same story had occurred another decade later, the official's own cell phone would have connected with the United States directly.

The point is obvious, and obviously important: new communication opportunities melted distance and time. People could reach each other, immediately, around the world. This made the experience of travel different from what it had been before – one could go a long distance and retain direct connection with family, friends and work, which meant that travel was less disruptive than ever before. The shrinking of communication gaps, at least technologically, made new types of collaboration possible: scientists for example could work on the same problem, in real time (impeded only by the intractable issue of different time zones), almost as if they were next door to each other. Connections among stock markets tightened as news could be exchanged instantaneously. Even student cheating took on new dimensions: students taking an Advanced Placement test in Egypt could use cell phones or email to tell friends in Los Angeles what was on the exam, hours before they actually had to take it – until the college board wised up and began preparing different versions of the exam for different international regions. The implications of new communication speeds were dazzling.

Technology was not the only story. As early as 1946 the International Labor Office, backed by powerful maritime unions in several parts of the world and their global federation, instituted an international minimum wage for all merchant seamen, regardless of nationality. Enforcement varied, of course, but shipping workers were able to extend the standard by refusing to handle ships from countries that defied the new minimum at national ports – so the international wage did spread widely in this unusual industry. The idea of a single international wage level for an important category of workers would have been unthinkable just a few decades earlier, but now it quietly became part of global life. Policies and organizations, and not just technologies, were creating a new world community, and this also reminds us that the contemporary phenomenon of globalization probably predates some of the most striking recent inventions such as cell phones and the Internet, which were called into being by new global needs and were not just independent sources of new contacts.

While historians did not invent the concept of globalization, we have noted that a vigorous group of "new global historians," including several leading scholars in the history discipline as a whole, have been using historical perspective to highlight how much is brand new about the global age of the past half century. Bruce Mazlish, for example, puts forth the idea that we should not just think of globalization as the most revolutionary development of the past several decades, but more grandly should accept the fact that we are entering a global epoch, as different from previous patterns as some of the great geological epochs earlier in the earth's history had been compared to prior patterns in terrestrial development. This means, obviously, that globalization is quite new: Mazlish and the other new global historians naturally recognize that there were earlier developments in international contacts, but they don't see them as coming close to the magnitude of contemporary globalization. If they are right, this also means that globalization is unusually sweeping in its implications for shaping human life, far beyond what is normally involved in defining a particular period of time.

Seeking to flesh out this far-reaching novelty, the new global historians offer a number of specifics, most of which are mutually compatible but which may also be subjected to separate evaluations. They see, for example, the global as a huge step beyond the mere "modern": modern meant industrial, it meant a new kind of state, and while these were important shifts, they differ from the wider-ranging implications of the global and they are also less significant as sources of change. Another venture (which again can be challenged, given the range of developments after 1850 for example): earlier international contacts revolved mainly around trade, but globalization is far more encompassing, with far more facets than commerce or even capitalism alone. Even the economic aspect is transformed: while a world economy has existed for centuries, a "global economy is something different: it is an economy with the capacity to work as a unit in real time on a planetary scale" (as Manuel Castells puts it). Yet another statement: globalization increasingly undermines both nation and state, for the process goes well beyond conventional politics; power shifts to more amorphous forces like communications networks or environmental impacts or to less fixed kinds of institution like multinational corporations or INGOs. The globalists point out that at least 52 of the richest entities in the world are multinational corporations, not governments – which means that over 150 nation-states are dwarfed by these economic giants (and there are over 60,000 multinationals in the world today altogether). They note further, connected with this, that inter-regional relations have shifted from conventional state-to-state diplomacy to the broader forces that are encompassed by globalization. Anxieties are redefined – another striking claim about the newness of globalization – as people realize that they are surrounded by vast processes, and as risks spread to global levels, well beyond the ups and downs of individual regions. And the new global historians urge that unless we turn to the huge changes that globalization has brought to the human experience over the past half century, unless we accept that globalization is revolutionizing human life as no mere contact patterns had ever done before, we will not have an adequate basis for shaping policies and perspectives to deal with the world around us – it's not just a matter of scholarly accuracy. Several of the historians, going beyond mere scholarly analysis, plead for new global ethics and humane standards to match and control the changes they see in organization and technology.

This chapter lays out some of the major developments that have unquestionably accelerated globalization during the past six decades. In the process, it allows further assessment of the claims of dramatic novelty. That important changes have occurred is incontestable, even if the current period is seen as the latest phase of a longer process (which is the argument of others in the small band of historians who have taken up this topic, like Robbie Robinson who sees recent patterns as the "third phase" of a transformation that began in the 16th century). The question is how fundamental the transformation, how radical the new directions human societies have embarked upon.

Four other preliminaries must be noted. First, even the most sweeping of the new global historians acknowledges the importance of interrelating local reactions and conditions with the mounting global forces. Indeed, balancing the local and the global is something of a mantra in this approach to history. Globalization obviously affects and limits diversity, but it does not erase it. Some of the diversity, in turn, relates to continuities from earlier relationships with inter-regional contacts.

New global historians express excitement about identifying the innovations globalization entails, but not blanket approval of the consequences these same innovations bring. They fully grant that globalization creates new problems and worries, even outright protests, and while they do not see the process turning back they are not blindly optimistic. One can accept the idea of fundamental change, in other words, without assuming that the world is better as a result; or one can insist on greater continuities with earlier phases of global interactions, but again with open evaluation of the quality of the results.

Potential debate might surface about exactly when the transformation (or next phase) began, and while the issue is less important than the discussions about the new period's relationship to earlier stages in the emergence of inter-regional connections it could warrant attention. Hence a third preliminary. After all, pinpointing a decade in which new or additional processes began relates to identifying the major causes involved in launching them. Casual observers might opt for recency, around some of the most dramatic new technologies such as the Internet. Most historians, however, including the new global group, opt for the mid-20th century as the point at which changes in policy as well as technology began to emerge, only to accelerate further, of course, as additional developments like satellite communications or the Internet factored in. There is some complexity here: it was in the same mid-century decades that the Cold War took shape, dividing much of the world along ideological lines, and this is not exactly consistent with the general processes we usually associate with globalization. But many historians believe that basic globalization features developed alongside the Cold War, and they also note that both the "free world" and communist sides in that conflict thought in global terms, even as they disagreed about what world they wanted to create. The end of the Cold War in the 1980s accelerated globalization further, but it was in fact almost certainly already under way.

Finally, the relationship of recent globalization to other commonly mentioned processes, notably Westernization or Americanization, deserves comment in advance. Americanization was a phrase much used in the 1950s – a French government official famously referred in that decade to the dangers of "Coca-colonization," and some of the concerns about globalization more recently have involved other American staples like McDonald's. American cultural as well as economic and military influence certainly plays a role in contemporary globalization. The broader process of Westernization must also be considered – one historian saw this as the central feature of the later 20th century, though he wrote before the globalization concept became current. Phenomena such as the global (though not uniform) spread of democracy owe much to ongoing Western influence. But the new global historians tend to downplay the role of this special type of regional outreach in the changes they identify, noting for example the increasing place of east Asian societies such as Japan, South Korea and now China in shaping many of the economic and cultural processes we associate with globalization. One of the new features of this globalization period, indeed, in contrast with the later 19th century, may well be the reduced hold of the West on the basic contours of change. After all, accelerating globalization occurred just as a host of regions freed themselves from Western colonial control – decolonization initially seemed to complicate globalization by introducing scores of new nations and new nationalisms, but this tension subsided. More recently, accelerating globalization has built on the rise of China, India, Brazil and other new manufacturing powers, reducing Western economic as well as political dominance in the world at large. Disproportionate Western influence still has something to do with globalization, but amid important changes and complexities – and the new global historians avoid the conflation of a now-diminishing Westernization and ascendant global change. Here, certainly, is a set of issues to be tested along with the broader probes of global transformations themselves.

The new framework: technology, policy and language

Developments in three areas combined to set the process of globalization in motion from the mid-20th century onward – or (less dramatically) to relaunch it after the tribulations of the world wars and depression decades. Two areas are familiar enough from the later 19th century, though they embraced very new features; a third area, language, had more obviously novel qualities.

The experience and outcome of World War II powerfully spurred this new framework. To be sure, the war caused great devastation. It helped lead to the new divisions that underpinned the Cold War between the Soviet Union and the United States and their respective allies. It hastened the dismantling of the Western empires, which had previously encouraged global contacts of a sort – though it is also important to note that the decolonization was itself a global movement, spreading rapidly from one colonial region to the next.

Three facets of the war most directly promoted new kinds and new levels of global interaction. First, the new position of the United States, even though it was contested, provided an additional spur to new connections – for example, in the growing importance of the English language in international communications. Second, the huge geographical scope of the war – far greater than that of World War I – promoted new technologies that would have implications well beyond the military. New types of aircraft and new communications systems had strong roots in wartime research. Finally, for many parts of the world, the shock of the war, on top of the previous dislocations of the Great Depression, caused many leaders to rethink earlier policies. American politicians, for example, realized that the fascination with isolationism had caused more problems than it was worth. New Japanese leaders, with American encouragement, obviously rethought their relationships with the wider world, and the collapse of Nazism had the same effect for Germany. Soviet policies became far more internationally oriented than they had under prewar Stalinism. Even more important, leaders from various countries, but particularly in Europe and the United States, vowed to create new international policies that would promote peace and economic growth. The idea of reforming global political structures was a key element in the globalization surge of the postwar world.

Transportation and communication

A series of developments in the second half of the 20th century speeded the movement of people, goods and, above all, information literally around the world. The primacy of communication was striking, but the contributions of global air travel were significant as well, allowing more people to go long distances for business, pleasure or migration than ever before.

Use of airplanes for regular transcontinental travel began in the late 1930s. Before that point, the need for frequent refueling prevented anything but occasional or very indirect, island-hopping flights. Pan American airlines established the first regular transatlantic route in 1939, but the advent of World War II obviously disrupted the service. Activity picked up after the war, when the utilization of jet engines greatly facilitated longer-distance flights, and at greater speed than was possible with propeller-driven craft. British Overseas Airways established the first regular jet service, from London to Johannesburg, South Africa, in 1952. A Convention on International Aviation, designed to help coordinate international flights under the administration of a United Nations Agency, was first signed in 1948. Quantas (the Australian carrier) developed the first nonstop flight across the Pacific in 1965. The effective birth of air travel and freight beyond national borders – staples of global connection today – is little more than a half century old.

Yet in that half century, the volume of global air travel has increased immensely, oscillating moderately according to economic conditions but trending steadily upward. By the early 21st century almost 100 million passengers in the United States were involved in over 800,000 international flights each year. A modest international airport in Copenhagen, Denmark, handled over two million intercontinental passengers each year (over 10 percent of its total activity), with over half of these heading to the United States, China and Thailand. Significant numbers of people – minorities of the total populations, but not tiny minorities – were traveling long distances every year, some of them repeatedly.

The rise of global air travel had its downsides, of course. The term "jet lag" was introduced in 1966, described as "a debility not un-akin to a hangover." For the first time in human history, hundreds of thousands of people every year were trying to do business or conduct diplomacy while feeling significantly under the weather and simultaneously coping with the strangeness of many foreign countries. Of course, experience brought some remediation, as the most frequent world travelers used various coping strategies and, at the highest level, luxurious airline accommodation might cushion the impact.

Air travel was not for passengers alone. By the 1970s, Flying Tiger Line, in the United States, was running regular package services to six continents, acquiring a fleet of jets in the process. This operation was acquired by Federal Express in 1989. Air transport became a major freight option, allowing perishables, urgently needed items, and legal and business materials to be carried, often overnight, literally around the world.

Key innovations in communications emerged during the same decades. Here, however, military needs, during World War II and particularly during the Cold War, provided particular stimulus, with resulting technologies quickly spilling over into more general global contacts. It was in 1945 that a British electronics authority, Arthur C. Clarke, wrote about the possibility of sending communications satellites into space, among other things to distribute television programs. By the 1950s, various firms were beginning to develop research in the area – one proposal particularly focused on the possible benefits (and costs) of satellites that would be able to carry intercontinental telephone calls in far greater volume than undersea cables could. It was the Soviet launch of the first space venture, Sputnik, in 1957 that really spurred activity. The American federal government began to collaborate with several corporations to build orbiting communications satellites. The first successful launches occurred in 1964, with the first regular network established the following year with the Early Bird satellite. Systems and participants expanded steadily thereafter. Global organization was provided by the establishment of Intelsat, which ultimately combined more than 130 governments and provided communications open to all nations. Individual countries, particularly of course from among the wealthier societies like Japan, Canada, Australia and ultimately China, Mexico, Brazil and India, established their own satellite systems as well.

The result was a literally revolutionary improvement in the number, clarity and low cost of international phone calls, and a brand new capacity to send television signals worldwide. Already portions of the 1964 Olympic Games in Tokyo were televised to western Europe and North America. Soon, transmissions from most parts of the world were possible, allowing news, sports and entertainment to be sent worldwide: audiences of a full quarter of the world's population for single events like World Cup soccer became a recurrent but heretofore unprecedented cultural phenomenon. On the phone side, by the 21st century facilities expanded to the point of providing hundreds of thousands of international or domestic calls at any one time, at less than 10 percent the cost of rates in the 1960s (and less than that when inflation is taken into account). Further, these services were available to regions regardless of levels of industrialization, assuming the ability to afford a cell phone or a television set – hence the west Africa story that began this chapter.

Building on satellite capacity was the emergence of the Internet as, again, an international device for the transmission of a massive amount of information and a tremendous variety of communications on a global basis. Research on the potential power of connecting computers began in the 1950s and 1960s, both in the United States and Europe; military and civilian sponsorships were concurrently involved. A number of small linkages developed, but the idea of a more unified network gained ground steadily. Initial goals focused both on communication and on enhanced information storage and retrieval capacity. Electronic mail opportunities emerged from 1979 onward. International connections were at first limited, because of disparate national systems and concerns about military secrecy. By the 1980s, however, greater standardization developed; in 1984 University College London began using Internet capacity to communicate with the United States, with computers talking directly with computers. Australian linkages developed at almost the same time as developments in Europe, and by the late 1980s Japan, Singapore and Thailand also gained global Internet connections. China introduced its first capacity in 1991. With some external funding, African connections developed from the mid-1990s onward. Clearly, a new global system had emerged with far wider information exchange capabilities, at almost instantaneous speed, than had ever before existed. There were of course limitations to this aspect of technological globalization: poor countries developed links, but with far fewer and less high-speed computers their participation was hardly complete. Other countries qualified their participation by introducing national content filters, a prominent feature for example of the Chinese system designed to limit any oppositional political impact. Various kinds of "digital divides" continued to define this aspect of globalization, sometimes adding to the more familiar global inequalities. Still, with email and the Internet (and by the late 1990s, pioneered by Japan, the ability to connect via mobile phones), opportunities for personal contact, scholarly and business interaction and other forms of exchange expanded beyond anything previously imagined in the experience of the human species.

Technological innovation had periodically contributed to trans-regional exchange before, with particularly striking developments of course in the mid-19th century. Arguably, however, the new possibilities for moving people, goods and information rapidly over long distances created a technological environment vastly surpassing any previous precedent. New organizational forms, like the multinational corporation or the instantaneous human rights appeals of contemporary INGOs, would have been inconceivable without this technological base.

Policy change

Two kinds of policy innovation altered the framework for globalization: some key new international institutions, and the values and functions they embodied, and, second and more gradually, crucial national decisions about relationships with global society. Launching the first category, in the later stages of World War II, two types of institutions were sketched, one for world politics, the other for the world economy, which reflected the wide desire to find global solutions for the kinds of problem that had torn the world apart in the previous two decades. The economic institutions also reflected the growing role of the United States in world affairs and its commitment to free market capitalism.

In 1943, at the height of the war, Great Britain, the United States, the Soviet Union and China issued a call for a new international organization to replace the League of Nations. A founding conference occurred in San

Francisco in 1945, and the organization began functioning in 1946, with its headquarters ultimately in New York. It was hoped that the new organization would be far more decisive in resolving conflicts and assuring peace than the League had been, and while the Cold War and later tensions disrupted this goal, the UN did in fact play an effective role in a number of trouble spots, winning agreements to send troops from member countries in many instances. United Nations agencies, assisting refugees, working for disease control, trying to promote economic development and technological cooperation have often proved even more constructive, constituting a major part of political globalization over the past sixty years. United Nations proclamations, beginning with the Universal Declaration of Human Rights and extending to statements on women, children, labor and other issues, have provided powerful political and humanitarian standards, helping to galvanize public opinion and influence local policies on a number of major topics. Hardly a world government, despite concerns from some critics, the United Nations has provided global influence. It has also served as a forum for the growing number of independent nations, almost all of them outside the West, thus becoming part of the redefinition of globalization away from almost exclusively Western dominance.

Meetings at Bretton Woods, New Hampshire, in 1944 established new institutions and policies to help regulate the global economy and prevent the kinds of instability that had marked the decades between the two world wars. The main goal of the conference was to win agreement from each participating country to maintain the exchange value of its currency in relationship to the price of gold (or, after 1971, the US dollar), in order to prevent incapacitating fluctuations that could disrupt international trade and domestic economic performance alike. Two specific institutions resulted in addition, the International Monetary Fund (IMF) and the International Bank for Reconstruction and Development which later essentially became the World Bank. Both organizations established voting rights for member nations, based on levels of economic contribution. The basic idea was to assure a free flow of trade and a commitment to collaboration in economic matters, to prevent the kind of selfish national separatism that had clearly exacerbated the depression. The IMF helped oversee the stability of exchange rates while advising countries on policies that might affect the international monetary system. The organization also had a fund that could provide loans to members to cover temporary trade deficits, while insisting on the adoption of economic policies it found suitable in return. What became the World Bank had the more straightforward task of providing investment money to help in postwar economic recovery (particularly in Europe), and, later, to aid developing nations in accelerating their economic growth and occasionally to provide debt relief.

International discussion also focused on tariff levels, with various agreements on lowering rates in the interest of freer trade from 1947 onward, and with another new institution, the World Trade Organization (WTO), ultimately set up in 1995 to encourage and monitor the process with even greater vigor. The result was hardly smooth sailing. A number of countries held back or were not admitted to the international organizations because of seemingly illiberal economic practices. Disputes over items like agricultural tariffs – where industrial nations tried to protect farming groups by limiting entry of foods produced, often more cheaply, elsewhere – were recurrent, and a number of international meetings ended in failure. Still, the effort was unprecedented and it had some obvious results. A number of countries, like China (admitted to the WTO in 2002), undertook significant reforms in order to participate fully in the global trading system.

This kind of global economic organization and policy had never before been attempted. Its global reach was imperfect, however. The communist bloc did not initially participate. Many developing nations, and other critics, argued that the new funds were excessively under American control and unduly committed to free-trade policies that interfered with local goals and often operated to the benefit of the industrial regions (particularly the West, but also Japan). While massive depression was avoided, periodic regional crises continued and certainly the funds did not manage to lift all areas up into sustained growth. Nevertheless, the effort to reduce the impact of regional problems on the larger global trading framework was real, and clearly differentiated this stage of globalization from the immediately pre- ceding decades. It was revealing that when in 2008–9 an unusually severe financial and economic crisis hit the world economy the leading nations (not now just the West, but rising stars in Asia and Latin America) actually sought to strengthen the IMF as a means of limiting national isolation and providing new levels of global financial monitoring.

The second type of policy change unfolded more gradually, but it involved not only reversing some of the isolationism that had developed earlier in the 20th century but also promoting levels of international engagement that were in some cases unprecedented. The United States, Japan and Germany moved, as noted, away from earlier policies quickly after the war, and became leading players in world trade and other global interchange – qualified only by some lingering suspicions of the former Axis powers (Nazi Germany, Italy and Japan). China underwent a massive shift in orientation in 1978, when communist leaders, though eager to preserve a separate and author- itarian political system, decided to embrace the world market and to open to unparalleled interest in hosting international visitors and in sending students and others abroad, with the broad goal of learning as much as possible from the rest of the world, and particularly from the industrial leaders. Never before had so many Chinese traveled so widely, even as China's role in the world economy and in other global sectors, such as athletics, expanded rapidly. Almost as dramatic was the decision by Russian leaders in 1985 to develop a more market-based economic approach and a more open political style, which also led to new levels of international exchange. The fall of European communism in 1989–91 destroyed the barriers between eastern and western Europe, including the Berlin wall, and embraced virtually the entire region in active global interactions. Even Albania, long isolated even within the communist bloc, soon joined the parade. By the early 21st century only a few countries, notably North Korea and Burma (Myanmar), stood apart from active international engagement, including extensive trade and travel. Other major regions had clearly decided that the costs of isolation, including missing out on the latest technologies and participation in potentially profitable world trade, were simply too great to bear. Never before had such a largely voluntary embrace of the importance of globalism occurred.

New policies and institutions committed to the free flow of goods and funds, and new national involvement in internationalism of various sorts set a policy context for globalization that was almost as significant as the technology revolutions. Indeed, the inquiry into faster means of communication was in part a response to the opportunities unleashed by policy change. The combination was powerful.

Language: global English

The spread of language had always been both a barometer and a facilitator of wider exchange. The extensive use of Greek in the eastern Mediterranean, well beyond the native Greek-speaking population, was a key example in the classical and post-classical periods. Arabic, fueled by the rise of Islam and Arab-led trade, probably came closest to the status of a world language during the post-classical period and beyond; but obviously many regions were uninvolved. During the colonial and imperialist eras, both Spanish and French spread widely, along with English. Always, language spread reflected the military and economic power of the linguistic source, and sometimes larger cultural prestige as well.

These same factors fueled the global spread of English in the decades after World War II, but now the whole world, and not just an extensive region, was involved. Earlier British imperial status and now the global surge of the United States explained why English was the global candidate. But it was the growth of new levels of interchange – the needs of a new phase of globalization – that explained why a common language was increasingly required for businessmen, athletes, scholars and others. And the spread of English in turn became a major factor in enhancing other aspects of globalization, completing the framework that decisively emerged in the late 20th century.

The globalization of English began with responses to some obvious new demands. International pilots almost inevitably needed a common language to communicate with airport control systems around the world, unless they visited a single-language area alone. English, in the postwar context, obviously fit the bill. Advancing technologies, like computers, inevitably generated new words, and while these could be translated – the French, fiercely, often tried to substitute for English in the information technology field – it was hard to resist the commonalities English provided. A key motive to learn English centered on the fact that, in many language areas, only English-language computer manuals were available. The increasing globalization of science, with researchers exchanging across borders, and the growing reliance on international conferences to exchange knowledge again promoted a single common tongue, and by the early 21st century 66 percent of all scientists in the world spoke English. While some of the new global organizations, like the United Nations, accepted several official languages, it was increasingly tempting – in places like the World Bank, with employees from all regions but a Washington base – to use English as the common denominator. Even linguistically divided India, or later the European Union, found this to be the case. By 2008, 80 percent of the electronically stored information in the world was in English – another huge inducement.

Both pressures and opportunities to learn English mounted steadily. New capacities, like global news services broadcasting in the language, increased exposure to English but also the expectation that certain types of people would be familiar with it if not fluent. In the process also, English tag lines became fashionable features in commercial advertising, making goods seem more desirable and cosmopolitan. The expansion of travel and tourism pressed many cities in places like South Korea, the United Arab Emirates and China to offer street signs and transportation directions in English as well as Korean, Arabic or Chinese.

Required courses in English became increasingly common in secondary schools, generally now in preference to any other foreign language – in contrast to a more traditional menu of options. Special English language institutes, offering short courses, proliferated. "Learn English in just 10 weeks!" More and more universities in places like The Netherlands, Russia and China offered regular programs in English to help their students link to the wider world and to attract international students for whom the language was the only common currency. By the early 21st century, with at least 100 million Chinese children studying English (more than the total population of the United Kingdom), the number of English users with other native languages vastly surpassed the number for whom English was their native tongue. Demand for Britons, or Australians, or Americans to teach abroad frequently surpassed the available supply. A forecast suggested that by 2015 over half of the world's people would have some grasp of English. As a 12-year-old self-taught student of English in China noted, "If you can't speak English, you're deaf and dumb." A Briton teaching a variety of international students, including a South Korean manager and a nurse from rural Japan, asks, "Do you want a lot of homework or a little?" And the unequivocal answer: "A lot." At a Japanese car plant in the Czech Republic, English was the only available working language for the multinational managerial team.

Countries where English has long been common, like India, prospered through this facility, piling up outsourced jobs that required phone services in English to the United States or Britain. Newer entrants, like Burundi, long accustomed to using French to supplement the native languages, now officially switched to English. The story was universal: English was becoming a vital entry to globalization, and its spread facilitated the process in turn.

Of course there were drawbacks, including worries about traditional cultural integrity and resentments over the prime position of a single language. Native English speakers became increasingly lazy about learning other tongues, which might hinder more sophisticated globalization in the long run. People who learned English as a second language might become more reluctant to learn a third: why bother, when "everyone" speaks English. But the momentum was unchecked.

Facets of globalization: trade and inequalities

Global trade levels soared during the half century after the 1950s, when postwar economic recovery was largely complete. With unprecedented transportation facilities and numerous international organizations and agreements encouraging relatively free trade, opportunities increased as never before, though of course there were significant national differences and also year-to-year oscillations depending on economic conditions. A number of nations depended hugely on exports. Established manufacturing countries like Britain, with exports accounting for 18 percent of the overall national economy, and Germany, at 25 percent, provided obvious examples. Newer-comers periodically enjoyed huge surges. Japan's exports grew 21 percent per year in the 1970s. Early in the 21st century, between 2002 and 2007, China expanded its exports by 400 percent. Key raw materials producers obviously depended massively on global trade, like the oil-producing states of the Middle East, and more recently Russia, selling almost all of their output abroad. Chile's rise as an economic power depended heavily on commercial agricultural exports of fruits and vegetables to North America and east Asia. The importance of global trade showed in certain product lines. The vast majority of the commercial airliners used around the world emanated from two companies by the early 21st century, Boeing in the United States and Airbus in Europe. Only a small amount of Russian production provided any significant alternative to the two global giants.

New trade levels and export dependence revolutionized certainly aspects of daily life. In wealthy countries, foods from around the world were regularly available, making unfamiliar products like New Zealand kiwis regular entrants to the more upscale fruit plates in the United States, Europe and east Asia. Along with the growing popularity of foreign restaurants in big cities almost everywhere, the opportunities for common eating experiences grew as never before, significantly modifying national food traditions at least in some countries.

Rising international trade meant, in other words, a growing dependence on the world economy for large numbers of regions, industries and workers. Even in a huge economy like the United States, up to 20 percent of the manufacturing labor force in states like Illinois depended directly on exports for their jobs. Rising trade meant, also, new opportunities for consumers, at least in the middle and upper classes, to obtain a broader range of goods, and sometimes cheaper or better-made items than were available through purely domestic auspices.

The global economy, even as it aggressively expanded, also brought new signs of regional economic inequalities – and sometimes new inequalities within individual regions, as between rural and urban areas in places like India. The problems were not, here, basically new: they had surfaced in earlier stages of trans-regional interactions. Some of the same areas were involved, in the deepest poverty or the greatest affluence, as had been defined as early as the 16th century – though there was some shuffling of the cast of characters.

Several factors pushed certain regions – many parts of sub-Saharan Africa, and portions of Latin America, southeast Asia and even the Middle East – into growing poverty, and they did not all stem, directly at least, from globalization. Rapid population increase was a problem in specific areas, as growth rates began to slow in the world as a whole. At least as important, however, was the fact that the prices for many raw materials and foods (other than oil) dropped massively (by over 50 percent from 1980 to the early 1990s), as production capacity outstripped demand – an old problem in specific areas, even in the dependent economies, now made worse by more intense globalization. International indebtedness trapped some regional economies also, causing financial crises that pulled regions down in the global framework. Technological change often advantaged existing industrial leaders, like Japan and the United States, giving them greater profit margins even in sales to the poorest countries.

Economic gaps were not just matters of statistics. They counted in human lives. People in some of the poorest regions faced massive unemployment levels – of 30 to 50 percent, particularly in categories like younger workers. In a few cases, like parts of Africa in the past few decades, actual rates of child mortality, improving slowly before, began to reverse direction, in part because of growing poverty.

By the early 21st century, though before the economic crisis of 2008–9, some inequality assessments became a bit more optimistic, mainly because huge countries like China and India began to participate more effectively in world trade and saw average incomes begin to inch up, and a substantial middle class begin to emerge. But this must not mask the fact that certain regions continued to suffer, if anything even more. China's emergence as a global production giant, for example, added new competition to manufacturing sectors in southeast Asia and Africa, providing an additional source of inequality along with the activities of the fully industrialized nations. Overall, by the early 21st century, 20 percent of the world's population, living in the richest regions, controlled 86 percent of overall global product; the lowest 20 percent had access to but 1 percent. The division was stark and, at the extremes, still growing.

Finally, of course, there were the recurrent economic crises themselves. Some economic nosedives did not fully spread to global levels. A sharp recession in the later 1990s thus affected parts of east and southeast Asia primarily. But major downturns clearly operated at the global level. A financial crisis in the United States, as in 2008, brought banks down in many other countries, because investments were global in scope. Reduction of American demand inevitably cut production rates in other countries, because so much depended on the huge and voracious American consumer markets. As credit dried up worldwide and unemployment rose in many regions (with the accompanying departure of many immigrant workers, back to often impoverished homelands), the fact of global interdependence, but also its obvious vulnerabilities, was starkly clear. While the crisis did not seem as severe as that of the 1930s, it was even more widespread geographically and far more rapid in its global manifestations than its predecessor – another sign of change, if a gloomy one.

Migration, travel and global communities

New travel facilities and new problems both helped prompt new surges of immigration. The big story was the movement of workers from impoverished parts of the world to centers of industry and urban growth. The United States received a rising tide of migrants from many parts of Latin America. Europe newly became a global immigrant destination, with huge numbers of Muslim workers and also people from Africa and the Caribbean. Even Japan, more resistant to immigrants, saw numbers grow from southeast Asia. Indian, Palestinian and Filipino workers poured into the construction projects of the United Arab Emirates, creating a population that was over 80 percent expatriate (non-citizen). Countries like Algeria (with workers particularly to France) and the Philippines (with unusual numbers of women working as waitresses, child-care givers and nurses literally all over the industrial world) provided especially large numbers of migrants, but the phenomenon was widespread. Long-distance movement, bringing people from dramatically different cultures into contact with each other and with the new host country, had never been greater, though the basic phenomenon was not novel. Advanced industrial regions, with low birth rates, often needed new workers, and clearly there were many people eager, or forced, to oblige.

The system was often exploitative. Some countries expelled workers as soon as they lost a job, adding displacement to economic shock. Western

Europeans called many of the immigrants "guest workers," but they were not always cordial hosts. Many workers in the Emirates had twenty-four hours to leave the country if their employment ended. Many women were seized as sex slaves, lured abroad with the promise of a service job which turned out to be mere prostitution. The global sex trade reached massive proportions by the 1990s. Overall, a 2005 report suggested that 600,000 to 800,000 people were being "trafficked" each year – that is, enticed to other countries where they would be virtually enslaved, often for sexual purposes. The steady growth of illegal immigration, pushed by poverty, left many workers vulnerable to demands from employers and roughing by police. Periodic violence against immigrants from such different backgrounds added to pressures, with occasional riots both against the immigrant tide and by displaced immigrants themselves. Again, many of these features were not brand new, but the scale was unprecedented.

Immigrants also had new opportunities to travel periodically from new home to old. One benefit the Emirates offered to international construction workers was an annual trip home. Latinos in the United States often went back and forth to their families of origin. Affluent immigrants, for example professionals from India, used the airlines to the same purpose. The result allowed new combinations of cultures, as old ways – like arranged marriages, for many Asian Indians – could be periodically recalled. One prominent Saudi diplomat, comfortable in his own country but also enjoying a mountain home in Colorado, referred to himself as "bicultural" – adaptive to both his main settings, despite their great differences. Returning immigrants, even on visits, could also bring new ideas and disruptions among friends and relatives who had not moved – another source of global change.

International travel now included tremendous waves of global tourism, often now seeking the distant and (on paper at least) the exotic – and the sun. Here, thanks to ready travel and a new zeal for vacation pleasure, the dimensions of change were substantial – though the results (on tourists and those who served them) not always easy to determine. Numbers were staggering: by 1990, millions of people were annually arriving someplace outside their home country as tourists; yet by 2004 the figure had already increased by 78 percent. Southern Europe was the largest single destination, but many regions participated, and growth was actually strongest in parts of the Middle East and southeast Asia, with good winter climates and the ability to attract visitors from Europe, east Asia and Australia; the Caribbean also enjoyed a huge boom. Japanese tourists headed in many directions, including Hawaii. The fall of communism led to some interesting new destinations, like central Asia. In some cases, regions suffering from the global economy in production sought to use climate and beaches, and cheap local labor, to create a tourist industry to compensate.

Global tourism came in various packages, with the extent of the global a bit of a variable. In 1950 a Belgian entrepreneur founded Club Méditerranée, or Club Med, initially to cater to single tourists interested in an experience abroad, later expanding to families. While the initial targets, in Spain and elsewhere around the Mediterranean, were not distant from Europe, in 1955 the company began to branch out, with a center in Tahiti. Soon, Clubs were scattered in Thailand, the Caribbean, Florida, Turkey and elsewhere – wherever there was sun (or for skiers, snow) to be found. The Club offered various activities and considerable assurance that basic (Western) amenities would be available. In dining, particularly, local cuisine was introduced only once a week – otherwise, standard European fare was offered. Except as service workers, locals were largely kept out as well. Visitors could arrange bus tours to see the sights, but they were carefully shielded from real local involvement. Resort hotels, springing up in Malaysia or Cancun, operated on the same principle: one might be abroad, but it should not be very different from home.

Indeed, international tourists were grouped into several categories. The largest by far, sometimes called package tourists, did not expect to endure much that departed from what they were used to. This included people who flocked to charter boats that only occasionally debarked passengers on local soil, usually to shop and then get back on the boat. As one tourist to a Spanish island put it, it seemed as though she was still in Germany because there were so many co-nationals around: "The nightlife is just like being in a Spanish theme bar back home." A smaller number of tourists, however, really wanted to get off the beaten track and experience local culture and deliberately escape the familiar. Often, a new destination – like central Asia recently, or parts of Indonesia – first attracted the explorer-type tourists, and only later drew in the big, amenity-filled hotels. How much of the experience, not to mention the motivation, was really global for the bulk of the new tourists was open to question.

Impact on the new tourist centers was also complex. There were obvious clashes of culture. German and other European tourists, from the 1960s onward, often expected to be able to enjoy topless bathing – locals were truly shocked but often acquiesced because of the lure of profits, and then found that young people began to relax their dress styles as well. Young men sometimes misinterpreted tourist costumes as an invitation to hit on female travelers – with varied reactions in response. On the other hand, some local tourist workers put in their long days and then went home with no particular change to report – it was just a job. Some of the most interesting consequences of tourism involved adaptations of local cultural products designed to combine traces of traditional styles with the features tourists associated with that particular site. Tahitians, for example, were expected to be sensual, and customary dances might be modified to live up to the expected image. Maasai warriors, on display for tourists in Kenya, were expected to wear certain kinds of costume – not what they currently wore, and not always really traditional – and to look fierce (while dancing before visitors sipping Western cocktails). In one Maasai performance, unusually adapted, dancers included evocations of the Lion King movie, including the phrase Hakuna Matata, and adding some Jamaican dances as well, just to broaden the appeal. Globalization, here, added up to a significant distortion of local cultural standards, whether for better or for worse. The process might make preservation of actual traditions increasingly difficult.

Tourism, but even more migration and professional travel, contributed to the formation of certain kinds of potential global communities, defined by common bonds (including globalized cultural productions) across national and cultural lines. A case in point, though only for a minority of those involved, highlights the growing interest in study abroad from the 1950s onward. Study abroad programs blossomed in the postwar decades. The number of Americans studying internationally, at least for brief stints, quadrupled between 1990 and 2007. Worldwide, by 2003, 1.5 million students were involved in programs outside their home country. Graduate students from Asia and Africa headed to training opportunities in science, technology and management in industrial centers. Undergraduates sought broader cultural experiences. China, Korea and Japan began sending large numbers of undergraduates abroad, either for full degree programs or for a semester experience. Many universities, as a result, boasted 10–15 percent of their student bodies from other nations. Study abroad programs did not automatically, of course, create lasting effects: many students stuck with colleagues from their own country, even if they also developed some new cross-cultural skills. But some students began to form friendships and professional ties, and sometimes romantic relationships, that would serve them lifelong, modifying, and in some cases replacing, the links to the home country.

Given travel, communication and study opportunities, it was not surprising that a number of transnational communities began to form, with members sharing an identity that might supersede their regional roots. Many scientists, for example, traveled almost interchangeably from one lab to another, regardless of nation, usually with English as the communication medium; global ties would be further renewed at frequent international conferences. In certain sports like tennis, touring athletes had the same experience, at least during their playing days.

The same sense of borderless community might develop among some of the crucial new organizations that sprang up from globalization, notably the multinational corporations and the INGOs. These groups, too, could form close ties among people from various national origins – professional links and social interactions as well. The possibility existed that new kinds of loyalty and identity, around professions or human rights or environmental commitments or simple profit-seeking, could begin to replace regional and national markers – not yet for a majority of people but for a growing cosmopolitan minority.

As always, however, some caveats apply. Many people could not or did not wish to travel – less than a quarter of all Americans, for example, even had passports. National loyalties burned bright for many people. A military confrontation between Britain and Argentina in the 1980s over a south Atlantic island controlled by the former brought out surprisingly fierce passions in two seemingly sophisticated countries. Another continuity from the past that not only persisted but increased in complexity involved passport and visa regulations. The Cold War prompted many countries to increase requirements for the permissions needed to cross borders. Growing terrorism early in the 21st century had the same effect in many places. Passports were supplemented by fingerprinting and eye scans, and many travelers who fit certain stereotypes were pulled aside for further interrogation. The process could be unpleasant and even insulting, and some people stopped traveling to certain destinations in consequence. The global community had a number of dead ends.

An organizational revolution? Multinationals and INGOs

Debate over how new contemporary globalization is can focus in part on a more precise issue: how new were the multinational corporations? To the new global historians, multinational corporations operate in distinctive ways and wield unprecedented power not just in the world economy, but in matters of the environment and in labor conditions and gender roles. But companies with international activities and great trans-regional impacts are not new, and questions can focus on how much – despite the novel term – has really changed.

Efforts at definition abound. Multinational corporations operate in many areas of the world simultaneously, with assets widely distributed as well. They can amass huge budgets, though scales vary. Their most characteristic feature is the installation of production processes in different regions, often with different specializations depending on the area. In the late 19th century, an international company might mine raw materials in one place and produce in another; or it might have factories in several places making whole products. The contemporary multinational, however, may make one set of components for a product in Indonesia (either directly or through a contractor), another set in Turkey and a third set in Kentucky, for assembly in Mexico. This new degree of specialization and international coordination allows the company to seek lowest labor costs, cheapest raw materials and most lenient environmental regulations, all the while taking full advantage of the new facilities in global transportation and communication. The same specialization allows many companies to shift locations fairly readily if costs begin to mount in one setting – and no government is powerful enough to stop them. All of this means, in turn, that the multinational corporation can have devastating regional impacts, in contrast to earlier trading companies that could certainly affect and exploit regions but were also more closely tied to particular localities.

Whether the multinational is a new animal or a somewhat redefined version of older international ventures is open to question. What cannot be disputed is the rapid increase in the number of global businesses: in 1914 there were roughly 3,000 real international companies; the number had doubled by 1970; but by 1988 the number was 18,500 and by 2000 it had reached 63,000. Multinationals were of course largely based in the United States, Western Europe, Japan and South Korea, but entrants began to emerge also from China and a few other high-growth economies.

The companies wielded huge power. Their directors were themselves a multinational group, but joined by great wealth and similar cosmopolitan life styles, punctuated of course by frequent travel. The organizations frequently affected basic policies, even in large nations – opposing labor reforms in China early in the 21st century, for example, that threatened to increase costs (often with the implicit threat of pulling out if pressed too far). They not uncommonly ignored environmental rules, using bribes as well as sheer influence to curry favor. At the same time, however, they brought jobs to areas with excess population, and in some cases their managers – often from the home country – were seen as offering better labor treatment than local firms generated. The trans-regional impact record was mixed.

Joining the multinationals, less powerful but sometimes providing a degree of counterbalance, were the INGOs, which were in some ways more genuinely novel than the business ventures, though with links to prototypes of the later 19th century.

INGOs varied greatly, but they all had some degree of international participation, on governing boards and among financial contributors, and they aimed at correcting problems in a variety of parts of the world. Often, they also appealed to "world opinion," by the 1990s using the Internet to call for massive email-writing campaigns to correct various kinds of injustice. Usually, they linked to local NGOs that helped provide information about problems and might help monitor responses. While mostly based in the West, they won attention from people in various places; and some other countries, like Japan, headquartered significant INGOs as well. The numbers and range of activity of the INGOs grew steadily, though probably not as rapidly as did the multinationals. Perhaps as many as 200 existed in 1900, up to 2,000 in 1960, and nearly 4,000 in 1980, with rapid further growth since that time. Many multinationals were directly linked to other global organizations: some consulted with the United Nations or the International Criminal Court, and many others were inspired by the United Nations Declarations of Human Rights.

While it had roots deep in earlier global history – including the humanitarian concerns of Quakerism and the passionate efforts against slavery – Amnesty International demonstrated many of the qualities of the contemporary INGO, and it served as a prototype for a host of other groups. Formed in 1961, with a London base, Amnesty initially sought to attack the political persecutions that were occurring within the framework of the Cold War. Its founder laid out the charge: "Open your newspaper any day of the week, and you will find a report from somewhere in the world of someone being imprisoned, tortured or executed because his opinions or his religion are unacceptable to his government. ... The newspaper reader feels a sickening sense of impotence. Yet if these feelings of disgust all over the world could be united into common action, something effective could be done." By 1977, when Amnesty won the Nobel Peace Prize, it had identified over 15,000 political prisoners in communist, democratic and developing nations alike, and had helped galvanize freedom for half of them. It promoted rights for famous detainees like Nelson Mandela in South Africa, for trade-union organizers in Central America, for prisoners in Northern Ireland, and for American civil-rights workers. By the 1980s the organization had 700,000 members from 150 countries, and offices in 50 different nations. Outraged public opinion was its stock in trade: Amnesty worked hard to publicize cases of human-rights violation, mobilizing massive petitions and urging voters to press their governments, using maximum publicity to prompt offenders to pull back.

Amnesty steadily expanded its definitions of rights and its own agenda. It attacked torture systematically, wherever it seemed to occur. It defended rights for workers. It began to pay growing attention to abuses of women, helping to define rape as a war crime but also moving into the area of domestic violence. And all of this depended on a capacity for reporting in virtually every part of the world, while maintaining standards for decency that were global in scope.

Amnesty's success prompted other human rights INGOs, like Human Rights Watch (formed in 1978), but also a host of other activist movements, effectively augmenting the range of issues covered by a global spotlight. The mid-1980s saw a burst of local rights groups, for example in Central America, coordinating with the key global organizations. Environmental INGOs began to form in the late 1960s. Friends of the Earth (1969) boasted over 700,000 international members by the 1990s, working actively to combat global warming and the reduction of the ozone layer; the more activist Greenpeace dated from 1971, and by the 1990s it had offices in over thirty countries and claimed over six million members worldwide. Like their human-rights colleagues, environmentalists sought to establish global standards for policy and behavior across national lines. Treatment of workers inspired yet another set of INGOs, often linked to labor unions: the Dutch-based Clean Clothes Campaign, for example, set up branches in all major countries to fight against sweatshop conditions by publicizing abuses and signing up millions of signatories on petition campaigns to press prominent companies to pledge reforms to address excessively low pay, forced overtime, and lack of safety on the job. Here, INGOs could, among other things, urge their sympathizers around the world to boycott the products of offenders.

Protection of consumer standards prompted another set of INGOs seeking to assure product quality. Originally in the West, global consumer groups frequently embraced tensions between moderate Western activists and leaders in other countries like Malaysia, who targeted Western countries for exploiting non-Western markets with substandard goods.

Despite occasional regional tensions, the INGO movement increasingly sought to provide some global balance against the power of the multi-nationals. In the 1970s, for example, global campaigns pressed the Nestlé Company to stop selling powdered milk in Africa, where its use amid unsanitary conditions frequently caused infants to die. A massive international boycott resulted, termed "the most devastating attack ever mounted on corporate advertising in the Third World." By the 1990s well-publicized pressures on companies like Nike produced promises to improve labor conditions in Vietnam and Central America. Links between local and global organizations produced similar corporate commitments to reduce environmental pollution in places like Indonesia. A global effort in the 1980s pressed the McDonald's restaurant chain to stop using non-biodegradable styrofoam cups and beef imported from the rainforest areas of Brazil: a company spokesperson had to admit, in 1990, that "because of our high visibility, the environment was becoming a monumental problem for us." Corporate exploitation, both of workers and the environment, continued, of course, and some responses to INGO tactics were either temporary or superficial – including environment-friendly publicity campaigns that had little to do with reality. Still, it was significant that global organizations were proceeding on several different fronts, moving well beyond the familiar emphasis on international trade and production, and that the whole process was generating some (partially) self-correcting features.

The expansion of global institutions, in number and in range of function, was clearly a key aspect of globalization more generally, reflecting the new framework in communication (and the use of English as a linguistic medium) but also pushing transnational exchange to unprecedented levels. A dramatic shift in scale was unquestionable, and, as the new global historians argued, it was certainly possible to interpret the result – the range of activities that now regularly exceeded the national level – as a revolutionary change in the nature and organization of human activities.

Global politics

Regular efforts at coordinating international policies on key issues and establishing functioning international institutions dated back to the later 19th century, but there was no question that, here too, the scope and intensity of activity ratcheted up many notches from the late 1940s onward. Policy efforts to encourage freer trade and international financial coordination, part of the framework for the new round of globalization, were direct components of the larger global political process. INGOs played their own role in spurring global attention to key problems, prodding individual governments and rousing larger public opinion to respond to issues across national lines. Examples of global political capacity multiplied. At the same time, the global political arsenal remained limited, and there were many constraining forces: nothing close to a world government emerged, despite hopes in some quarters and fears in others. The political side of globalization was a glass half empty – compared to the needs generated by the welter of world problems – or half full – compared to responses just a half century before.

International conferences abounded on virtually every imaginable issue of global policy, some sponsored by the United Nations, others prompted by groups of individual nations. Trade issues, obviously, were a recurring topic; so were labor conditions. Spurred by the United Nations, an international convention was forged on various rights for children, including a prohibition on treating children who committed crimes as adults or subjecting them to capital punishment; only the United States and Somalia refused to sign on. Economic development and agriculture, women's issues, treatment of refugees, labor conditions, and, as we will see, environmental concerns also focused international attention. The conduct of war remained a key topic: various international meetings sought to define and punish acts of genocide, others dealt with efforts to limit the spread of nuclear weapons, another urged a ban on landmines (another international treaty that was widely approved, though which the United States refused to sign), still others tried to ban the use of child soldiers.

Supplementing global politics per se was a steady expansion of global charities beyond the formal foreign aid supplied by governments in most industrial nations (though at widely varying levels). Natural disasters like earthquakes or tsunamis called forth massive giving, as well as short-term efforts by many nations to provide emergency assistance. People in the United States alone contributed over a billion dollars for relief in the Indian Ocean tsunami disaster in the early 21st century. The idea of charity for strangers, across borders, operated in many directions. Thus while attention focused most obviously on disasters in poorer regions, a calamity like the flooding associated with hurricane Katrina in the United States drew voluntary gifts from groups and individuals in many countries, from Europe to Saudi Arabia to Japan.

A variety of campaigns, some under official sponsorship of key governments, and others from private groups, sought to define a host of global policy standards, expanding what was often referred to as "world opinion." From the late 1940s onward the United Nations regularly issued proclamations on the equality of women, and then from 1965 onward began sponsoring recurrent conferences to spread the word. Large numbers of governments did, in response, add assurances of equality to their national constitutions. In 1975 the Organization of African Unity recognized "international standards of general application designed for the protection of rights of women." African courts in a number of countries began to rule in favor of women's property rights, citing the fact that governments had agreed to international conventions on equality. On another front: in 2006 the United States Supreme Court ruled against capital punishment for children, citing among other things the international standards on this subject.

Not infrequently, the idea of global norms significantly affected national policies, even on core issues. During the 1950s, wide public concern responded to above-ground nuclear testing and its spread of certain cancer-causing pollutants in the atmosphere. Various groups in the West and Japan, in the Middle East (particularly against French testing in the Sahara), among Buddhists and other religious constituencies generated marches, petitions and letters that finally caused major governments, including the United States, to agree to a test ban treaty. Another broad opinion movement in the 1980s, particularly in Europe and the United States, pressed businesses to withdraw investments from South Africa in protest against the racist policy of apartheid and the attendant police repression, and along with intense local agitation finally caused the changes in law that collapsed that system in favor of democracy and legal equality. Never before had this kind of global pressure played such a role in military or internal policy, implicitly trying to define types of health threats or racial inequalities that had simply become unacceptable according to a potent if ill-defined global community. American President Dwight Eisenhower acknowledged the force in 1958, in response to a scientist who urged him to continue nuclear testing: "the new thermonuclear weapons are tremendously powerful; however they are not ... as powerful as is world opinion today in obliging the United States to follow certain lines of policy."

The importance of global governance, even if informally organized, showed up interestingly in response to the economic crisis of 2008–9 – in striking contrast to the absence of effective global response to the depression of the 1930s, when narrow national policies predominated, including raised tariffs, and almost certainly made matters worse. Quickly, late in 2008, a new "group of 20" was formed, to include economic powers in Asia and Latin America as well as the more familiar cluster of Western industrial nations plus Japan. While disagreements persisted, literally every major leader recognized that transnational coordination was essential and that the crisis also demonstrated the need for new global rules over the behavior of financial institutions. Globalism was no longer almost entirely Western, and it was seen as the only approach that could possibly master economic problems that were themselves worldwide in scope.

But the global political glass was also half empty. Many nations, having signed global conventions, pulled back in fact. Several African courts, for example, began after 2000 to revert to more customary law in arguing that women should not own property, despite formal adherence to equal-rights pledges. Some global goals, like the abolition of child soldiers, were simply ignored by rebel groups that had no interest in international standards. Negotiations about the environment often foundered on the unwillingness of the United States to sign major agreements. Japan tried to resist the global efforts to limit the harvest of whales. Ambitious hopes to get agreement on banning child labor proved overreaching, as a number of south Asian countries, dependent on growing amounts of child labor (against the larger global trends), simply held back. While a global approach to the economic crisis of 2008 largely prevailed, a few countries, like Ecuador, raised tariffs in an attempt to isolate the national economy from the larger crisis.

Global intervention in crises proved inconsistent. World opinion and the interests of several key states helped prompt action against civil strife in the former Yugoslavia and East Timor, but it largely held back from anything but ineffective laments in some of the bloody African clashes like the genocide in Rwanda in the 1990s. Media coverage highlighted some tragedies more than others, public opinion proved somewhat fickle, and motivations for action in some places, like Africa, were simply less acute than in other instances. Some observers worried that racist biases helped explain why certain crises were essentially ignored.

Despite sincere hopes, no uniform standards emerged for internal politics. From the 1970s onward liberal democracies did begin to spread widely, encouraged by support from existing democracies and from the relative success of democratic forms in the West, Japan and India. Democracy gained fairly uniformly in Latin America, in places like the Philippines and Indonesia, and in a large minority of the states of Africa, as well as in most eastern European countries after the fall of communism. But much of the Middle East held back, aside perhaps from minor concessions such as elected local councils; China put down a major democratic movement in 1989; Russia's commitment to democracy seemed to falter somewhat after 2000. It was not clear that agreement on basic political principles was going to be part of the global future.

Finally, other trends raised complications for political globalization. The formation of the European Union, designed to overcome the limits of national divisions and to make Europe more effective economically in the larger world, was a crucial innovation of the post-World War II decades. The move was not anti-global. But a focus on building greater European unity and identity could in fact distract from full support for larger global institutions. Europeans sometimes worked more on the creation of their own identity than on global standards.

Overall, it was clear that political globalization, while measurably moving forward, was not in the main keeping pace with some of the other facets of globalization. The capacities of the multinationals or the surge of global environmental change outstripped institutions designed to oversee at a global level. It was clear as well that some essentially political claims from the most enthusiastic proponents of globalization were, at the least, premature. Thus one series of arguments held that since democracy was becoming a universal political form and since democracies did not go to war with each other, war would become a thing of the past. A variant involved claiming that all societies were becoming consumer focused, which would also inhibit war since conflict damaged living standards. There was, simply, no sign as yet that these sweeping consequences, however desirable, could be seen as part of the innovations globalization would bring.

Global health

Developments on the global health front were in some ways unexpected. The rapid increase in the pace of trans-regional contacts should, by traditional standards, have led to a corresponding surge in the spread of epidemic disease. But while there were some signs of this, new methods of control, expanding from the international public health efforts of the later 19th century, actually constituted a greater change. What had been tentative, disputatious conferences turned into systematic global-organizational efforts.

The SARS (Severe Acute Respiratory Syndrome) epidemic of 2002–3 was a particularly interesting case in point. The outbreak, which would ultimately kill 774 people, began in China, whose government initially sought to conceal the problem lest it disrupt international contacts of other sorts and embarrass the regime. A Canadian electronic health-warning system, operating under the auspices of the World Health Organization (WHO), picked up news of the problem in November 2002, and this began to galvanize a further international response. The disease did spread rapidly, which is what one would expect with globalization: transmissions that in the 14th century took years, or in the 16th century months, now operated within a matter of days. SARS quickly hit a total of thirity-seven countries, mainly in Asia but also including Canada. Under guidance from the World Health Organization, affected countries began to organize quarantines of affected areas – WHO at one point advised against any non-essential travel to Toronto – and also screened airline passengers for signs of disease. Governments in Singapore, Canada and (under new policy) China actively enforced coordinated measures of protection. By summer 2003 the disease had been contained, with surprisingly little overall damage. The SARS episode testifies, thus, both to the vulnerability to disease transmission that is part of contemporary globalization, and to unprecedentedly effective, though not flawless, global response.

The more important contemporary global disease, AIDS, had a less happy history. First developing in Africa, AIDS spread fairly rapidly to the Caribbean and elsewhere, transmitted above all by sexual contacts. Some incidence would develop in almost every part of the world, and in the 1980s it was feared that a global health catastrophe might result. Global efforts developed to conduct research on possible therapies and to persuade governments and individuals to take measures that might limit the disease's spread. Considerable foreign aid and private philanthropy were aimed at those African states, mainly in the east and south, where the disease remained particularly acute. Expensive treatments available in the wealthier nations did limit the disease. Government responses varied in the world as a whole, causing variations as well in the incidence and prospects for the disease. Overall, the problem was partially contained but not resolved.

A new global disease scare erupted in 2009, with an outbreak of a new kind of swine flu in Mexico that quickly spread to several other countries. World agencies mobilized quickly to monitor air travel and to help fund Mexican medical intervention. But there were also clear possibilities of a rapid global pandemic. The report card in the area of global health, like that for global politics more generally, remained mixed.

Cultural globalization

The intensity and range of global contacts inevitably spilled over into values and beliefs, modifying without erasing local cultures for many people. Cultural globalization, not brand new, took on new dimensions, and of course created new resistances in turn. Many people – particularly young people – found a real need to feel connected to a larger cultural world. The young man in a McDonald's restaurant in Shanghai, who noted that he came there not because he liked the food, which was to his mind worse than Chinese food, but because it linked him to global tastes and to youth in other countries, expressed precisely that new kind of thinking.

Global cultural currents flowed heavily, but not exclusively, from the United States and to a lesser extent western Europe. It is vital, however, not to overdo the Western sources of global cultures: Japan was also a key center for cultural entertainments (which by the early 21st century comprised the largest export sector for the nation in terms of value), and China, Brazil, India and many other countries contributed actively as well. Global culture moved, in other words, in several directions, including to as well as from the United States. Americans picked up music crazes from Europe, passionate toy and game fads from Japan, medical interests from China, and movie styles from India – the list was long.

Different kinds of people were variously exposed. Some regions were more receptive to global culture than others. Wealth was a factor – global cultural products cost money – but so was prior cultural conditioning. Rural areas had far less access to global culture than urban centers did; even in 2009, only about a third of the world's population had any contact with the Internet, to take one striking example of cultural constraints, though access to television and radio were more widespread.

Global culture had many shapes. Relatively few efforts tried to bridge among the major religions on anything like a worldwide basis. The Roman

Catholic papacy did reach out for discussions occasionally with other Christian groups, but also with Jewish, Islamic and Buddhist leaders, but it periodically antagonized some of these faiths as well. A few other agencies sponsored wide-ranging interfaith dialogues. But, other than continued missionary activity by individual religions (particularly active in Africa and Latin America), there was no real move toward a more global religion.

In contrast, something like global science and medicine did emerge. Scientists from many nations collaborated in major laboratories, even when sponsored by a single national agency. Researchers in Singapore established such a powerful center for research on liver diseases that virtually every regional effort tried to link in; the same applied to Dutch research on breast cancer. On a more popular level, access to standard medical treatments and hospitals became increasingly common, at least in urban areas, so the question of what to do if you fall seriously ill, increasingly had a global answer. Of course there were compromises: many people in Taiwan combined traditional rituals with recourse to modern medicine. But the modern medical component was quite real nevertheless. Equally important, exchanges moved in other directions as well. The rise of global roles for China included growing popular interest in Chinese medical approaches including acupuncture, with centers widely available in many countries outside east Asia. Acupuncture began to spread in the United States in the 1980s; by the early 21st century almost nine million Americans had received treatment, a major example of mutual flow in science, broadly construed.

The most obvious emphasis for global culture, however, rested on increasingly widespread and pervasive consumer interests. The spread of movies and television showed created international audiences for common fare; the same applied to the growing popular passion for certain sports, now including basketball along with earlier staples which themselves became more widely known. Globally shared consumer items, like Hello Kitty merchandise (from Japan) or Barbie dolls (from the United States) or Sudoku puzzles (Japan again), created other common denominators for consumer interest. Even such an initially American item as the Disney theme park proved widely exportable, with successful ventures in Japan and (after some initial adjustment) Europe, while parks in the United States drew almost as much eager attention from middle-class Latin Americans as from Americans themselves as places to which one must take the family if one was a self-respecting parent.

Global consumer culture showed in many ways. The spread of American fast-food restaurants to cities in a whole variety of societies was a case in point. McDonald's moved across borders first in 1967, with outlets in Canada and Puerto Rico; in 1971 a restaurant opened in Tokyo as "makadonaldo" spread to Japan. The globalizing Soviet Union accepted a branch in 1990, and by 1998 the chain was operating in 109 countries. Other fast-food outlets were not far behind, along with many local imitators, significantly modifying the way many people ate and the kinds of food they found interesting. A few concessions proved necessary: beer at McDonald's in France, more vegetarian fare in India, teriyaki burgers in Japan, and special meals during Ramadan in Morocco. But the basic concept remained the same, as the experience, once American, now became global.

Beauty contests sprouted almost everywhere as well, from American origins in the 1920s (a few predecessor events dotted the later 19th century, also mainly in the United States but with a beach pageant in Belgium in 1888). Globalization began in 1951, with the establishment of the Miss World competition, followed by Miss Universe the next year. Later on Miss International (1960), Miss Earth (2001, with a purported environmental focus) and Miss Tourism Queen International (2004) joined in. Equally to the point, regional and national contests spread in India, many parts of Africa, Australia and elsewhere. The idea was to sell a global standard of female beauty in venues that would have wide popular appeal – and the concept clearly caught on. While many people disapproved of the contests, on grounds of traditional morality or feminist concerns about exploiting women's bodies, there were women in virtually every region willing to participate. Middle Eastern interest grew, with a Lebanese winner of Miss International in 2002, Miss Turkey gaining Miss World and a Muslim from Bosnia winning the first Miss Earth title. A Pakistani woman won Miss Bikini Universe in 2006, though this caused great controversy.

The commercial aspects of Christmas spread widely, even in non-Christian areas like Turkey and the United Arab Emirates; having an excuse to shop and offer gifts to the family increasingly knew no borders. The notion of sending commercial greeting cards, initially a Western innovation, entered the celebration of Ramadan, the Muslim month of fasting and prayer. Birthday parties spread widely, and the American jingle "Happy Birthday" was translated into every major language.

Other global consumer currencies included the adoption of blue jeans, at least for young people. Comic books spread widely, though they had somewhat different content and emphases in different cultures; Japanese contributions to comic books and related animation were particularly important. Shopping malls fanned out in many places: a mall in Dubai charmingly took the name Ibn Battuta, connecting current globalization with earlier world travel. Most cities also sported essentially similar types of luxury hotel, often run by chains such as Hilton or Marriott, another way in which consumer culture seemed to unite the (urban) world around many common standards and around a commitment to material comfort.

Shared consumer forms and products could be misleading. Not everyone was interested, and of course many people lacked funds to indulge in consumerism of any sort, whether global or local. Consumer interests might overlap but offer different particulars. Japanese use of the national Disney Park included elaborate commitment to buying gifts for others, which was less prevalent at the American version where souvenirs for the attending family were more important. Europeans were notoriously far more interested in using much of their extra income for long vacations, in contrast to Americans who placed greater emphasis on buying material objects. Global consumerism existed, in other words, but it had significant regional translations.

Critics abounded, of excessive materialism and loss of local identities as well as what seemed to be clear violations of traditional Christian or Islamic morality. Interesting efforts emerged to combine global consumer patterns with local customs. Thus a beauty contest in Kerala, in southern India, tried to reward contestants who wore traditional costumes as part of their display and also could demonstrate knowledge of local epics; the effort misfired somewhat, because real traditionalists were not willing to enter any beauty contest while the women who were eager knew little about Keralan language and literature. More successfully, the popular Indian film industry, called Bollywood, quite vigorously blended Indian themes and styles and Holly-wood glitz; interestingly, by 2008, Bollywood approaches began to win Western audiences, which showed once more that global culture was moving in several directions.

Global culture also helped create clear new problems, even aside from the concerns of traditionalists, though the problems also measured the importance and impact of the global standards. The advent of American television programming in some of the Pacific islands caused an increase of bulimia and anorexia among some teenage girls, eager to make their figures look like what they were seeing on the screen. More commonly, new types of food, often fattier than local fare, plus the use of computer games along with sedentary school work, helped prompt a literally global epidemic of obesity among middle-class children. While places like the United States had the highest obesity rates, the problem demonstrably hit urban families in China, India and elsewhere. Global standards could alter lives in fundamental ways, another aspect of the process that was unprecedented.

The global environment

The aspect of globalization that was most completely brand new to the later 20th century involved environmental impacts. Humans had altered, and often dramatically worsened, the environment before, from the rise of agriculture onward, but mainly on a local or regional basis. With industrialization in the later 19th century, the needs of factories or consumer in one place could prompt changes in other regions that in turn deteriorated the environment. Thus trying to meet Western demand for vegetable oil or coffee led to the expansion of plantations in west Africa or Brazil that reduced local vegetation and damaged water supplies. The spread of rubber plantations in Brazil had the same effect. Clearly, the Western-dominated global economy was beginning to introduce serious environmental change. The fact that decisions in one region could affect environments in another was environmental globalization of a sort, meshing with the idea of the 1850s as the launch pad for modern globalization.

But more literally global environmental deterioration awaited the later 20th century. Attempts to curb local factory pollution by creating tall smokestacks helped spread pollutants to distant areas – to Canadian forests from the United States Midwest, or to Scandinavian forests from the German Ruhr, through the phenomenon of acid rain. Use of various chemicals for consumer products in various parts of the world began to reduce the ozone layer to a dangerous degree, another global result. Reduction of the rain-forests to meet global demand for beef and other products, plus growing carbon emissions from expanding factories and automobile use, began to create the phenomenon of global warming and an attendant reduction in the icecaps in the Arctic and in Antarctica alike. Never before had such widespread climate and pollution impacts resulted from human activity.

And of course regional impacts from global activity accelerated as well. The later 20th century was dotted with oil spills from wrecked supertankers that could foul water, shores and animal life in places like Alaska or Spain or Malaysia. Many foreign-owned manufacturing plants spilled chemical pollutants in Mexico or Indonesia. An American factory in Bhopal, India, exploded, causing tremendous local maiming and loss of life. A nuclear accident in the Soviet Union spread radiation to a number of surrounding countries.

International political efforts, as well as domestic regulations, fanned out to try to deal with what was effectively an environmental globalization. Discussions of environmental controls increased from 1997 onward. A major conference in Kyoto, Japan, set limits on carbon emissions in order to curtail global warming, but several key nations refused to sign on and it was not clear that the limitations would be effective in any event. At the same time, vigorous debates occurred about how great the crisis was – there was some scientific dispute – and about who should take the lead: developing nations wanted the wealthy nations to pitch in first, without impeding their own growth plans, whereas the older industrial centers hesitated to push too far unless other significant polluters (like China, which took second place to the United States by the 21st century) faced up as well. Environmental impacts and responses constituted one of the clear question marks of the newest phase of globalization.

Global protest

Contemporary globalization brought one final innovation, from the late 1990s onward: an attempt to develop protest forms that would directly confront the major features of globalization. Obviously, all sorts of group worried about major aspects of globalization or about the process as a whole. Many labor unions were concerned about the loss of jobs to lower-paying regions. A number of INGOs tried to tackle environmental standards. Culture critics bemoaned the inroads of foreign influences on local traditions: a key theme of many writers, from Japan to Mexico to west Africa, involved a loss of identity as meaningful cultures gave way to faceless and shallow consumerism and sexual exploitation. Fundamentalist religious groups, whether Christian or Islamic or Hindu, often directly combated global cultural standards, while also often feeding from groups that were suffering economically from foreign competition. A host of local nationalisms gained new strength – the surge of Scottish nationalism is an example – not just because of the appeal of a glorious regional past but because the local identity might counteract global forces. Globalization as a source of protest and concern was hardly new.

Nevertheless, it was a testimony to the new power and sweep of globalization that an explicit protest movement also emerged. Extensive riots erupted in Seattle in 1999 around meetings of the WTO designed to lower barriers to international trade. Protesters came from many parts of the world. They included environmentalists, opponents of consumerism, advocates for the protection of workers and working conditions, and partisans of traditional identities. They embraced many who saw globalization as a means of exploiting the poorer regions of the world while exacerbating economic inequalities. As one participant put it, "protesters included: French farmers, Korean greens [environmentalists], Canadian wheat growers, Mexican environmentalists, Chinese dissidents, Ecuadorian anti-dam organization, U'wa tribes people from the Columbian rainforest, and British campaigners against genetically modified foods." Motives were diverse, and not always entirely compatible: but there was agreement on a globalization target and a specific focus on institutions that seemed most responsible for the acceleration of the process.

At least in the short run, the protests had little impact other than to provoke massive security arrangements at subsequent global gatherings. But the efforts persisted: most meetings of the World Bank, or by 2009 the Group of 20, saw major local demonstrations, drawing people from various places united in their sense that globalization was moving the world in the wrong direction. The efforts, stemming from so many different parts of the world, were themselves of course a backhanded illustration of globalization itself.

Global accumulations and innovations

Contemporary globalization – or the contemporary phase, depending on how one views historical antecedents – involved two clearly novel elements: the global environmental impact and embryonic global protest – and a massive acceleration and expansion of more established patterns, notably in the areas of technology, language and culture. Significant changes in organization and global politics added in, and there were some redefinitions of earlier staples like migration and disease transmission. Even global food access, though not new, now expanded its impact through the global epidemic of obesity. The overall combination provided powerful arguments for those – whether historians, other social scientists or simply ordinary observers including of course the protesters – who felt that a fundamental transformation was under way that would measurably differentiate the world's present and future from its past. Global innovation could be welcomed by optimists who saw in it a source of greater overall prosperity and of political counterweights to traditional evils like the oppression of women or the denial of basic human rights. It would be bemoaned by those who identified both economic and cultural deterioration. The two groups might clash endlessly over their evaluations, but they would ironically agree that something massive was in the works.

Was there any cause to hesitate, not about the fact of significant change but about the claims of radical and systematic novelty? Was there any reason to look to history as more than a benchmark against which the colossal changes of contemporary globalization could be measured?

Further reading

Andrews, Maggie and Talbott, Mary, eds. *All the World and Her Husband: Women in Twentieth Century Consumer Culture* (London and New York: Cassell, 2000).

Bascu, Juanita-Dawn. "Measuring Citizen Attitudes toward Globalization." Thesis submitted to the College of Graduate Studies and Research, University of Saskatchewan, June 2007.

Block, David. *Globalization and Language Teaching* (London and New York: Routledge, 2002).

Boli, John and Lechner, Frank J. *World Culture: Origins and Consequences* (Oxford and Malden, MA: Blackwell Publishing, 2005).

Castells, Manuel. *The Rise of a Network Society* (Malden, MA: Blackwell Publishers, 2000).

Connelly, Matthew. *Fatal Misconception: The Struggle to Control World Population* (Cambridge, MA: Belknap Press, 2008).

Cowan, Tyler. *Creative Destruction* (Princeton, NJ: Princeton University Press, 2003).

Doremus, Paul, Keller, William W. Pauly, Louis W., and Reich, Simon. *The Myth of the Global Corporation* (Princeton, NJ: Princeton University Press, 1998).

Friedman, Thomas L. *The Lexus and the Olive Tree: Understanding Globalization* (New York: Farrar, Straus and Giroux, 2000).

Guha, Ramachandra. *Environmentalism: A Global History* (Upper Saddle River, NJ: Longman, 2000).

Hilton, Matthew. *Prosperity for All: Consumer Activism in an Era of Globalization* (New York: Cornell University Press, 2009).

Kleinman, Arthur, ed. *Medicine in Chinese Culture: Comparative Studies of Health Care in Chinese and Other Societies* (Washington, DC: U.S. Government Printing Office, 1975).

LaFeber, Walter. *Michael Jordan and the New Global Capitalism* (New York: W.W. Norton, 2002).

Lauren, Paul Gordon. *The Evolution of International Human Rights: Visions Seen* (Philadelphia: University of Pennsylvania Press, 2003).

Lew, Alan, Hall, C. Michael, and Timothy, Dallen J. *World Geography of Travel and Tourism* (Oxford and Woburn, MA: Butterworth-Heinemann, 2008).

Mazlish, Bruce. *The New Global History* (New York: Routledge, 2006).

Mazlish, Bruce and Chandler, Alfred D. *Leviathans: Multinational Corporations and the New Global History* (Cambridge: Cambridge University Press, 2005).

Moore, Karl and Lewis, David. *Birth of the Multinational: 2000 Years of Ancient Business History – from Ashur to Augustus* (Copenhagen: Handelshojskolens Forlag, 1999).

Orlove, Benjamin. *The Allure of the Foreign: Imported Goods in Postcolonial Latin America* (Ann Arbor, MI: University of Michigan Press, 1997).

Pennycook, Alistair. *The Cultural Politics of English as an International Language* (Upper Saddle River, NJ: Addison Wesley Publishing Company, 1995).

Rees, Stephen. *American Films Abroad: Hollywood's Domination of the World's Movie Screens from the 1890s to the Present* (Jefferson, NC: McFarland, 1997).

Robertson, Robbie. *The Three Waves of Globalization: A History of a Developing Global Consciousness* (London: Zed Books, 2003).

Stearns, Peter N. *Global Outrage: The Impact of World Opinion on Contemporary History* (Oxford: Oneworld Publications, 2005).

Steger, Manfred B. *Globalization: A Very Short Introduction* (Oxford: Oxford University Press, 2003).

Von Laue, Theodore H. *The World Revolution of Westernization: The Twentieth Century in Global Perspective* (New York: Oxford University Press, 1989).

Watson, James. *Golden Arches East: McDonald's in East Asia* (Palo Alto, CA: Stanford University Press, 2006).

Wells, Alan. *Picture-tube Imperialism? The Impact of U.S. Television on Latin America* (Maryknoll, NY: Orbis Books, 1972).

Chapter 7

Conclusion

The historical perspective

Globalization has a complex history. It does not sail smoothly from some earlier point in time, like 1000 CE, though there are connections among the different phases of trans-regional contact over the past millennium. It does not emerge brand new from the heads of policy innovators and communications inventors 50 years ago. There are good cases to be made for several key junctures in the history of globalization (or protoglobalization or archaic globalization – the various terms show how hard it is to pinpoint a single date of origin). Ultimately, it's the complexity that emerges as the key finding, not a need to make a decisive selection of one particular episode.

Analyzing globalization's origins and phases encounters several cultural sticking points in the history discipline and in contemporary attitudes alike. Historians, as we have seen, do tend to like to push things back in time, to claim that what seems new actually started earlier. After all, the past is their stock in trade, and lending the past undue contemporary significance is an occupational hazard. The tendency does not mean that any particular claims – for example, about developments around 1000 CE or before – are wrong, just that they deserve scrutiny.

Lots of people tend to fall victim to inevitability arguments, that is, to arguments that once one particular pattern developed, later patterns inevitability follow. Globalization certainly asks students of the process to try to figure out at what point inter-regional contacts were so intense – even with far different technologies from those available today – that later amplifications followed naturally, without much need for additional causation. (Or a variant: globalization is new but now sets an inevitable path for all regions.) Historians usually caution against too much inevitability, against a tendency to look for straight-line connections between past and present (this wars against the impulse to find earlier-than-expected origins). Globalization calls for some sorting through of the inevitability aspects: at what juncture did the process become essentially self-sustaining?

Contemporary culture, perhaps especially in the United States, tends to exaggerate recent change, to argue that far more transformation, and more fundamental transformation, is occurring than is actually the case, and to minimize continuities from earlier points in time. The claim of revolutionary developments in this or that area is almost constant. Globalization is a massive invitation to this kind of hyperbole, to the temptation to dismiss the past and enshrine the present, and historical analysis, even if not always conclusive, is desirable particularly to guard against over-facile assumptions. The fact that contemporary culture exaggerates the novel does not mean that claims of groups like the new global historians are wrong, just that – like the push-things-farther-back impulses of many conventional historians – they deserve sensitive analysis.

The history of globalization may invite, as part of its complexity, a more nuanced view of the whole process than most globalization theories have emphasized. We suggested earlier the possibility of breaking it into constituent parts, before recombining the whole, and historical analysis facilitates this approach. Certain aspects of globalization go way back in time, and while they did not have contemporary shape early on, there are certainly some connections between then and now. Migration and disease transmission are the most obvious aspects that begin to set a trans-regional stage early on. Extensive and regular trade, despite important anticipations fairly early, may have a slightly later origin, though it certainly developed intensely enough several centuries ago, along with the business organizations to match, that a purely recent date is questionable. Political and cultural globalizations, though again they offer some earlier hints, seem to begin decisively in the later 19th century. But full environmental globalization is a recent product. Current globalization not only reflects recent policies and technologies. It also interweaves the many strands that began to take shape early on. One of its telling features, in fact, is its multifaceted quality, its blending of trade with culture, innovative politics with old–new patterns of disease transmission. Historical perspective is central to understanding this process, and how it departs from, yet builds on, the past.

While pointing to partial origins well before the contemporary era, history also shows the oscillating quality of globalization. Globalization or proto-globalization has not moved forward steadily. There are periods of relative stability punctuated by new factors that begin to accelerate change, and there are periods of at least partial retreat. The second quarter of the 20th century – not that long ago – is a particularly important case in point. Serious globalization had blossomed in the later 19th century, but it did not bring uniform benefits and it suffered from excessive Western dominance – and it caused widespread pushback after World War I. This pattern could, after all, be repeated again in the future, despite the more recent intensification of the process. Within China today, for example, intellectuals divide over whether globalization is a benefit or a curse, with some claiming that China can find greater world voice as well as prosperity through participating in globalization; but others damning the process as a Western-capitalist plot that will force China into a foreign mold – and this in a country that, many observers might argue, has profited particularly from new global contacts over the past two decades. On a wider scale, depending on what aspects of globalization are emphasized, polls show that upwards of 53 to 79 percent of all people in the world oppose globalization today. Economic globalization is widely feared, because it brings too much inequality and so many factors that escape regional governance, but cultural globalization is even more resented (by up to 70 percent of those polled) on grounds of loss of identity; only political globalization wins (bare) majority support, apparently because many people hope that more effective political agreements will help keep other aspects of globalization under control. To be sure, there is regional variation: people in North America (particularly the Atlantic and Pacific coasts), western Europe and Japan – especially young people – like cultural globalization, by a 4–1 margin; but all generations in most other regions disagree vigorously. Interestingly, however, people in the United States, against the global majority, seem to fear political globalization above all, though there are also concerns about economic dislocation and immigration (and, among some groups, about culture as well). Worldwide, women are slightly more likely to favor most aspects of globalization than men are – which makes sense in terms of the history of at least recent globalization and its bearing on traditional gender alignments, but which adds another dose of complexity. With attitudes and mixtures of this sort, with so much division and hostility, can we be sure that another retreat might not occur?

The historical perspective certainly shows why there are so many arguments among scholars, activists and ordinary people alike about the pros and cons of globalization. Problems with protoglobalization surfaced early, particularly in terms of regional economic inequalities and undue dominance by certain societies. All phases of globalization have left some groups feeling they were losing control or were being challenged if they hoped to retain cherished cultural identities. Many of these problems have continued to dog the process, often accelerating as globalization itself becomes more intense, creating great sensitivity to the economic drawbacks for many groups and encouraging the perception that globalization is simply a fancy name for Western or American economic and cultural imperialism. Globalization has marched forward anyway, though sometimes amid interruptions and ongoing regional disagreements, but the hostilities remain important as well. One of the intriguing aspects of the contemporary era is the effort, still tentative, to figure out how best to express concerns directly about the process itself, how to give voice to people otherwise ignored except by conscientious pollsters. This aspect of globalization history is still being written.

Globalization, despite all the debate about it, is not an abstraction. As it has unfolded in key phases, it has affected what people in many regions ate, what they valued in life, what kind of education they sought, what diseases they might contract and of course what kinds of goods they bought. It has stimulated a sense of adventure and the excitement of encountering different cultures, and it has created a fear that risks were too great and that one's own ways of thinking about things must be protected from outside contagion. It has defined key political issues for leaders and voters alike, even when domestic issues seem easier to grapple with. The daily meanings of globalization are more important now than ever before, but they are not brand new. The unfolding of globalization over time is a story of changes people encountered in many aspects of life, of new stimulus and new anxiety alike. This mixture, too, continues to unfold.

Index